WHEELERS, DEALERS, PUCKS & BUCKS

A ROCKING HISTORY OF ROLLER HOCKEY INTERNATIONAL

by Richard Neil Graham
Toluca Lake, California, USA

Published by Inline Hockey Central

Graham, Richard Neil, 1958-
Wheelers, Dealers, Pucks & Bucks:
A Rocking History of Roller Hockey International / Richard Neil Graham

Printed in U.S.A. by CreateSpace
ISBN: 978-0-9834060-0-6
LCCN: 2011924425
Cover Design: Andy's Printing of Burbank, Breck Wilson & Richard Graham
Cover Photo by Wen Roberts Photography Ink

Table of Contents

In Memoriam

Jack Armstrong, Craig Charron, Phil Chiarella, Jerry Diamond,
Carl DiPietro, Bruce Hammill, Wild Bill Hunter, John Kanel,
George Mikan, John Murphy, Stu Nahan, Walt Poddubny,
Barry Potomski, Phil Randolph, Wen Roberts, Red Rush,
Maury Silver, Norman Silver, John Spoltore

Photo by Wen Roberts Photography Ink

Acknowledgements

So many people had a hand in making this book possible. First, I must thank my father, E. Lloyd Graham, for giving me the space and time to write this book. The book could not have been finished without his unending patience, love and support.

There's something called an angel in the publishing world; someone who goes above and beyond to make a book happen. In this book's case, it is Jeanie Buss. Jeanie's support for this book at a critical juncture inspired me and renewed my energy. Her incredible Foreword also helped to revive my energy in the final months before publication. Jeanie, you're the best.

Bob McKillop of the Anaheim Bullfrogs offered to do "40 interviews, if that's what it takes" for me to get the book done, but he was so sharp that I think we nailed it in one. Thanks, Killer.

John Lyman of JohnLymanphotos.com graciously offered me the use of many of the excellent photographs used in this book. Thanks, John. Your patience is amazing.

Rob Krier went over the manuscript with a sharp eye at the last minute to eliminate a lot of my errors, poorly constructed sentences and idiosyncratic style choices. I hope that the Kings' game I took him to was payment enough for the incredible job he did.

Chuck Schiele, a longtime friend, excellent graphic designer, fine artist and songwriter/musician/record producer jumped in at the last minute to design the book's inner pages.

Breck Wilson, another talented graphic artist, also came into the process very late and did a wonderful job finalizing the front and back cover designs.

Steve Pona patiently answered hundreds of my questions about the inner workings of Roller Hockey International's offices, the league's economics and many other topics. Steve also pushed me to improve several chapters that I'd thought I'd already finished. Only later could I see that Steve was correct and that those chapters were immeasurably better than they had been before his suggestions.

Rich Sedlisky, a buddy and New Jersey Devils' fan from New York City whom I've never met, but have had as an online friend for more than a decade, was a great sounding board. He lent a layman's ear, ensuring that I was writing for a wide audience and not just people who knew RHI intimately. Thanks, Rich.

Others who deserve a mention include Ellen Adderly and Jared Adderly, Andy's Printing of Burbank, Michele Arnesen, Davis Barber, Robert Basile, Jeff Buma, Matt Caputo, Cliff Chi, Mike Conroy, Warren Ettinger, Bradmond Fikoby, Jim Fox, Paige George, the entire Graham family (you know who you are), Robert Grandy, Laura Harvey of CreateSpace.com, Harvey the Bartender at Hotel Amarano in Burbank, Taryn Johnson, Stan and Louise Jones, Isabelle Harris, Laura Kittiko, Titia Leisz, Dan Lilie, Jamie Scott Lytle, Jeri Lopez, the Los Angeles Kings, Peter Lyons, Donna Mack, Bob Makela, Todd McCormick, Sonny Miller, Jon Niola, Timmy Nolan's of Toluca Lake, Jay Piz, John and Jodie Potter, Dr. Jonathan Rand, Rui "Bobby" Russo, Tony Richardson, Dan Roberts, Mary Roberts of Wen Roberts Photography Ink, Tracy Robinson, Mark and Kirsty Salvetti, Matt Savant of the Honda Center in Anaheim, Sierra Nevada beer, Jim Singer, Victor Smith, Starbucks of Toluca Lake (my office and home away from home), Karin Tobiason, David Tseng, Karl, Catherine, Pierre and Savannah West, Anno Willison, Bill Wechter, Breck Wilson, Vivian Wong, and Terry, Jill, Jeremy and Jenna Young.

To everyone who took the time to talk to me for this book, thank you. Your stories are what made it special for me, and what kept me going when I hit difficult stretches in writing. I also want to thank the founding fathers of RHI – Ralph Backstrom, Alex Bellehumeur, Larry King and Dennis Murphy – for creating the league and for speaking to me for this book many years later. A special thanks to Dennis for continually supporting this project and for becoming a very close friend. God bless you, Dennis, and "don't take any wooden nickels, big guy!"

David McLane, who joined RHI in 1994, helped me to better understand the workings of ESPN and the nature of its dealings with the league. David also provided moral support when the chips were down, which I appreciated greatly.

I'd also like to thank the readers of Inline Hockey Central who have been so supportive of this book from the beginning, and whose positive comments and support often came at just the right time to renew my energy and steel my resolve. Ultimately, this book's for you.

Author's Note

Governator-to-be Arnold Schwarzenegger and Glenn Frey of the Eagles were just two of the famous people who dropped their children off at a karate-for-kids studio in the building in Santa Monica, California, that housed InLine Hockey News, the print publication that I worked for from 1994-1997. One day, I'd heard that Ray Mancini, a famous boxer, was in the building, so I asked IHC's assistant editor, V. Wade Contreras, to invite him up so I could meet him.

About 15 minutes later, Wade said, "Hey, Rich. Ray 'Boom Boom' Mancini is here to see you."

I said, "Send him in. I'll kick his ass."

I was having a lot of fun as the editor of InLine Hockey News, and it showed. The satisfaction, confidence and fulfillment that I derived from covering a small but growing niche sport in the mid-1990s was immense. The day that Ray Mancini walked into our inexpensive (earthquake-retrofitted) office, I had no idea of the changes that were coming to the sport and my life. Ignorance can definitely be bliss. I had fallen into a sport (popularly known as roller hockey) that perfectly mirrored my first love – ice hockey. Sure, it was played on asphalt, concrete, wood or several different types of plastic court rather than ice, but it was hockey. And for someone like me, born in Canada before the advent of computer games, the Internet and American Idol, there's nothing more natural than a love for hockey.

Before I came to InLine Hockey News, I'd written a column on the growing inline game for Hockey Player magazine. That's when I met Street Hockey magazine publisher Mark Brown and associate publisher Robert Dean Hoffberg, both of whom played pick-up roller hockey at the beach parking lots in Santa Monica, California. Mark always cracked me up with his understated humor. At one Los Angeles Blades' game in 1993, a beautiful spectator walked by past us in the stands.

"She reminds me of a dream I'm going to have tonight," Mark deadpanned. Robert, who co-founded the magazine with Mark, was also a professional magician who worked under the name Robert Dean.

It wasn't long before I was that magazine's editor (soon to be renamed Roller Hockey magazine). As I took over the reins from Kurt Helin, Street Hockey's first editor, the wheeled version of the sport exploded onto the contemporary sports scene with a sonic boom. As a member of the small niche media covering the sport, my colleagues and I were fairly bullish about the prospects of the league, hoping that as the league grew, so would the stability of our jobs. Unfortunately, the league didn't survive, and the magazines eventually disappeared along with it. I have documented the amateur game and the intermittent stabs at creating professional roller hockey leagues since then with my web site – http://www. InlineHockeyCentral.com – but without Roller Hockey International to cover, it's never been quite the same.

However, there are still spots where roller hockey shines brightly. Many current inline hockey tournament series boast hundreds of teams per event. And on Wednesday, March 2, 2011, Bobby Ryan scored on a penalty shot in overtime against the Detroit Red Wings. Ryan was an elite youth roller hockey player who played under the name Robert Shane Stevenson. (The story of his name change is worth a book in itself.) Other former roller hockey players in today's NHL include the Pittsburgh Penguin's Brett Sterling, Lee Sweatt of the Vancouver Canucks, and Devin Setoguchi of the Minnesota Wild.

At one game I attended in March, the Anaheim Ducks played the Vancouver Canucks, and a woman sitting behind me criticized the Vancouver VooDoo jersey I was wearing, saying it was the ugliest jersey design she'd ever seen. I happen to love the design, and I told her that back in the mid-90s, it outsold Vancouver Canucks' jerseys by a margin of 8-1. She wasn't impressed, but neither was I with the Ducks' pedestrian jersey design.

I wrote this book to recapture a seven-year stretch from 1993-1999 when I covered RHI (as well as Major League Roller Hockey and Pro Beach Hockey). My goal was to try and record a small slice of history that might otherwise fade away if someone didn't document it, and to recount as many interesting and humorous stories about RHI's players, league administrators, team owners, coaches, writers, photographers, referees and fans as I could to try and capture the spirit of those years.

If I've accomplished that, I'll consider this book a success.

Rock and roll!

Richard Neil Graham

To my father, E. Lloyd Graham, for hockey;
to my mother, Harriet Evelyn Nielsen Graham, for words.

Foreword

By Jeanie Buss, Executive Vice President, Los Angeles Lakers

Wheelers, Dealers, Pucks & Bucks. Could there be a more titillating title? I sat down with author Richard Graham in November of 2008, when he was already two years into his attempt to chronicle the fast rise and fall of Roller Hockey International. He had a gleam in his eye that reminded me of when I first met him as a beat writer covering the burgeoning sport of roller hockey. He always had a way for getting his story.

And what a story he got. Countless hours of research, interviews and off-the-record conversations have paid off for Mr. Graham and the reader. We meet the wheelers (the players), most of who were minor-league ice-hockey journeymen. These players were propelled by a new sport to take center stage at major NBA and NHL arenas during the summer months, fulfilling their dreams of fame and not so much fortune. Next are the dealers like Dennis Murphy, with connections so strong he can gather the top 10 sports moguls in a room with a single phone call. The disappointing saga of the puck specifically designed for roller hockey, which was counted on to supply the bucks to bankroll the league (imagine if the NBA earned a royalty for every basketball sold in the entire world), is a lesson that even today's big-league commissioners should heed.

All sports fans and especially those who want to understand the operations of a league and its teams will benefit from this read. As a former Roller Hockey International team owner and a current executive for the 16-time NBA Champion Los Angeles Lakers, I still relate experiences from those six seasons in the craziest – yet – I – still – cannot – believe – it – is – gone league. My prediction is that this book will be optioned for film rights and that we will see the next great sports movie produced featuring characters even the greatest scriptwriters couldn't create. I'd personally like to thank Richard Graham for telling a story just waiting to be told.

CHAPTER 1

We Never Had an
Opening-Night Crowd that Big

"COME ON, BOYS. SHOW THESE PEOPLE WHAT WE'VE GOT!"

Bob "Killer" McKillop exhorted his teammates from the bench as the
Anaheim Bullfrogs lined up on a slate-gray concrete floor across from
the Utah RollerBees for their Roller Hockey International home opener on
July 2, 1993.

It wasn't the very first game of the season – the Los Angeles Blades had
traveled north to play the Oakland Skates the night before and there were two
other league games that night – but it was definitely the most high-profile tilt.
It was the first sporting event in the $123 million Anaheim Arena, already
nicknamed "The Pond" in anticipation of the imminent arrival that fall of
one of the National Hockey League's newest franchises, the Mighty Ducks of
Anaheim. More than 200,000 square feet of Italian marble lined the arena's
walls and inside concourses. The Orange County Register and the local
television network Orange County News were in the house. The new espn2
television network was taping the game, Sports Illustrated was there to cover
it, and a contingent from Japan watched from a private suite. For star power,
Sylvester Stallone, fresh off the opening of "Cliffhanger," was in the stands
along with 13,141 other fans, making it just 4,000 short of a sellout.

As in ice hockey, the game that Roller Hockey International was modeled
after (albeit with major tweaking), players could substitute for each other
during the play. It was known as "changing on the fly," and that's what
McKillop and teammate Christian Lalonde did a little more than a minute
into the game. Hopping over the boards from the Bullfrogs' bench, Lalonde
picked up a loose puck in the middle of the rink and saw McKillop streaking

toward the Utah net. Instantly, Lalonde zipped the puck to McKillop.

"He fired a pass right on my tape and I one-timed it into an empty net," McKillop said. He had scored just 79 seconds into the game. "I put my arms up in the air and waited for the boys to come and celebrate with me," McKillop said. The near-capacity crowd gave a thunderous ovation. To McKillop, it was electric. "I was thinking, 'Wow. I think you made the right decision,' (to play in the fledgling roller hockey league). We all knew it."

About an hour before the game, Dennis Murphy, one of the four founders of the new Roller Hockey International league, stood outside of the Anaheim Arena with Bullfrogs' owners Maury and Stuart Silver. (Nelson Silver, Stuart's older brother, had yet to arrive.) The three men watched as the crowd filtered in.

"We've got a good crowd," said a gleeful Murphy to the Silvers. The effusive Irishman was seeing the hard work he and his partners had done in the past two years come to fruition. Later Murphy said, "We never had an opening-night crowd that big in the World Hockey Association."

The Anaheim Bullfrogs' inaugural season opener was only the second event ever to be held at the Anaheim Pond. The first? A Barry Manilow concert. The Bullfrogs papered the house with two-for-one ticket sales and giveaways, and it was unclear just how many people showed up simply to see the ritzy new arena and wound up hooked on the Bullfrogs.

"We gave a lot of freebies away to get people in," said Maury Silver, a Montreal native who had moved to California to start Avon Car & Truck Rental. "But we made a lot of money the first night. Not everything was comped. There was a two-for-one, and we did very, very well the first night. At that time, we thought we had a gold mine. I really did." The Bullfrogs' owners cleared $34,000 that first night. "It was going great," Silver said. "We were the first team to ever play in the Pond. We had the girl dancers – the Polliwogs – and everything. We put on a nice show. We really did. We were doing very, very well."

Chris Palmer, the Bullfrogs' assistant general manager that night, well remembers the day. "It was chaotic," Palmer said. "That day was *crazy*. We were driving around giving tickets to all the youth teams, all the rinks, just making sure that all the tickets got out there. We handed them out at the

Chamber of Commerce. We worked it pretty hard."

The Bullfrogs' staff was nervous because they didn't know how many people would show up, but they knew that they had the beautiful new Anaheim Arena on their side.

"People wanted to come, regardless of what was there," Palmer said. "I'll never forget walking in that building when they were about to drop the puck, and we had 13,000 and change. It was awesome. All that hard work was worth it; we almost packed the building. It was a great feeling of accomplishment."

In the Bullfrogs' locker room before the game, coaches Chris McSorley and Grant Sonier prepared the players for the contest.

"We didn't know anything about our first opponent, obviously," Sonier said. "We talked about what we felt were going to be our strong points – getting the puck to the net, typical hockey stuff, then went out for the warm up. Ten minutes before the game started, we talked about motivational things that were going to make us win: 'Guys, we don't know what the officiating is going to be like, we don't know what the floor is going to be like; we're just going to go out there and do whatever it takes to win the hockey game. It appears that there's going to be a big crowd, so get ready for a fun night.'"

"That was the coming-out party for all of us," McKillop said. "We didn't know what to expect. 'How physical is it going to be? How intense is it going to be? How much better are we? Is anyone going to come? Are we really worthy of playing in this facility?' Our practices were so upbeat and physically demanding. They paid us well, and as a result they demanded a lot from us. Chris and Grant made sure that we were ready to play. We were going after a championship."

McKillop said that the Bullfrogs players were handpicked to come, and could be handpicked to leave. "This was just like ice hockey," McKillop said. "A lot of people were expecting a lot out of us. We came to play. We practiced for a month and a half before that first game. That night really set the tone for the entire season."

When the lights were turned down for player introductions, an expectant hush settled over the crowd, and Ann Victor, a Bullfrogs' public relations coordinator, tapped Rob Laurie on the shoulder.

"The cheerleaders are going to go out, and then we're going to announce you one by one, starting with you, Rob, because you're number 1," Victor told him. "I want you to skate out there about where the blue line would be and stop and stand there."

"There were a bunch of people wearing headsets – in ice hockey, you might see one – coordinating everything," Laurie recalled. "You could see the spotlights swinging around, and wherever the spotlights hit, there were people. We were amazed, standing there about to go out on the floor, knowing that the place was just packed."

When his name was announced, Laurie skated out with speed, forgetting in his excitement one important detail. "I was thinking, 'I don't know how to stop,' " Laurie said. "I'd only been on Rollerblades for a couple of weeks, and I didn't know how to stop yet."

As Laurie approached the line of Anaheim Polliwogs cheerleaders on the floor, he had to make a quick decision.

"I'm thinking, 'Oh, no. I'm in the spotlight and I don't know how to stop here. If I try something I'm not really good at, I may fall.' "

Performing a pirouette in bulky goalie gear, Laurie spun in a circle at the last moment and bumped gently into the boards on the opposite side of the rink. Disaster averted.

After McKillop's early goal, the Rollerbees tied the game in the first period before the Bullfrogs' Kevin Kerr scored the first of his three goals to start a seven-goal run that put the game out of reach. Anaheim pulled away and cruised to a 12-4 win. In addition to Kerr, McKillop also scored a hat trick, Brad McCaughey had two goals and four assists, and defenseman Joe Cook chipped in two goals. Laurie, despite not knowing how to stop on wheels, was solid in net.

Four players scored for the RollerBees, including team captain Todd Harkins, who also had two assists.

"Two of the RollerBees wore quad skates," McKillop remembered.

The RollerBees had Rich Chernomaz, the all-time leading scorer and long-time team captain of the Salt Lake Golden Eagles, as well as Brett Harkins, Todd's brother. Chernomaz and Harkins were "a couple of great ice hockey players," but the RollerBees simply "didn't have the depth we had," McKillop said.

"You've got guys who are all from the minor leagues, and we play in front of anywhere between 3,000 to 7,000 people," Bullfrogs' forward Savo Mitrovic said about the opening-night crowd. "When you see a 17,000-seat arena with a lot of people in there, it certainly gave you goose bumps. For us in the minor leagues, it was 'The Show.'"

CHAPTER 2

The Malevolent
Vacuum-Cleaner Attachment

On July 1, the night before the Bullfrogs' smashingly successful home opener, the Los Angeles Blades played the Oakland Skates in the Oakland-Alameda County Coliseum Arena.

The Coliseum had hosted the NHL's California Golden Seals from 1967-1976, but it had been years since hockey of any kind had been played in the building. The Blades defeated the Skates, 11-9, in front of about 3,000 fans, many of whom were nearly ejected for littering. When Oakland's Chris Robertson scored his third goal of the game, Skates' fans began throwing their hats into the rink.

"The ushers went around ejecting people because they thought they were throwing trash," Blades' owner Jeanie Buss said. "They had no idea what a hat trick was! They hadn't had hockey in so long, that they were throwing people out. We were like, 'No, no, no, it's OK. That's how you celebrate a hat trick. It's a tradition!' "

An ice hockey tradition, to be sure, but Roller Hockey International was fresh and new, like the inline skating craze. As a result, the league benefited from press coverage from the very start. Sports Illustrated's Kelli Anderson attended the home openers of both the Oakland Skates and the Anaheim Bullfrogs, mentioned that the Skates' players were towed onto the rink by Harley-Davidson motorcycles, and described Oakland's logo as "a bottom-feeding fish that looks… like a malevolent vacuum-cleaner attachment." To add injury to insult, the Skates suffered a big loss in the first five minutes when star player Aldo Iaquinta went down with a damaged knee.

Jeanie Buss, who shared ownership of the Los Angeles Blades with her father, Dr. Jerry Buss, the owner of both the Los Angeles Kings and Lakers at the time, attended the Blades' first game in Oakland. She would see many

6

more games in the ensuing years, but this one was special.

"At the start of the game, when the team came out, skating in their uniforms, with 'Blades' on their chest, the sense of pride that I got in my chest…" Buss said, and then paused. "It was a great moment. I'll never forget it as long as I live."

In addition to the Bullfrogs, Blades, RollerBees and Skates, there were eight other teams that first season – the Calgary Rad'z, Connecticut Coasters, Florida Hammerheads, Portland Rage, St. Louis Vipers, San Diego Barracudas, Toronto Planets and Vancouver VooDoo. The teams were divided into three divisions – named Buss, King and Murphy – after Jerry Buss and two of the league's three founders.

There were two other games on July 2, 1993. The Vancouver VooDoo took on the San Diego Barracudas at the San Diego Sports Arena, while the Toronto Planets met the St. Louis Vipers in front of 7,908 fans at the St. Louis Arena. The Vipers won, 12–9, with Scott Rupp and Myles Hart each scoring hat tricks, and former St. Louis Blues' winger Perry Turnbull scoring two shorthanded goals in the fourth quarter. (RHI games consisted of four 12-minute periods.)

The Planets' Christian Skoryna, a 20-year-old from Elgin, Ontario, Canada, couldn't help but notice that the coach of the Vipers kept yelling at him, perhaps trying to get him off his game. "He was yapping at me and yapping at me," Skoryna said, "So I finally said to him, 'Who the hell are you?' "

The coach pointed up into the rafters of Checkerdome, as the St. Louis Arena was affectionately known at the time.

"That's who I am." The coach, NHL Hall-of-Famer Bernie Federko, was pointing at his retired #24 jersey from his 14-year career with the St. Louis Blues. Skoryna said, "I didn't say another word. I just put my head down and skated straight to my team's bench."

The next night, the Vancouver VooDoo hosted the Los Angeles Blades at the 3,500-seat PNE Agrodome. The Agrodome was filled to capacity, with 300 people paying for standing room only, and 200 plopping down bucks just to get into the building. The VooDoo were up by three goals, 6-3, late in the game, and the hometown fans were happily anticipating a celebration when the Blades staged a comeback and tied the score. It took 13 players per side in the tie-breaking shootout before L.A. ultimately prevailed.

VooDoo administrators said later that one could have heard a pin drop after the Blades' game-winning shootout goal. On the bright side, by 8:30 a.m. the next day, 40 people had called and purchased season tickets for the VooDoo.

Three days later, in their home opener, the Blades scored another narrow victory, defeating the Calgary Rad'z at the Great Western Forum, 7-6. What many remember more than the score, however, was something that happened before the game began. The Blades skated through fog to a song by Metallica as they were introduced one by one… and several of the players slipped and fell as their urethane wheels made contact with the condensation from the fog on the floor.

"It was important to us from day one that we were going to treat this as major league and with respect – our fans, our players, the product," said Jeanie Buss. "Everything was important to us. So we brought in a fog machine, and at that time, by '93, they had found that the best surface was Sport Court. Well, Sport Court doesn't handle moisture very well. The fog machine, while a great idea, was a disaster."

In that very first week of Roller Hockey International's inaugural season, there were big crowds and small crowds, down-to-the-wire games, a flair for the dramatic and unexpected accidents. But where did the league come from?

CHAPTER 3

Dennis, I've Been Expecting Your Call

The driving force behind Roller Hockey International, Dennis Arthur Murphy, might be the most unlikely, least known and most influential visionary in North American professional sports history. Visionary, because he saw possibilities where others only saw obstacles; least known, because he concentrated more on creating leagues than in bringing attention to himself; and unlikely, because he was never a great athlete. In fact, he was rather short and round, when you got right down to it. He was a second baseman on the varsity team at University High School in West Los Angeles – notable alumni include Judy Garland, Marilyn Monroe, Elizabeth Taylor, and Nancy and Frank Sinatra Jr., – but his love for sports and building new leagues greatly surpassed his own playing skills. Despite his rather Leprechaun-like stature, "Murph" had tall dreams, a gift of gab, and the ability to bring together a diverse group of people to work toward a common goal. When he wanted to, he also had the remarkable diplomatic ability to avoid being pinned down on any point of contention in an argument or discussion.

"He's a round man in a round room," said John Black, who coached the Los Angeles Blades in 1993. "You just can't corner him."

Born in Shanghai, China, in 1926, to a father who worked for Standard Oil and a housewife mother, Murphy and his family moved back to the United States a year before the Japanese attacked Pearl Harbor in 1941. A staff sergeant in WWII, Murphy joined the reserves after the war and came out of the Korean War as a captain. Murphy attended the University of Southern California on the GI Bill majoring in economics, but did not spend any time in that field. He was a one-term mayor of Buena Park in Orange County, California, before becoming a marketing executive for one of California's biggest civil engineering firms, Voorheis, Trindle, and Nelson.

An Irish-American with a politician's eye for opportunity, Murphy became the creative mind behind the American Basketball Association (1967-1976) and the World Hockey Association (1972 to 1979). He was also a co-founder of World Team Tennis along with Larry and Billie Jean King prior to co-founding Roller Hockey International. The WHA and the ABA competed directly with the entrenched National Hockey League and the National Basketball Association. Murphy and company enticed Bobby Hull to flee the NHL to the WHA with an unprecedented $1 million contract. "Mr. Hockey," Gordie Howe, was soon to follow. Murphy was the commissioner of the WHA for three years. Both the WHA and ABA eventually merged teams into the more-entrenched leagues, showing the merit of Murphy's ideas.

Murphy had also worked with Alex Bellehumeur, the owner of State-Wide Developers, a Southern California real estate development firm, a past president of the Port of Long Beach, and a governor's appointee to the World Trade Commission. Patrician, well-dressed, and with every hair in place, Bellehumeur met Murphy in 1980 when Bellehumeur was working with football coach George Allen to bring an NFL team to the then-vacant Los Angeles Coliseum. Outmaneuvered by the Oakland Raiders, Bellehumeur then hired George Allen as a consultant with the goal of creating a new professional summer football league.

"We put together 12 teams and were all ready to go, but the television company that had granted us television exposure was closed by the Internal Revenue Service," Bellehumeur said. "I opted as chairman and founder to recommend to all of the teams that we pull back. That's what they agreed to; without television, it was too big a risk. As a result, George Allen took that business plan to Dave Dixon and the IFL morphed into the United States Football League. During this process, I needed someone to run the show, and Dennis Murphy was recommended. I had never met him before. He came wobbling into my office, and I hired him as the president. And we became very close friends. We have worked on several professional leagues, including RHI."

In his autobiography, "MURPH, The Sports Entrepreneur Man and His Leagues: ABA, WHA, WTT, RHI, IFL, GHA, and Bobby Sox Softball," self-published in 2002, Murphy described Bellehumeur as "stubborn, very opinionated, tough, charming and a great dresser. He is also a person who understands people better than I. We had some real battles over people. In retrospect, Alex was right on most of his observations." When he discussed the idea for Roller Hockey International with Bellehumeur, "he liked it and wanted in," Murphy wrote. "He said he would allow us the use of his office space; provide us with secretarial help and the use of the telephones. This sounded great to me."

As Murphy told it, one day in 1991, he was a passenger in future RHI CEO Larry King's car in 1991 when they were delayed on a side street and saw some kids playing roller hockey. "I said, 'That's what we ought to be doing,'" Murphy said. "We thought that it was a sport that could become a professional league."

In "MURPH," he wrote that upon returning from the car ride with King, he told his brother John what he had seen: "He informed me that inline skating was a hot ticket and people everywhere of all ages and sizes were playing roller hockey in parks and playgrounds. This immediately appealed to me. Imagine hockey being played on cement [concrete] rather than ice. Imagine being able to play hockey anywhere in the world, rather than being limited to ice arenas. Wow! What a way to finish up my career."

It made for a good story, but both Alex Bellehumeur and Larry King later said that it wasn't actually as Murphy had remembered, though the gist of the tale was true.

"Dennis called me one day and said, 'Larry, I saw these kids playing roller hockey,' and 'What do you think about doing a roller hockey league?' I said, 'Dennis, I know nothing about roller hockey. If you want to do it, I will help you."

Perhaps it was the result of a faulty memory, or Murphy's desire to enhance the story, but in the end, it really doesn't matter. Murphy, then 66 years old, was inspired to begin working to develop a new sport and was off to the races.

He invited King to join him and Bellehumeur in developing roller hockey at a professional level, and King accepted.

King, born in Ohio and raised in California, was an attorney by trade as well as a sports entrepreneur. In addition to helping create World Team Tennis and womenSports, which eventually became Women's Sports Magazine, King helped develop the Women's Sports Foundation and the Kauai-Loves-You Triathlon in Hawaii. Scott Tinley, a top professional triathlete at the time, recalled this about King: "I did play tennis with him at his place in Kauai a few times and he's a keen doubles player with a crisp cross-court volley. He seemed to be a hard worker, always dabbling in a variety of sporting ventures."

In person, King seemed pleasant, if reserved, and hard to read. Described as enigmatic, aloof, sarcastic and bright in turns, King was once married to tennis star Billie Jean King. As Roller Hockey International began to take shape, King was married to the vibrant and friendly Nancy King, who did communications work for the league in its early days. Murphy was named RHI's president, Bellehumeur was the chairman of the board, and King became the league's general counsel.

Murphy, Bellehumeur and King were now well on their way, converting Bellehumeur and Murphy's preexisting corporation, World Sports Management, Inc., into RHI, Inc., and the two men retained controlling interest in the new entity, with King as co-founder and part owner.

"We were missing one thing – a high-profile hockey man," Murphy wrote. Ralph Backstrom, who had won six Stanley Cup Championships with the NHL's Montreal Canadiens, was hired as the new league's commissioner. Murphy had known Backstrom from his days as a player in the WHA following his NHL career. Then living in Denver, Colorado, Backstrom was the National Hockey League's Rookie of the Year for the Canadiens in 1959. He was an inspired choice to oversee the league's rules and style of play. A speedy skater, Backstrom was known as much for his relentless pursuit of loose pucks as he was for his gentlemanly play. Classy and kind, he was voted Most Valuable Player of the second Canadian/Russian series, which featured WHA players against the Russians. He later coached the University of Denver Pioneers' ice hockey team for six years.

"He knew that I was involved in inline skating back to the '70s, so when he was contemplating starting a new league, I was one of the first persons that he contacted," Backstrom said. "He asked if I would be interested in getting involved in roller hockey. I said, 'Dennis, I've been expecting your call.' "

Murphy, King, Bellehumeur and Backstrom captured the imagination of roller hockey players and fans around the world for a good chunk of the '90s. The four men who deserve the most credit for founding Roller Hockey International were a diverse group with a variety of personalities and drives. Those personality differences, however, would lead to the fissures that would hamper RHI greatly in the years to come.

CHAPTER 4

As You Know, I Invented the Rollerblade

Maury Silver, who purchased RHI's Anaheim Bullfrogs with his sons, Nelson and Stuart, was an early adapter and tinkerer of modern inline skates. One of his claims, however, was eyebrow-raising.

"As you know, I invented the Rollerblade," Silver said, matter-of-factly.

Silver said that Stuart had a choppy ice-skating stride as a youngster compared to his older brother, Nelson, so he built the skate to improve Stuart's stride.

"Stuey was playing hockey at [California's] Culver City Ice Rink," Silver said. "He wouldn't actually glide on skates. Stuart was very fast on his feet, but it was like running. If he would glide, he'd have been twice as fast."

So Silver took the wheels off an A&P shopping cart, "nailed a pair of boots onto a piece of wood," and attached the whole conglomeration to a thick board, with the wheels at the bottom, so that his son could practice taking fuller strides. Silver initially staggered the wheels under the board.

"I put one here and one here and one here and one here," Silver gestured with his hand, mapping out the wheels' placement in a zigzag pattern, "so he could take full strides, to glide. Maybe that would help," Silver said. "I figured I'd start it that way. Make him practice on the street because the wheel was thicker. But it wasn't right, so I decided to put 'em [the wheels] in a row. Make it a little smaller, and try to get thinner wheels. That's what I did. I have the first skate, the first skate ever built. It's in the trunk of my car; I'll show it to you."

While there's no doubt that Silver's story is true – and he's got a patent to prove it – he certainly wasn't the inventor of "the Rollerblade," by any means. Inline skates have a long and well-documented history. Designs and patents were developed by many people over the course of nearly 200 years, and inline skates were a direct descendant of the first ice skates.

According to the National Museum of Roller Skating in Lincoln, Nebraska, John Joseph Merlin was "the first recorded person to invent a roller skate, doing so in the 1760s in London, England."

The *first* documented inline skate design was created by one Monsieur Petitbled in 1819 in Paris, France. The National Museum of Roller Skating credits a New York resident, James Plimpton, with the development of the modern "quad" roller skate, with wheels attached side by side, in 1863. So, in between Petitbled's 1819 patent and Maury Silver's home-made design were scores of patents for inline skates, as Scott Olson would later discover. But we're getting ahead of ourselves.

Silver met Ralph Backstrom shortly after he was traded to the Los Angeles Kings from the Montreal Canadiens in 1971 and showed him his ideas for an inline skate.

"I still have that first pair," Backstrom said. "It was an old pair of L.A. Kings' skates; we took the blades off them and added wheels." Backstrom would skate around his Los Angeles neighborhood and get stares: "I could see neighbors peering around corners – this crazy Canadian," Backstrom said.

Silver received a patent for his version of the inline skate in 1972, incorporating Backstrom's idea to rocker the skate (raising the heel and toe wheels to better simulate an ice-skate blade). He and Backstrom talked about offering the invention as an off-season piece of training equipment.

"It was the same stride as an ice hockey skate," Backstrom said. "Going down and coming up hills was a tremendous help. I felt I'd be in pretty good shape going into camp."

[A five-minute video on the Internet features Backstrom playing for the World Hockey Association's Chicago Cougars. The final minute of the clip shows Backstrom skating around his neighborhood while wearing his Super Street Skates (Look for the video on YouTube). With Backstrom's enthusiastic support for inspiration and his credible hockey name for authenticity, Silver had expensive dies and molds made to create the frame for the Super Street Skate.

"At that time it was really costly, because we were making the skate frame out of steel," Silver said, as many of the materials used in current-day inline skates didn't exist.

In 1972, Gimbels, once the largest department store chain in the country, wanted the skates, Silver said. "They gave me an order, but they wanted us to go on television and make commercials" before they would buy the skates. "We'd have had to lay more money out than we were going to make on the thing, so the dollars didn't add up."

Silver and Backstrom bought Bauer skate boots to put on top of the frame and had meetings with various manufacturers to convince them to produce the skates for the mass market.

According to Backstrom, "We went to Bauer, CCM and Voit, and everyone said, 'Thanks, but no thanks. Nothing will ever replace the four-corner roller skate.' I knew in my heart that they were wrong. We might have been 15 years ahead of ourselves at that time. I could blackmail some of those companies," by threatening to embarrass them with proof of their shortsightedness. To this day, Backstrom regrets not continuing with the Super Street Skate. "I should have stuck it out, but I was still playing hockey and got traded to the Chicago Blackhawks, and that kind of ended it."

The end for Backstrom was just the beginning for another hockey player, Scott Olson, a native of Minneapolis, Minnesota. Olson was playing minor-league hockey for the American Hockey League's Brandon Wheat Kings in Manitoba, Canada, in 1978 when he saw an advertisement for the Super Street Skate in The Hockey News. The ad showed a photograph of Backstrom wearing the skate – with his Los Angeles Kings' jersey on backwards because of trademark issues – and Olson was intrigued. Once he returned home after that season, in 1979, Olson discovered that his brother Brennan had already purchased a pair of Super Street Skates.

"I'm going, "Holy cow, man!" Olson said. "I was always into fitness; I always wanted to train harder than anybody because I wanted to be one of the first American goalies to make it to the AHL. So I was looking for anything that I could do to get to that level."

There were three pairs of the Super Street Skates left at a local sporting goods store when Olson got there. He bought them all, put one pair on his ice hockey boots, and sold the other two pair the next day at a party. His next move was to call the Super Street Skate Company and order 1,000 sets of the skates – sans boots. The skates were "on some really inferior skate boots that had no support," Olson said. "I just want the bottoms." By the time the Super Street Skate frames had arrived in Minnesota, Olson had already pre-sold 12 pair, and "it just kind of snowballed from there."

Though the Super Street Skate's boot came in various sizes, the frames were one-size-fits-all, and that wasn't good enough for Olson, who began tinkering. He devised a way to make the blade length adjustable and more maneuverable, but Super Street Skate wasn't interested in his innovations. Olson wasn't going to do a patent search until his patent attorney suggested it. "We did the search, and lo and behold, 100 patents came back with the inline skate," Olson said. That's how Olson discovered the Chicago Roller Skate Company's inline skate design that was retractable and adjustable. He hitchhiked to Chicago to get a first-hand look.

"It was perfect," Olson said. "It was really a clean design, and it would fit every size. I could adjust them and make a kids' skate" as well as adult sizes. Another design feature of the Chicago Roller Skate Company's patent was dual-bearing wheels – the Super Street Skate had single-bearing wheels – so he developed a dual-bearing wheel of his own that made the skate even faster. "Once I did that, I was going from skating a few miles an hour to 15 miles an hour, and saved a lot of effort," Olson said.

The skate that Olson created with inspiration from the Super Street Skate and furthered with the Chicago Roller Skate Company's patent "became the first Rollerblade design," Olson said. Olson marketed the skates as an off-season training device for ice hockey players, assembling them with his brothers in his parents' basement.

"I think the improvements I made certainly helped get it to the recreational level, and that was always my goal, too," Olson said. "I knew that we could make a viable and profitable business selling to hockey players, but I really wanted to make it much bigger than that, and that's really true – we came up with the faster wheels and the better boot. That really took off, and of course, the marketing – that's everything, you know."

Many individuals can take credit for creating a version of an inline skate, including eventual RHI commissioner Backstrom and his longtime friend Maury Silver, but it was Olson's version that would catch the eye of sharp Minneapolis businessman Bob Naegele, Jr. In 1984, Naegele purchased Olson's fledgling company, now called Rollerblade, and effectively marketed the skates to the general public. Once the skates became ubiquitous on city streets, sidewalks and tennis courts, and along beach bike paths and parking lots, it was only a matter of time before it caught the attention of sharp-eyed sports entrepreneurs like David McLane and Dennis Murphy.

The game of roller hockey wasn't created to coincide with the improvement of the inline skate, though it may have seemed so to all but the biggest roller hockey aficionado. According to the National Museum of Roller Skating's website, "the first official roller hockey game, called roller polo, was played in 1878 at the Denmark Rink in London, England." In 1924, the International Roller Sports Federation (FIRS) was founded in Montreux, Switzerland, and one year later, FIRS established the first European Championship for roller hockey. In 1936, FIRS produced the first World Roller Hockey Championships in Germany.

The game was also popular in the United States. In an article in the November/December 1992 issue of Street Hockey magazine entitled "Roller Hockey – Turning Back the Clock," Irwin Hoffberg – the father of that magazine's associate publisher Robert Dean – wrote that "in the Bronx during the 1940's … our equipment consisted of the skates with metal wheels and clamps that fastened the skates to our street shoes. The clamps attached over the soles of the shoes… the puck we used was a .25 cent roll of electrical tape." Hoffberg excerpted a letter from George "Doc" Yoder, owner of Doc's Roller Rink in Middletown, PA, who first played roller hockey in the 1930's: "I remember in the '30s using Liberty and other magazines tied to our legs as shin guards. We also made our own hockey pucks. We used bowling pins. Using a wood lathe, we cut them down to the size of an ice hockey puck and then drilled a 3.4 inch diameter hole halfway through the thickness of the puck and inserted hot lead into the hole. This kept the puck from rolling on edge and also weighted the puck so it did not rise too much…"

All those games over all those years were played on quad skates, two-axle skates with two wheels per axle, the same configuration seen on most modern-day cars. However, it was the creation of the modern inline skate, improved by Maury Silver, the Chicago Roller Skate Company and Scott Olson, and marketed strongly by Rollerblade, Inc., that led to the founding of Roller Hockey International.

CHAPTER 5

Who is this Bizarre Human Being?

The founders of RHI wanted to jump-start the league with an exhibition tour in 1992 to help generate fan interest and exposure leading into its inaugural season in 1993. Former St. Louis Blues' general manager Chuck Catto coached Team Canada and picked his team at RHI summer tryout camps in Toronto and Vancouver before the tour, while Team USA, coached by John Black, was put together after tryouts in Los Angeles, Phoenix and Las Vegas. Team USA also scouted for players at the USA Confederation of Roller Skating National Championships in San Diego that July.

Dennis Murphy wrote to Dr. Jerry Buss, asking if he would be interested in hosting the tour's first game at the Great Western Forum in Inglewood, California. Buss forwarded the letter to his daughter, Jeanie, and said, "Dennis is such a good friend of mine; I want you to handle this."

Jeanie Buss remembered thinking, " 'Oh, this is a disaster! How are they going to be able to play hockey on concrete?' It made no sense to me, but I worked for Dr. Buss; I do what he tells me to do. I thought we were going to get those really good rollerbladers [sic] that you saw at Santa Monica Beach and teach them how to shoot a puck – as opposed to being [ice] hockey players that would learn how to rollerblade. So, there was a different concept that I hadn't accepted."

The first game of the Roller Hockey International Exhibition Tour was held at the Forum on August 13, 1992, and drew close to 6,200 fans. Team USA won, 7-3. Jeanie Buss was shocked "that we could draw that many people" with no advertising. Her instincts about the floor were correct. It *was* a problem.

"We played right on the sub floor of the Forum," Buss said. "At that time, nobody really knew what the right surface was. I mean, you thought of parking lots in Venice or Santa Monica. That's where people were playing roller hockey. So, we figured the concrete floor would be fine. It wasn't fine. They tried to add different powders and stuff just to try to get some grip for the players' wheels."

(According to Paul Chapey, a longtime roller hockey aficionado, Scott Accongio, John Black's assistant coach, convinced the operations people at the Forum to spread Pepsi syrup on the concrete to make the floor stickier.)

Jeanie Buss felt that the playing surface "was kind of a disaster, but the turnout of the crowd… Instantly, the light bulb went on: 'This is what kids were playing, and this had a chance to really be something big.' I was excited by the possibilities." Once Buss and her father saw the positive reception the game received from fans, they decided to buy a team. "It was important to my dad that I be named co-owner along with him," Jeanie Buss said. "That's how we got ownership [of the Los Angeles Blades]."

The first game of the tour was shown locally on tape-delay on CBS, with play-by-play by longtime sportscaster Red Rush and commentary by Bauer Hockey's Director of Marketing Peter Davis and Los Angeles Kings' forward Luc Robitaille. All the tour's players used Bauer ZT7 skates with plastic frames and stock urethane wheels. Tim Conyard of Team Canada drew first blood, scoring six minutes and 59 seconds into the game.

Advertisements were jammed into the television broadcast at every pause in the action and included such companies and products as Bauer Supreme Custom 3000 ice skates, Upper Deck collectible cards (with Bugs Bunny and Elmer Fudd united with sports stars like Jerry Rice and Dan Marino), Raging Waters, Phil Rizzuto shilling for the "Money Store," Paul's (I *am* the King) big screen TVs, Pacific Telephone cellular phones, Supercuts (Robitaille could have used a trim; he sported an mullet on the broadcast, a sign of the times), Family Fitness Centers (only $49 a month!), the Good Guys, and Jacoby & Meyers Law Offices.

"Solid hitting out there, Red; I wouldn't want to be out there," Robitaille said, after Rush described a player going "ankle over tea kettle" after an opponent's check.

Team USA's Daryn Goodwin got a kick out of Robitaille calling him, "a big farm boy from Visalia, California," and he recalled sweat dripping through his

21

Bauer ZT7 skate boots – so much so he had to blow dry them at halftime.

After the Laker Girls performed a halftime dance routine, local sportscaster Bob Elder (and eventual Anaheim Bullfrogs' general manager) came onto the rink to interview Peter Davis, Dennis Murphy and Ralph Backstrom. Davis was enthusiastic about the demand Canstar Sports, Bauer's parent company, was receiving for protective gear for inline hockey. Murphy, sporting a wide grin, noted the size of the crowd and said, "I hope from here on, it's up, up and away." Backstrom's facial expression communicated relief and delight. "We knew it was a great sport all along, but to have it confirmed by the fans here in L.A. makes me feel awful good," Backstrom said.

For game two, the two teams were bused to Phoenix, where they played at the Arizona Veterans Memorial Coliseum. Team Canada won, 8-7, in overtime, for its only win of the series, in front of 4,000 fans.

"After we won the first game, on the way to Phoenix, the Canadians sat in front of the bus and goalie Don Thompson was lipping off so much to them that it made us all sick," said Team USA's Daryn Goodwin. "He won the first game and got yanked in the second. Karma!"

Stephane Desjardins, though Canadian, played with Goodwin on Team USA. Desjardins also remembered the long road trip from Phoenix to Vancouver, as he very nearly missed the bus. After the game in Phoenix, a local woman offered to show Desjardins the town. After driving him around for a while, she dropped him off nearly an hour's drive away from the team hotel, and he had to take a very expensive cab ride back to find Team Canada and Team USA players impatiently waiting for him.

"It was a long trip to Vancouver," Desjardins said. "Team Canad took crap all the way from L.A. to Phoenix, but we had to take crap all the way from Phoenix to Vancouver. That was a little bit harsh." What made it harsher for Desjardins was that he'd collided with Team Canada's Mike Kennedy in the first game in Los Angeles. "I played with a charley horse all the way through the tour," Desjardins said. "My leg was so bad on the bus. When my leg was straight, it cramped up, so I bent it. Then when I'd try to bring it straight, I'd get a big cramp. It was bad."

The teams played games three and four at the P.N.E. Arena in Vancouver, produced by Mike King, the soon-to-be owner of the Vancouver VooDoo. The U.S. won both games in overtime by identical 6-5 scores, before a combined crowd of about 7,000. A severe thunderstorm that weekend may have kept the numbers down. Game five, originally scheduled for Caesar's Palace in Las Vegas, and organized by Mike Talkington, was switched to the Santa Fe Casino, where Team USA won, 13-4, on August 29.

RHI's founders contacted Sport Court in a panic when the Caesar's Palace venue didn't materialize. Ten days before the event, Sport Court provided the floor that covered the ice hockey rink at the Santa Fe Casino. That gave Sport Court – a company founded in 1976 by Dan Kotler to provide families with a multi-use backyard recreation court – a foot in the door RHI and the inline skating industry in general. Kotler would become the owner of the Utah RollerBees in RHI's first season.

The tour finale was shown live on CBS in Los Angeles and Las Vegas on August 29 at 9 p.m. Desjardins scored two goals and two assists in the finale and was the tour's leading scorer, with 10 goals and 10 assists in the five games. Of all the players on the tour, Desjardins would go on to play the most RHI games – 43 over the course of four seasons. Team Canada forward Mike Kennedy, from Vancouver, eventually played the most NHL games of any player who participated in the tour, at 145, mostly for the Dallas Stars. Team USA forward Jim Hau of St. Paul, went on to play two RHI seasons, for the 1994 Minnesota Arctic Blast and the 1995 Minnesota Blue Ox, and scored 83 points in 39 games. His teammate on the tour, forward Rob Hrytsak, of Saskatoon, Saskatchewan (the rules on nationality were fairly loose; a player didn't have to be from America to play for Team USA in that tour), played 30 RHI games for three teams – the Connecticut Coasters in 1993, and the Sacramento River Rats and Vancouver VooDoo in 1994. John Black, who coached Team USA, became a well-respected coach for the Los Angeles Blades, Portland Rage and Sacramento River Rats over the course of several RHI seasons.

In "Professional Roller Hockey Gets Off and Rolling," an article in the November/December 1992 issue of Street Hockey magazine, Editor Kurt Helin made what might have been the first mention in print about RHI's new, and eventually, controversial puck: "Roller Hockey International also developed a new puck for the tour. It is a hard plastic puck with a spoke design that slides on six metal braids. It is lighter than an ice hockey puck, but heavier than most street pucks. Most of the players felt it was a good puck, although no one has developed a puck that glides as smoothly as an ice hockey puck. However, RHI told us that they have made further improvements to the puck which will make it the 'smoothest street hockey puck available.' " The puck, called the Jofa SpeedPuck, would cause much angst and anger to many people in the ensuing years.

According to "RHI's Exhibition Series," Eric Colby's article in Hockey Player magazine's November 1993 issue, there was some fairly stiff checking in the tour games: "Not only was offense the rule of the night, but some Team USA players were a little surprised, most of them pleasantly, by the hits being delivered by both teams. 'The good thing is we get to ride on the bus with 'em,' joked Jeff Furlong, a 24-year-old defenseman from Yorba Linda, California. 'It'll ebb and flow,' said Black. 'The guy you knocked down tonight will be the one you're playing cards with on the bus tomorrow.' "

The tour gained exposure and interest for the upcoming league, and perhaps even more importantly, it broke even. The players got free equipment and were paid – the winners took home $300 for each win, the losers, $200. Coca Cola, Frito Lay, Kellogg's and Albertsons provided the financial backing for the television coverage for the tour opener at the Forum in Inglewood. The exposure from that and later televised games from the tour helped RHI to be seen as a legitimate sports league.

Dennis Murphy credited Patrick Mulcahy with much of the tour's success. Mulcahy, the owner of Mulcahy Sports Group, a sports television broadcast company based in Newport Beach, wrangled television coverage for the series opener. His accomplishment proved to be about as easy as performing a shutout in the high-scoring game of roller hockey. Mulcahy had known Murphy since 1988, and his company had produced 150 events in eight nations in 11 years when he agreed to pitch the RHI tour for television.

"I did what a sports-marketing company is supposed to do," Mulcahy said. "I secured sponsors and venues, wrote marketing proposals. I'm feeling pretty good, walking down the street. I've got all the big names – Jeanie Buss, Ralph Backstrom – a lot of heavy hitters. I figured, 'Shit damn, it's going to be a slam dunk.' I got turned down by *everyone*."

Mulcahy was dumbfounded.

"All I had to do was fax what I wanted on my play date on my schedule and how many reruns I needed, and I was never turned down, ever," he said. "Not only was I rejected by ESPN, I couldn't even get it on espn2. So I went to local television affiliates. I knew we could probably put 12,000 butts in seats there. We had good promotion monies and I went to ABC and was rejected. I went to NBC and was rejected. My moment of last resource was my buddies at Channel 13. They rejected me. I'm in the parking lot of KTTV and I'm so angry, I'm so pissed off, I'm kicking the tires of my car, I'm pounding the trunk of my car. People are looking at me asking, 'Who is this bizarre human being?' I looked across the street and I saw CBS. I said, 'Screw it.' I went to CBS and into the lobby and said, 'I need to see the GM now. Here's my card and my credentials.' I'll be damned. Steve Gigliotti, a really nice man, he gave me 30 minutes. After about 40 minutes, he calls in Jim Hill and Jim sits down. I said, 'Look, because of Jeanie Buss, we've got the Laker Girls to perform, all-star teams, a new sport, a breakthrough sport.' They all looked at me and said, 'OK. We'll give you your play date.' I said, 'OK, how many reruns?' I needed that money so we wouldn't lose our butts. You can't count on revenue from butts in seats; you've got to have broadcast and ad revenue or you're dead. That's how RHI made it."

The league didn't make money from the broadcast, but it received enough exposure to help make RHI look like a legitimate sports league. "It was three weeks of fun. I'm going to miss it," Team USA player Jim Hau told Eric Colby of Hockey Player magazine after the tour. "Who knows, maybe this will turn out to be the sport of the nineties."

CHAPTER 6

These Quad Skaters are Driving Me Up the Wall

If you were ever in close proximity to Dennis Murphy and had any talent at all, he could probably find you a job. His brother John was the league treasurer. Jerry Dovin, Alex Bellehumeur's accountant, became the league controller. Anno Willison, whom Dennis met at the Los Alamitos Race Course, became the league's tryout camp coordinator.

"The RHI office was across the street," Willison said. "Jerry Dovin was Bellehumeur's accountant, and we'd been friends since 1986 or so. I'd give racing tips to Dovin; he'd give 'em to Dennis, and Dennis would win. One day, Dennis and his brother John were at the races – like Mutt and Jeff. Dennis, a USC alum, has the temperament of a boiler on a steam engine train. John, a Notre Dame alum, was like the agitator in a washing machine."

The Murphy brothers, both wearing their alma maters' team caps and jackets, didn't know who Willison was as he sat behind them and listened as they argued over the merits of Notre Dame and USC.

"I'm a Trojan," Willison said, "But I decided I'd tell Dennis I was a 'Domer', and I got him going. His face got redder and redder until it matched his USC jacket. Then I let them know that I was a Trojan, and John got pissed."

After the encounter at the track, Dennis Murphy and Willison discussed RHI, and Murphy offered Willison the position of running the tryout camps.

"He did that to get even with me," Willison said later, grinning. Willison, directed by Ralph Backstrom, took care of the marketing, hotels and lodging for the tryout camps throughout the United States. The camps, which took place in the months just before the season started, produced some of the players for the league, but perhaps more importantly, brought in funds to get the league going. Thousands of players across the country paid about $40 to $50 each for the chance to show off their skills and perhaps make a team.

(Some later complained about having to pay to tryout, arguing that most of the teams had already solidified their rosters with minor-league ice hockey players. However, some players at the camps *were* selected by teams, and how many players who tried out and didn't make a team ended up with a fun story to tell their grandchildren for a measly $50?)

Roller Hockey International used the camps to prove the sport's allure and viability to prospective owners – and to help the league founders sell areas of dominant influence to those owners. The first tryout camp was in Bricktown, New Jersey, not long before the season started.

"It was the only arena on the east coast that Bauer was affiliated with, and Bauer was going to be a sponsor of the league," Willison said. "We could get players from New York, Pennsylvania, New Jersey, Virginia, Maryland and the Washington, D.C. area. Jerry Dovin, Dennis Murphy, Ralph Backstrom and I were there. It was a great turnout… and a fiasco. Dennis was supposed to show up with a cashier's check to pay for the arena, and he didn't. Dennis called Peter Davis of Bauer to get rink credit, but we couldn't play the f rst day. There were hundreds of people lined up ready to try out. It was a nightmare. Dennis was arguing with the lady at Bricktown about it and was pounding on her desk… and she had a fishbowl on her desk. I was trying to make him settle down.

"She said, 'If you knock that fishbowl off my table, you won't play here even *with* a cashier's check.' A banker friend of Dennis's from Florida finally guaranteed the check, and when he did that, they let us try out Saturday and Sunday."

In his autobiography, Murphy wrote about butting heads with old-school roller hockey players during the league's early tryout camps: "We did encounter one initial problem with the hockey purists who believed the sport should be played wearing 'four wheeled' skates. We were convinced that inline skates was [sic] the future. I had to utilize my best political skills to get over that hurdle. I pushed the inline skates at our tryout camps while allowing the quad skates to be used. I remember our tryout director, Anno Willison, saying in desperation, 'I can't wait until we decide to use the inline skates for our league. These quad skaters are driving me up the wall.' "

Some veteran roller hockey players also complained about the puck RHI planned to use.

"At a tryout camp at Whittier, some guys came in on quads, and some guys came in on inline; most were on quads," Dennis Murphy said. "We put our puck out there, and some of the guys were moaning about the puck. We said, 'If you don't like the puck, you can walk out the door.' Some of the guys walked out the door. Some of the traditionalists, it was hard to get them to conform. You can't blame 'em; they grew up that way and wanted to stay that way."

The tryout camp participants played by the rules that RHI Commissioner Ralph Backstrom put together. To differentiate RHI's game from that of the NHL and ice hockey, Backstrom decreed that RHI would dispense with ice hockey's blue lines. The center red line and offsides calls would remain, however. To avoid offsides, players were required to carry the puck over the red line before passing to a teammate who was already in the zone. (Most amateur tournaments had already dropped the offsides and illegal clearing rules completely, opening up the game, making long breakout passes and breakaways possible, and cutting down on stoppages of play.) Backstrom also decreed that tied games at the end of regulation time would go straight to a shootout. He chose to go with four 12-minute quarters rather than the three 20-minute periods of ice hockey, not only to set RHI apart from the NHL, but also to obtain more TV timeouts for potential broadcast advertising.

As a skilled former NHL player, making the rules and providing skating room for the danglers in the fresh new sport of inline hockey inspired Backstrom.

"With my background in the inline skate, it really appealed to me – I could live my dream all over again," Backstrom said. "Dennis asked me to write the rules and make it a really creative game. All of the ice rules I didn't like, I eliminated. I said, 'Dennis, we've got to get rid of the blue line. American fans have a football mentality, and they like two zones.' No blue line and four on four, it's really going to open the game up, and there will be very few offsides. We averaged anywhere from 90 to 100 shots a game, and 10-12 goals a game. People want to see goals. They didn't want to see a 1-0 roller hockey game. It was wide open, four on four; you didn't need as much overhead, less players, less travel expenses. We finished games in less than two hours; it wasn't dragging into the middle of the night if the game was tied – we had the shootout. Now the NHL is doing that. A lot of things that we did were ahead of our time. In NHL's overtime, they play four on four. I wanted to shorten the game, have more shots, more goals, fewer whistles – and a game where a goalie could have six or seven goals scored and still be the star of the game."

Joe Tamburino was an 18 year old with just one year of ice hockey experience when he went to the RHI tryout camp in Bricktown. He'd been playing roller hockey in a full-contact league in Fort Rockaway, Queens, New York. He saw a poster promoting the camps at a tournament, so he and a friend drove to Bricktown for the two-day tryouts.

"There were a lot of coaches and scouts," Tamburino said. "They divided us up into teams like any other weekend tryout. We had maybe three games on Saturday and one game on Sunday. I remember players being on quads. The quad thing was just fading out, and the inline thing was the next big move in roller hockey. The guys that were real sturdy on their skates were wearing the quads. The tryouts were pretty competitive and physical. They were still experimenting with the four quarters and the offsides rule, carrying the puck over the center line. There was no Sport Court; it was on the concrete flooring underneath the ice."

Tamburino remembers tryout camp participants who received rude awakenings when they stepped out onto the playing surface and weren't prepared for the checking and hitting.

"You'd get players that would go out there for one game, thinking, 'I'm a good hockey player,' but they'd never played any full contact," Tamburino said. "They'd go out there and take one or two good hits and that was it – they'd pack their bags. There were a few guys that probably didn't make it through the weekend."

Berkley Hoagland, who tried out for the Connecticut Coasters, had never worn inline skates, so he went to K-Mart and bought a pair of Rollerblade Lightnings.

"I had no idea what the hell I was doing, and I just started skating up and down the street," Hoagland said. "I couldn't stop. I was in my regular hockey gear. I put on my hockey pants, my helmet and my knee pads, and I would skate up and down the street, falling down a lot of times, because they've got that frickin' brake in the back. I had no idea what to do. When I actually showed up to the tryout, these guys had the Bauer skates with a plastic blade on them with no stopper on the back. It was like a regular ice hockey boot, but it had inline wheels. I kind of took the whole thing as a joke, you know? So I skated, and I was just kind of jousting and sticking guys, because I really couldn't move all that good."

Both Hoagland and Tamburino did well enough at the tryout camps to garner invitations to specific teams' camps – Hoagland by the Coasters and Tamburino by the Florida Hammerheads.

"The next thing I knew, I got the phone call to go down to Miami," Tamburino said. "When I first went down to Miami for the tryout, my luggage came in, but my equipment was lost. It wound up on a plane going to Peru. My roommate had an extra pair of skates – 9-and-a-halfs – and I wear 11-and-a-halfs. So I crunched my feet into them. I don't know how I got my feet into those things; I was dying. I was lost without my equipment; it was broken in and comfortable. My grandfather was a politician for his local union here in New York and he was good on the phone. He called the airline and said, 'My grandson got a tryout for a professional hockey team in Miami. If you don't get his equipment to him, there's going to be a big issue.' The next thing I know, I come back that afternoon and it was there in my room."

Tamburino said that he loved the experience of being a professional roller hockey player so much that he would have done it for nothing.

"I would have played for free that year," Tamburino said. "If they had said, 'We can't pay you, but we'll put you on the roster,' I would have stayed."

CHAPTER 7

Sell the Sizzle and not the Steak

Like Dennis Murphy of RHI, David McLane was a promoter through and through. As an adolescent in Indianapolis, Indiana, McLane was a fan of televised wrestling, with its semi-scripted action and obvious heroes and villains. At just 15, McLane created a fan club to promote William "Dick the Bruiser" Afflis, one of his favorites. He also sold mail-order photographs of the Bruiser and other professional wrestlers, and was eventually hired to promote and market Bruiser's World Wrestling Association. McLane then became the ring announcer and match commentator for the company's television broadcasts. He also became a concert promoter, yet found time in the midst of all this to earn a BA in telecommunications and a BS in business from Indiana University. His first real claim to fame came when he launched the Gorgeous Ladies of Wrestling (GLOW), featuring Jackie Stallone, the mother of Sylvester Stallone, in 1986. GLOW, like many of McLane's future productions would, leaned heavily toward high camp, humorous gimmicks and personalities. After selling GLOW, McLane was ready for something new, and he found the spark on the sidewalks of San Diego and the driveways of Los Angeles in 1990.

"I was having lunch in San Diego and saw a guy and a girl wheel by the restaurant on inline skates, which I had never seen before in my life," McLane said. He went outside and asked the couple about their skates, and the man explained that he also used them to play inline hockey. McLane walked away, thinking, "Those skates are marketable." Driving home the next day to Los Angeles, he saw a youngster in a driveway hitting a ball against a garage door with a hockey stick, wearing the newfangled skates with all the wheels in one row. McLane drove into the driveway and asked the kid what game he was playing. "Roller hockey," was the child's reply. That's when, McLane said, "The seed was planted to create a roller hockey league."

McLane's research at a Beverly Hills library introduced him to inline hockey's antecedent, street hockey, which had been played in the schoolyards and parking lots of New York for decades. Already knowledgeable about the steps it took to bring new sporting events to television, McLane completed a business plan and pursued a television partnership.

"ESPN, through the help of Miami business contacts John Zoder and Nick Buoniconti, became my partner, and together we created the World Roller Hockey League (WRHL)," McLane said. "With a television deal in pocket, I set out to secure a venue. I knew operating in an arena would be too expensive and we needed a facility which would provide valuable marketing push."

Walt Disney World joined with McLane and ESPN, and offered its Disney-MGM Studios Theme Park near Orlando, Florida, as the venue. McLane's WRHL was actually the very first deal between ESPN and Disney, and it would lead to ESPN launching its first ESPN Zone restaurant at Walt Disney World. In 1995, Disney became the parent company of ESPN.

All McLane needed now was a sponsor to help pay for the expenses not covered by ESPN and Walt Disney World. He flew to Boston and met with Larry Franklin, the owner of Franklin Sports, the largest independently owned sporting goods company in the U.S. McLane convinced Franklin to supply uniforms, equipment and cash for the new World Roller Hockey League, the first made-for-television roller hockey league in the United States. (Though the World Roller Hockey League used the same four-on-four player format as Roller Hockey International, checking was prohibited in the WRHL, something that would separate it greatly from RHI's rock-'em-sock-'em game.) Eight teams competed from May 5 to June 1, 1993, in front of television cameras and guests who wandered in from other attractions at the theme park.

In "Follow the Bouncing Puck: The WRHL's Rocky Start," a freelance article in the September 1993 issue of Inline magazine, I wrote that the new league "had set out to make a big splash in the roller hockey world," but that things were "just a little bit, well, Goofy. The games were to be played on an experimental plastic surface made by Sport Court Inc., of Salt Lake City, Utah, but the players slid all over the court as if they were skating on banana peels instead of inline skates. Players who could normally make a hockey stop on a wood floor in six inches slid 20 to 25 feet when they tried to stop on the Sport Court. Before any games were played, the flooring was ripped out and replaced with a tennis court surface. That too was jettisoned after a few games and replaced with a second Sport Court surface – one that finally did the job."

Other issues included the players' concern about the flimsiness of the Franklin gloves and the bouncing Franklin puck, which made it difficult to control and decreased scoring. To solve the equipment problem, the Disney prop department attached the Franklin logo to 80 pairs of Sherwood gloves. To counter the difficulty in scoring, the goals were widened one foot from NHL-regulation size 4' by 6' to 4' by 7'.

According to San Diego Koho Hosers' captain Jim Hatch, his team quit the event because "we knew that the hockey was not going to be its best under the conditions they had. I've been involved with roller hockey for five years, and I couldn't stay and watch the game take a step backwards."

David McLane disputed that story, saying that when the Hosers asked for more money, he refused and had them locked out of their hotel rooms.

Pat Brisson, a Hosers' player who stuck around to play with the Express, the eventual champions, said that because the league was brand new, problems were to be expected.

"The first week was more of an R&D situation for the WRHL," Brisson said. "David McLane wasn't expecting all the problems that came up. He sold the deal to ESPN – he had the right idea, but he doesn't know anything about a puck or a stick or inline skates. He'd never been to a hockey game. So you have to understand where he's coming from. Toward the end of the competition, it was great, it was fun and everybody had a great time. Next year, if they have a better surface, a different puck and different equipment, it's going to be much better."

Rich Garvey also switched from the Hosers to the Express, telling his former teammates that if they felt they were the best team in the world, "then that means you beat anyone, anywhere, under any circumstances." Garvey said that he wasn't going to walk away from ESPN "on principle." When the Hosers flew out the next morning, Garvey stayed in Orlando and played with Brisson and his newly formed team.

ESPN telecast 33 games of the taped WRHL competition beginning July 21, including the best-of-five championship series.

In the November 1993 issue of Hockey Player magazine, Paul Chapey, whom McLane had hired as a consultant and who recruited all 80 players, wrote about the league in his column: "The World Roller Hockey League was disappointing. And I played a part in it." Chapey had great respect for McLane, "a class guy who [had] great instincts, quick decision-making ability and a very likeable personality… [but] knew nothing about hockey." However, he derided the league's play as "sloppy, but with plenty of scoring. Sell the sizzle and not the steak."

In an interview years later, Chapey said that McLane's heart was in the right place, but that the WRHL was a disaster.

"He paid me as a consultant, but he paid me better than he listened," Chapey said. "He was very honorable and we parted ways in the middle of the whole thing. He wanted to do things his way. I wasn't going to have the sport embarrassed by McLane. They had flooring problems. They brought in Sport Court, but the best floor in those years was Roll-On, because the wheels weren't designed for Sport Court. Guys would be falling down. Guys on a good Roll-On floor could stop on a dime and fly. McLane never did get the floor right."

"This was really the year that the ice guys embraced roller hockey, mostly due to the fact that it paid their bills," recalled Daryn Goodwin. "In the spring, teams were picked for the World Roller Hockey League. This got the attention of my ice buddies, who laughed at me for playing roller hockey. All of a sudden, a month's vacation at DisneyWorld and a chance to make more than they did playing ice sounded pretty damn good."

Goodwin said that it was a bittersweet experience.

"The rink sucked, the equipment we had to wear sucked, and the game looked bad on TV," Goodwin said. "The good news is that we had fun in Florida, made some money playing, and were on espn2. Ron Duguay played, and his supermodel wife Kim Alexis was roaming around. Ron complained until he got the league to sign off on the helmets, because he didn't want to wear one. So on top of it all, many of us were helmetless and sporting shades."

Goodwin also praised the league commissioner, Pierre Larouche. The bad news?

"Dave McLane owned the venture and screwed everyone that went to play in RHI later that summer by not paying us the remainder of what he owed us, stating it was a breach of contract," Goodwin said. "A real screw job, considering our work for him was complete and we were independent contractors. After interest, I think that $6k he owes me is up to about $126k."

Scott Rupp, who also played in both the WRHL and RHI, concurred.

"McLane was trying to protect the league so that you didn't play in any other professional league. Well, so then the question was, 'Do you play in RHI and give up that money,' you know? Guys had to make those decisions. I know that myself and Myles Hart did."

"It was an exciting time and not without its problems," McLane said later. "I recall one team arriving to Walt Disney World and the night before they were to play they asked for more money or they weren't going to play the game. A note was slipped under my door at 11:00 p.m."

McLane didn't mess around. By 2 a.m., the Hosers' players had been notified by the hotel they were no longer under the policy of the WRHL and that they needed to vacate the hotel the next morning or post a credit card.

"The next morning executives of ESPN showed up and I was faced with explaining to them that one game that was to be filmed that day would not be, and the team was sent home," McLane said. "That act cemented a relationship with ESPN and created a new one when I called current NHL hockey agent Pat Brisson in Los Angeles and asked him for help in fielding a new team. Within five days Pat Brisson arrived in Orlando with 11 new players that would now play under the team name the Express."

Brisson and the Express finished the league's regular season in fourth place, and then won a single-elimination game against the Fury, 9-4, receiving four-point efforts by both Brisson and his teammate Stephane Desjardins. In the second round of the playoffs, there were two best-of-five series, with the Titans playing the Typhoon, and the Express lining up against the undefeated Blast. The Express received brilliant goaltending from Jason Maxwell, who had the league's worst goals-against average during the regular season, and knocked out the Blast. Meanwhile, the Titans had knocked out the Typhoon, setting up their finals matchup against the Express. The Express won game one, 9-7, and this time, both Brisson and Desjardins scored hat tricks. In game two, Brisson and teammate Eric Le Marque each scored three goals, as the Express won, 11-5. In game three, the Express received two goals from Desjardins, his 12th and 13th in the playoffs, and the Express won the game, 4-2, blanking the Titans three games to none.

Desjardins remembered that the Express got shellacked "17 to 3 or something stupid like that" in their very first game of the tournament. Made up of several other French-Canadian players besides Desjardins, the Express also included Le Marque, Brisson (the agent for Los Angeles Kings' star Luc Robitaille), and former NHL player Ron Duguay. Duguay had played 864 NHL games for the New York Rangers, Detroit Red Wings, Pittsburgh Penguins and the Kings.

"Guys like Duguay and Le Marque, they'd never played roller hockey before, so it was pretty hard for them," Desjardins said. But the Express began to come together as a team, "and by the end of the tournament, we were unbeatable," Desjardins said. "Duguay was my linemate. He's a disciplined guy; he picked up roller hockey pretty fast." The night before the championship game, Desjardins said that the Express went out drinking with the Titans.

"They were buying us shots, trying to get us drunk," Desjardins said. The Titans' strategy worked, at least on Desjardins, who showed up late at the Disney Studios the next day, and without his pass. So he jumped the turnstile at the security checkpoint and ran to the Express locker room with Disney security guards in hot pursuit. His teammates explained that he was with them and that everything was OK, but they certainly weren't pleased.

"I go in the locker room and everybody's so mad at me," Desjardins said. "I smelled like alcohol, but I ended up scoring the winning goal. I played out of my mind."

Though David McLane had lots of hopes and plans for a second WRHL season in 1994, RHI's momentum from its 1992 Exhibition Tour and the problems of WRHL's first season would also make it the league's last. In fact,

Ron Beilsten, who'd been invited by Chapey to Florida to coach the Blast, was already receiving "the vibe" about RHI while he was in Orlando.

"I got a call while I was down there," Beilsten said. 'Hey, these guys, Bernie Federko and Perry Turnbull, want to talk to you when you get back.' "

Federko and Turnbull were former players for the National Hockey League's St. Louis Blues, and Federko was slated to be the coach of the newly formed St. Louis Vipers of RHI. Turnbull was going to play. When Beilsten returned to St. Louis, he was coaching an amateur team practice when Federko and Turnbull told him that some of his players could conceivably play for the Vipers. They asked him if he'd like to be an assistant coach for the Vipers.

"Hockey's in my blood," Beilsten said. "Am I going to pass this opportunity up? No way. That was it. So from day one, I was there."

CHAPTER 8

A Convergence of Opportunity

"Jesus saves. Gretzky Gets the Rebound and Scores."

That was just one of the bumper stickers seen around town when Wayne Gretzky led the National Hockey League's Los Angeles Kings to the team's first and only Stanley Cup Finals appearance in the spring of 1993 against the Montreal Canadiens. Coupled with the growing popularity of inline skates, the success of the cinematic The Mighty Ducks at the box office in late 1992 and the imminent arrival of the actual Mighty Ducks of Anaheim NHL franchise in the fall of 1993, the cool sport of ice hockey was suddenly hot – and hip to play outdoors. Everywhere you looked, formerly "normal" people were gliding and swooping around on the speedy contraptions like seagulls on wheels. Addictive as snack chips but 10 times healthier, roller hockey took over parking lots, tennis courts and nearly every imaginable flat surface.

"The timing was just right in Southern California at the time," said Anaheim Bullfrogs' assistant coach Grant Sonier. "With Gretzky in Los Angeles and the Ducks starting that year in the brand-new Pond, the whole inline skating craze was like a perfect storm. It all just came together. It was a really unique time."

The sport's popularity wasn't limited to Southern California. According to the National Sporting Goods Association, inline skating was the hottest sports activity in 1991 – it estimated that there were approximately 6.2 million skaters at the time.

"Inline skating was growing from a $300 million industry to a billion dollar industry in the first three years of RHI," said Steve Pona, who directed RHI's equipment supplier pool at the time. "The NHL expanding into Sun Belt states was huge. There was a convergence of opportunity that validated the RHI entrepreneurs."

So did the fact that RHI's 12 teams had drawn some 356,000 fans during the 1993 season.

In putting RHI together, Dennis Murphy had written to hundreds of his sports associates, inviting them to purchase territorial licenses to promote league games in their city. From those contacts, Murphy received enough qualified interest to assemble 12 teams in key markets at $55,000 a piece. Each team promoter was also required to pay $4,000 per game (14) for player prize money.

An article in the October 25, 1993, issue of BusinessWeek claimed that Murphy, King and Bellehumeur put up an initial investment of $300,000 to $400,000 to form RHI.

"That's one of those ludicrous stories that has no relationship to anything," RHI's CEO Larry King said later. "It's not real. There was no money ponied up. It's like every other time that Murphy started a league. He might get one guy to put up 10 or 15 thousand dollars to print up the materials… Murphy puts all the materials together to start up the league; the league will pay for the promotional pieces, and he goes out and hustles a couple of guys into the project, and the first one that buys a team really funds the league."

King said it was "a total shell game" until five or six franchises were sold and enough money was collected to hire people to run the league offices and teams.

"Then you have enough money to hire all these people who've been hanging out on the off chance that they might get a job, and the money guy never puts up a nickel," King said.

The Original 12

One of the original 12 franchises was the Anaheim Bullfrogs, owned by the father and sons' team of Maury, Nelson and Stuart Silver, respectively. The Silvers were partners in Avon Car and Truck Rental, the largest transportation agency serving the entertainment industry in Los Angeles. The Silvers hired Chris McSorley as coach, who insisted that Grant Sonier be hired as his assistant coach as well. McSorley had coached the Toledo Storm to the East Coast Hockey League championship that spring, while Sonier had coached the Detroit Falcons of the Colonial Hockey League. Between them, they'd bring ice hockey players they'd coached to RHI and have a powerful and instant impact on the league. The Bullfrogs owners paid a heavy price for playing in the glitzy Anaheim Pond – between $14,000 and $16,000 a night for rent. The Bullfrogs' mascot was named Zeus, and its cheerleaders were called the Polliwogs. Instead of singing "We will rock you" to Queen's "We are the Champions," Bullfrog boosters chanted, "We will croak you."

Lawrence Ryckman, who purchased the Calgary Rad'z, was coming off a successful season as the owner of the 1992 Grey Cup Champion Calgary Stampeders of the Canadian Football League. The Rad'z played in the Calgary Saddledome and were coached by Morris Lukowich.

The Connecticut Coasters were put together late and in a hurry by RHI's leadership when the league had trouble finding an acceptable arena in Orlando. The team, added at the last minute and owned by the league, played in the New Haven Memorial Coliseum, which had recently lost its main tenant, the New Haven Senators of the American Hockey League. Dennis Murphy's brother, John Murphy, was installed as the team's general manager. He had been involved in sports for the previous 10 years in the World Hockey Association and the American Basketball Association, as well as being the general manager of the San Francisco Shamrocks of the Pacific Hockey League. Coaster's Coach Jim McGeough, the brother of former NHL referee Mick McGeough, had played in 57 NHL games. The team's name was chosen after a preseason contest that drew 2,000 entries. New Haven was the league's smallest city. Money was tight, and Anno Willison, who was dispatched by Dennis Murphy to assist many early RHI teams, recalled borrowing his daughter's credit card to hire a bus to take the Coasters to a game in Toronto that first season.

Julia Neal, the editor of the Garden Island daily newspaper in Kauai, Hawaii, was the full owner the Florida Hammerheads, who played in the Miami Arena and lived in the fashionable Clevelander Hotel. Dennis Murphy recalled that Neal was "a very dedicated gal. She worked awfully hard and she was a very good owner, always attempting to make her team better and be competitive."

Dr. Jerry Buss and his daughter Jeanie shared ownership of the Los Angeles

Blades. Coach John Black, who had coached Team USA in RHI's inaugural tour, gave up a successful law practice to coach the Blades. The first true professional roller hockey coach, Black had played on numerous national champion roller hockey teams in the previous decade. The team played in the Great Western Forum, which was also the home of the Los Angeles Lakers at the time. An added perk for the players – the basketball team's cheerleaders, the Laker Girls, performed at Blades' games.

The Oakland Skates, owned by Murray Simkin, Gail Bettinelli and Bill Schoen, played at the Oakland-Alameda County Coliseum Arena. Simkin, the son of a former owner of the NHL's Winnipeg Jets, owned Tony Roma's restaurants in Canada and would eventually become the CEO of a series of Wayne Gretzky's Roller Hockey Centers. Schoen owned "Hockey & Skating," a tabloid publication that covered ice and, eventually, inline hockey. Coach Garry Unger was famous at the time as the National Hockey League's "Iron Man," having played 914 consecutive games in the regular season from 1968 to 1979.

The Portland Rage played in the Portland Memorial Coliseum and were owned by Bill Conyard and his sons Tim and Joe. The Conyards owned the Sport and Hockey Hut in Portland, and Tim and Joe played for Team Canada in RHI's exhibition tour. "They did a very good job," recalled Dennis Murphy. "Bill was always there for me. He was a real good guy. He was friendly and he was always working with his team and was dedicated to make it happen." Anno Willison remembered that the Rage were the first RHI team to leave the league. "I tried to get the lumber people up there to come to the games," Willison said. "They [the Conyards] didn't have the financial wherewithal to make that team run. They had the background in roller hockey, using that little rink in Beaverton. The Conyards were really super, super people, but they were the first to fold."

The San Diego Barracudas were owned by Fred, Bill and John Comrie. Team President Fred Comrie was also the owner of the San Diego Gulls ice hockey team, and the Barracudas would play in the same venue as the ice hockey team, the San Diego Sports Arena. Bill Comrie owned the Canadian Football League's British Columbia Lions, and the three brothers built "The

41

Brick," Canada's largest furniture retailer. Mike Comrie, Bill's son, would go on to play more than 500 games in the NHL and marry American actress and singer Hilary Duff. Robbie Nichols, the team's general manager and coach, was co-MVP for the Gulls in 1992.

Keith Blase, the owner and president of the St. Louis Vipers, was a former executive director for USA Hockey, the governing body for amateur and Olympic ice hockey in the United States. Coach Bernie Federko played 14 seasons with the St. Louis Blues and Detroit Red Wings, while assistant coach Perry Turnbull was Federko's teammate on the Blues from 1979 to 1984. The Vipers' assistant coach, Ron Beilsten, was deeply involved in amateur roller hockey and was a great help to the Vipers as they composed their roster, partly with local talent. The Vipers played in the St. Louis Arena, and Beilsten remembered going to Vipers' practices, walking around the hallways and hearing the gruff voice of Brett Hull coming out of the Blues' office.

The Toronto Planets were owned by David Barr, who had spent 12 years in the Israeli Air Force. Dennis Murphy said that Barr "was a real character. He liked to call me in the evening to bug me... but he was a dedicated guy, too. He was always calling on the phone at the odd hours of the night." Head coach Dan Cameron once coached NHL star Eric Lindros. The Planets played in Varsity Arena. The team's roster boasted goaltender Manny Legace, who would go on to have a long NHL career with the Los Angeles Kings, Detroit Red Wings, St. Louis Blues and Carolina Hurricanes.

Dan Kotler and Cal Coleman purchased the Utah RollerBees, and the team played most of its 1993 season games on Kotler's patented plastic Sport Court surface in a 4,700-seat outdoor arena called "The Hive." Blowing sand, heat and wind caused problems, however, and that's when 49 percent owner Larry Miller, the owner of the Utah Jazz, stepped in and moved the team to the Delta Center in Salt Lake City. According to an article in Utah's Deseret News, in the first week of their existence, the RollerBees had the dubious distinction of having played before RHI's largest and smallest crowds in the first week of the 1993 season: 13,148 at Anaheim on Friday, July 2, and 1,917 on Saturday, July 3 at home against the Portland Rage. According to RHI co-founder Dennis Murphy, Kotler was "one of our strong guys. He worked awfully hard for the league through Sport Court. He benefited by it, but was dedicated to make our league happen."

Vancouver VooDoo Team President Mike King was the captain of Team Canada in RHI's inaugural tour and was so impressed with the potential of the league that he bought a team. "We feel very strongly that RHI will address a neglected segment of the market – the real sports fan," he said. "Most pro sports have become too expensive for the average fan. RHI will provide exciting, affordably priced entertainment which the whole family can enjoy." The VooDoo's vice president and coach was former Toronto Maple Leafs' enforcer Dave "Tiger" Williams, the NHL's all-time leader in penalty minutes. The team played its initial season in the PNE Agrodome.

The 1993 regular season ran from July 1 to August 15, with each team scheduled to play seven home and seven away games. The top four teams from each division would make the playoffs, a three-game series to take place from August 16 to September 1. Unique to RHI was how the league paid its players. In an attempt to keep salaries financially feasible for team owners, all players were paid the same $314 per week salary. However, the players also chased after $672,000 in prize money. Players on teams that were successful in the playoffs could make as much as $7,917 for the two-month season.

Larry King said he based RHI's prize-money formula on the system he had used in World Team Tennis.

"Having contracts like all other leagues did was just a stupid way to do business," King said. "It was bad for the players, it was bad for the owners, and it was bad for the fans, for the same reason that contracted players are bad for baseball, football and basketball. If you have a good team, all the players are worth more to break up and give their services away to other teams, and so the fans are never going to see a winning team return. The owner is going to take the player that's worth nothing, build up his name, and the kid's going to sell it by going to another team."

While RHI's founders were putting together the league, the mass media was taking note of the growing popularity of all things inline. Sports Illustrated for Kids portrayed the wheeled game as the sport of choice for kids in St. Louis and the surrounding suburbs. Having Brett Hull as a local star for the St. Louis Blues certainly didn't hurt the sport's popularity.

Even traditional American sports like baseball had to be wary of the roller hockey explosion. Signups were so dramatically affected that one regional director for Little League Baseball in Southern California requested that a local youth roller hockey league change the dates of its season.

The boom drove many companies to attempt to cash in on that popularity. Some of the new products released included Aura Omnitrade's "Online skates" that inflated at the heel and sides of the foot, Bauer's expanded line of inline hockey gear, Branch's new Street Sticks, Brown's "Thunderball" ball hockey equipment, CCM's inline skates featuring "The Pump" technology from Reebok, Louisville's Road Work line of off-ice hockey gear, Koho's Street Revolution line, Mil-Mar Engineering's stiffer aircraft-grade aluminum inline skate frame, Cooper's Streets hockey gear, and Easton's new line of SH 4500 Street Hockey gear.

Ken Schneider was one of the first roller hockey players in Santa Monica. In late 1988, soon after Gretzky hit Tinseltown, Schneider was a Rollerblade tech-rep who introduced people to inline skating. Rollerblade ran clinics on Tuesday nights in a beach parking lot, teaching people how to inline skate. Roller hockey players soon showed up on the scene.

"We'd have 15 to 20 guys showing up religiously and playing in the dark," Schneider said. "We got some friendly games going, and suddenly we were playing every night of the week."

Then someone got the bright idea to show up on weekends, and the Santa Monica roller hockey boom was on. Passersby stopped to watch, and then more and more people donned skates to give it a try.

In an article in the August/September 1993 issue of Street Hockey, "Hockey Hot Spots, Los Angeles' Outdoor Roller Hockey Heaven by the Beach," I wrote:

"Next to the Pacific Ocean, in a place famous for G-string Gidgets, wrought-iron weight lifters, radical surfers, sexy sun worshipers and peaceful palm trees, the Southern California version of Canada's national sport is the hottest thing going… On any weekend it's easy to find four to six pick-up games going, with a crowd of extra players waiting to get into a game.

Occasionally, NHL players (such as the Kings' Luc Robitaille) and other dignitaries stop by to play. It's a far cry from just four or five years ago, when skating around this beach with a hockey stick was about as popular as an offshore oil spill."

Things had changed in the North American sports landscape, and for a while at least, RHI was to lead the way.

Chapter 9

We Were Just Winging It

"Killer, come on. We gotta go."

Grant Sonier, assistant coach of the new Anaheim Bullfrogs professional roller hockey team, tapped Bob McKillop on the forehead and eyed the assortment of empty beer bottles and other evidence of a wild night of partying strewn around the room. Sprawled on his bed in the Ramada Anaheim on Katella after a night out carousing with his teammate Savo Mitrovic (who lay in a similar condition on the other bed), McKillop opened one bleary eye to Sonier, who had pushed open the unlocked and not fully closed hotel room door. McKillop had forgotten that he and Savo had been invited to go golfing that morning with Sonier and Stuart Silver, one of the owners of the Bullfrogs.

"What time is it, coach?" he asked.

Perhaps in a different situation, McKillop would have sprung out of bed, full of apologies, but he'd played for Sonier with the Detroit Falcons of the Colonial Hockey League, and Sonier wasn't an old-school coach of curfews and curmudgeonly complaints. In fact, it was a reunion of sorts, as Mitrovic had flown into Anaheim the night before, and he had been McKillop's teammate under Sonier with the Falcons.

"It's 6 a.m., Killer," Sonier replied. "Enjoying California so far?"

All three men had come to Anaheim at the behest of Bullfrogs' coach Chris McSorley, the younger brother of Marty McSorley of the NHL's Los Angeles Kings. McSorley had actually spent his *honeymoon* in the Bahamas on the phone, trying to build the best possible team. McSorley, 31, was coming off a successful coaching season, leading the Toledo Storm of the East Coast Hockey League to the championship in the 1992-1993 season. He had to be convinced to take the coaching job with the Anaheim Bullfrogs. Once he was certain that ice hockey players could be successful on wheels, he was very confident about his success with the Bullfrogs. Grant Sonier was in Anaheim welcoming the players while McSorley was away. (McSorley's new bride was presumably fuming on a Bahaman beach.)

McSorley's instincts told him that it would be easier to teach ice hockey players how to skate on inline skates than it would be to teach players with a non-check roller hockey background how to play his style of physical hockey. McSorley's strategy was a double-edged sword – it would provide jobs for many minor-league ice hockey players, but it would put the squeeze on many passionate inline hockey players who'd never played the checking game. Many wannabe RHI players found out quickly in training camps that stepping from the streets into the rinks would be harder than they imagined; a few suffered separated shoulders or worse when checked into the boards by a 200-pound ice hockey player for the very first time.

That the players McSorley brought in were tough is evidenced by a story told by Savo Mitrovic. Mitrovic and Bob McKillop had became fast friends in a unique, archaic, painful and, apparently, effective manner. Playing together on the Detroit Falcons during the 1992/'93 season, McKillop, a pure goal scorer, was in a slump and had been benched, and Mitrovic was also out of the lineup with an injury. So Mitrovic took McKillop to a bar.

"We had a couple of drinks, and then I hauled off and I drilled him in the head and knocked him off the stool," Mitrovic said. "He got back up, and he popped me and knocked me off the stool. We did this all night. I can recall the coaching staff coming in the next day and looking at Bobby McKillop and saying, 'What the heck happened to you?' And he looked right at the coach and said, 'Savo hit me.' They come in the trainer's room, and they look at me, and I'm the same way; I'm all black and blue. They ask me, they say, 'What happened to you?' And I say, "Bobby hit me.' And that was it. And they were flustered. They didn't understand what was going on. That night, Bobby went out there and scored four goals and three assists, and he was on fire. So, it's just basically letting a buddy know, 'Hey, I'm a buddy.' You know? 'I'm there.' A buddy's a buddy when a buddy can take a punch."

Many of the ice hockey players found it challenging to get used to playing on wheels. Brad McCaughey of the Bullfrogs remembered his first day on inline skates. He couldn't stop, and he ran into the boards several times.

Entering the offensive zone and taking a shot, he'd realize, "Wait a minute, I can't stop." Playing defense, McCaughey found a different problem. Skating backwards on a 2-on-1 rush, he realized that he'd skated right in front of his goaltender and needed to do something. So, he pivoted, skated into the corner, and left his startled goaltender with a 2-on-0. "A normal defenseman would be able to put the brakes on," McCaughey said.

Trying to find creative ways to get around the difficulty of stopping on inline skates, McCaughey eventually came up with a move that dazzled assistant coach Grant Sonier. "In roller hockey, you couldn't stop on a dime; you'd have to make a big turn," McCaughey said. "I came up with this move where I would start going around a defenseman, and then drop down on a knee – which would stop me – and spin around. The defenseman [with his momentum] can't really stop and follow me the other way. So I remember working on that move a lot in practice. I don't know how much I did it in a game, but I did it in practice quite a bit. It was just one of those things – how can I stop and go the other direction real quick, 'cause I knew the defenseman couldn't do it."

Kon Ammossow, known as "The Skate Doctor," owned several skate shops called Inline Rollerworks, and when a Bauer representative told him about the formation of Roller Hockey International, Ammossow called the Anaheim Bullfrogs and offered his services. The Silvers, who knew a good deal when they saw one, quickly snapped up Ammossow to do skate tech for the team. Ammossow, who had all the riveters and other tools he needed at hand, set up the Bullfrogs' Bauer ZT7 skates with wheels and bearings, and even realigned the frames on some players' skates.

"I sat up many nights remounting roller chassis on to old ice boots and stuff like that," Ammossow remembered. "Whatever needed to be done. This team was set up, man," Ammossow said. "They looked really good, like they were on ice. All the other teams looked like they were on rollers; they were limited in what they could do."

Bullfrogs' coach Chris McSorley called Ammossow his "secret weapon," and it's no wonder. Ammossow researched all the available skate wheels on the market, tested them on the players, and scored a bonanza when he made a deal for wheels that no other team had.

"We had an in with Hyper," Ammossow said. "They gave me a whole bunch of different wheels and I tried them on a couple of players, and I picked 72 millimeter wheels that they only sold in Europe for indoor speed skating or something like that. I said, 'How many of these wheels do you have in stock,' and they said, 'Oh, about 5,000 of them,' and I said, "I want them all.' So I took every single one of their wheels, which did us for the rest of the season. And nobody else had those wheels or could get them. They were probably pissed off about that, too, but you know what? We were there to win."

Despite the inherent difficulty in making the transition from ice to inline hockey, the Bullfrogs' coaching staff continued to bring in ice hockey players.

"We had the premier players of the minor ice hockey leagues," said Bob McKillop. "We had a team that could have competed in the AHL – Victor Gervais, Brad McCaughey, Kevin Kerr, Devin Edgerton, Rob Laurie, Mike Butters… When we started skating at Rollerplex in Northridge (we didn't have a training camp facility of our own), the team was hand picked. As guys started rolling in, we had bodies, but they were roller hockey guys. We started whittling them down. Gervais and Edgerton came in. First there were five of us ice hockey guys, then eight, then 10. I remember watching L.A. practicing. 'Oh boy,' I thought, 'Are they in trouble.' They watched us practice and guys we cut – Brett Kurtz, Mike Ross, Mike Callahan – went to L.A., because after watching us, [L.A. Blades coach] John Black said, 'Holy shit.' "

"I still remember that first practice, because the first couple practices were no-contact, and then, when it went to contact, it was a little scary," Bullfrogs' forward Ken Murchison remembered. "It's tough. For guys who grew up down here who didn't play contact, it's a tough game to just all of a sudden be thrown into and adjust. There were some guys with the old 'deer-in-the-headlights' look. There were a few guys that didn't come back."

"Our very first practice was in Orange in a public roller skating rink and it had a mirror ball on the ceiling," remembered Anaheim Bullfrogs' assistant coach Grant Sonier. "Maury and all the other owners had already had all those tryout camps all over the country – our team was already picked. Maury said, 'We've got 112 guys,' and I'm like, 'Are you kidding me?' I immediately just went in and divided them into groups of 20 and we had 25- or 30-minute practices – I just wanted to see what the guys could do and started to evaluate. I remember talking to Chris and saying, 'You know what, I'm not very good and I'm a lot older than some of these guys that are playing. I think if we bring in some ice hockey players, we might be able to do something really neat.' And I remember having a conversation with Maury and his two sons, saying, 'I want to cut all of the players and bring in 15 ice hockey players.' They thought I was absolutely off my rocker."

When Maury Silver saw the ice hockey players Sonier had brought in stumbling around on inline skates for the first time, Silver said, "Well, it's a good thing we have boards on the rink, or those guys would end up in L.A. County."

"I'd never really been on roller hockey skates before," said Bullfrogs' defenseman Joe Cook. "I went down on my first rush down the rink, took a slap shot, went to the corner and had no idea how to stop and went face first into the chain-link fence."

Sonier tried to convince Silver that the ice hockey players would get the hang of it.

"I'm like, 'Maury, you gotta trust me," Sonier said. "Give these guys three or four days and they're going to be fine. And they practiced and they practiced and then they could start to turn, start to cut one way and cut the other way, and do the other stuff that they were good at – because they were professional hockey players. That stuff all came on once they got their wheels underneath them. Then we just brought in more players and more players."

"I was the first to show up," McKillop said. "Sonier said, 'If you're going to do it, I need you out here ASAP, like next week. Worst-case scenario, you have two weeks in California and then you can go home.' So I said, 'Sure, send me an airline ticket.' I flew out, brought my Rollerblades with me, and I go out there and play with these guys. We're shooting at a garbage can, playing pickup games, and I'm in my shorts and T-shirt with skates, a stick and gloves. I figured out that this was just like ice hockey, except for learning how to stop on those damn things. I called Savo Mitrovic, a buddy of mine and said, 'The weather's beautiful and the women are phenomenal.' "

Mitrovic flew out from Toronto three days later to join the ever-changing Bullfrogs' tryout camp roster. Playing in full gear with long-pant Cooperalls, the roster was whittled down to about 25 players.

Sonier told the ice hockey players that the Silvers were going to show up to watch a tryout and said, "Lay the body" on the roller hockey players to show the owners that "there was a big difference between the ice and roller guys."

"Well, I can't stop to save my life, and I'd just lost in the playoffs in ice hockey, so I was playoff ready," McKillop said. "My mentality is that way, anyway. So some guys are skating up the floor with their head down, and me and Savo just would level them. Then we'd hammer them in the corner. Before long, we could basically do anything we wanted. I was introduced to Maury and Stuart Silver. Maury looked at me and Savo and said, "Yep, I see where we need to go." Grant said, 'We got a whole bevy of these guys.' "

Mitrovic said that the team would play against each other day after day, improving incrementally: "We would scrimmage. What better than to go down one-on-one against Joe Cook or Darren Perkins? I'm going against the best. I can't get by him, I'm in trouble. Guess what? I figure out how to get by him. And you know what? He wants to stop me from me going around him. So, I'm practicing against Victor Gervais, Kevin Kerr, Brad McCaughey, Bobby McKillop, players of that caliber, guys that you might meet three or four times during the ice hockey season – but we got the luxury of practicing with each other every day. So we became really, really good."

From the very beginning, the Anaheim Bullfrogs' ownership had the players participate in local promotions and meet the people whom they hoped would become fans of the team. One day, the Bullfrogs had to do a team promotion while wearing full equipment on a hot day at a local school's basketball court. Grant Sonier told the assembled students, "These guys are really accurate. When they shoot the puck, they can hit anything that they want. For example, Christian [Lalonde] can hit that basketball rim with a wrist shot."

Lalonde remembers his jaw dropping. "He just set me up to fail, right?" I said, 'Why'd you do that Grant?' So I wind up and I shoot that puck – and I could shoot it a million times and never hit it – and I hit it right on target. It sailed and hit the thing, banged right off the rim. I couldn't believe it, and the guys couldn't believe it, but the kids thought we could just do that on command."

Lalonde illustrated the popularity of roller hockey at the time with the following story.

"We weren't making that much money, but we were popular," Lalonde said. "I remember we went to a promo at a Target in Rancho Cucamonga. They had some football players and some people from a soap opera that pulled up in a limo, and then you had the Bullfrogs table with me, McKillop, Savo and [Steve] Beadle, and we were signing Bullfrogs' stuff. At the soap opera table, there were a couple of old ladies. There weren't many people at the football table, either. It was upside down. Everybody came to get our autographs, not the football players' and the actors'. I was kind of embarrassed for them."

In addition to the promotions, the Bullfrogs' players had lots of time for golf, and back at the golf course in Encino on Savo Mitrovic's first day in Southern California. McKillop was by far the best golfer. "I'm a four or three handicap, Stuart's not real good, Savo's not real good, and Grant's a seven or eight handicap," McKillop said. "We end up at the Braemar Country Club. We played four or five holes, and came to about a 165-yard par three, and Stuart says, 'I got a bet for ya. If you can hit this green, I will give my watch.' He's got this Rolex watch, diamonds all over it. Then he says, 'If you don't, you'll play the season for free.' I looked at Grant. I'm a good golfer. I'm going to hit that green seven or eight times out of ten. That's probably a $20,000 watch. I said, 'Are you going to feed me, Grant, if I miss? Who's going to feed me?' To make a long story short, I said, 'No, no, no.' Stuart had an NHL Stanley Cup ring that he'd taken off a guy on a bet."

It was the first time McKillop and Mitrovic had met Stuart Silver. "He was flamboyant," Mitrovic said. "He rolls up in a Rolls Royce. I'm not a golfer. Bobby's the golfer. And I'll tell you what, Stuart Silver is a terrible golfer. He is probably the worst golfer I've ever seen. And he cheats. I saw more golf balls drop out of his pocket... He hits a bad shot and he ends up finding it. It certainly comes out of his pocket. He's a great guy, but the game of golf is about honor, and there was no honor."

Sonier laughed at the story.

"We were making putts for his diamond-loaded Rolex watch. He'd bought somebody's Stanley Cup ring, and he was a horrible golfer, and Killer was a great golfer, I was an OK golfer, Savo was below me, but Stuart was like another five levels below all of us. He just kept wanting to putt for this and that. I remember on the 18th green, we were giving him like two strokes a hole… it was just hilarious… we had some great times. He was a complete shyster. Honestly, it was like we were involved with our own Montreal mob."

CHAPTER 10

I'm Definitely Not Laughing Now

The Los Angeles Blades, the Bullfrogs' natural rival just an hour to the north up the Golden State Freeway, also had training-camp stories. Steve Bogoyevac had just traveled back to California after a road trip with his East Coast Hockey League Dayton Bombers' ice hockey teammate Rob Laurie. When he and Laurie visited Bogoyevac's grandparents, Bogie's grandfather asked, "Hey, have you guys heard about this new professional roller hockey league?" Bogie and Laurie laughed, thinking it was a joke.

A week later, Laurie called Bogoyevac from Michigan, and said, "Hey, I'm playing roller hockey in California!"

"Great! Me, too!" Bogoyevac said. "I'll see you next week."

A week went by and Bogoyevac hadn't heard from Laurie and figured he wasn't coming after all.

"At the end of the training camp, we actually finally got in contact with each other and realized that we were on different teams," Bogoyevac said. Laurie ended up with the Bullfrogs, a team that would become L.A.'s greatest rival.

In "A Player's Perspective," his column in the December/January 1996 issue of InLine Hockey News, Bogoyevac remembered his earliest days with the Blades: "A week into training camp, when I finally learned how to inline skate and play hockey at the same time – what a blast! And I would get to play at the Great Western Forum. At that point, I was still unsure of who was in the league, the name of the league, who owned our team and how many games we would play. But I did know how much fun I was having playing hockey on inline skates… 'I'm in 'The Show,' I thought to myself. There aren't any higher leagues, we have television and newspaper coverage – I must be in 'The Show.' To top this all off, I get to live at home, play in front of my family and friends, and this is my summer job."

crashed the tryout.

"Every time I shot, I fell flat on my face, and everyone started laughing," Hoagland said. "I was playing defense at the time, and during the tryout, I got in about 10 fights. I was fighting anybody that even looked at me wrong, and Mugger [Coasters' coach Jim McGeough] liked it. I think they saw it like… 'Hmmm, black dude, playing hockey – we're going to have this guy as the first black player in RHI.' I took that and I ran with it. The next thing you know, I'm doing all these interviews, and all this stuff around town."

Todd Johnson, who would become a teammate of Hoagland's on the Connecticut Coasters for a time in the first season, remembered an exhibition game the Coasters played prior to the 1993 season, against a team from New York City led by Jimmy "V" Vivona. Johnson said they looked liked they'd just came out of a scene from "The Warriors," a 1979 movie about a New York gang's battle to cross the territory of rivals and escape to the safety of their own turf.

"They're all these scrappy guys and they have these quad roller skates on, and we're laughing our asses off," Johnson said. "They looked like a gang. They've got their shin pads taped up, and they look like they just got off some movie lot. They proceeded to kick our ass, like 24-3. They killed us. We were supposed to be the pros, but we were just learning [the inline game]. These guys were a national championship team, and they could stop on a dime [while] we would go for a 30-foot radius curve to turn around and go back the other way. They just proceeded to school us and had the last laugh."

"They had all this news in New Haven about this new professional league," said Hoagland. "They broadcast it a lot and gave away free tickets, and about 2,300 people showed up. These guys were downtown New York, and they had been together for years. They shit-kicked us. McGeough cut every single guy that played in that game except two or three guys," said Hoagland, who didn't play because of an injury. "He cut everybody and then took like four of their guys and said, 'You guys gotta come play for us.' So, our first year, we had three guys who were on quads. Our goalie, Neil Walsh, wound up being on quads. So, they had to call Dennis Murphy and ask if the quad skaters could be allowed in."

"I remember that game like it was yesterday," said Jimmy Vivona. "It was my New York Bauer Cyclones team, coached by Rich Richie, against all the guys who were trying out for the Connecticut Coasters. I actually played against my own Bauer team that night. In all fairness, the vast majority of guys that Jim McGeough knew he was picking on the team were scratched that night. He was only looking to add one or two more guys to his Coasters team, and I was fortunate enough to be one of those guys. I knew before the game even started that my team was gonna kick the shit out of the guys who were trying out for RHI. I even told Jim McGeough before the game that with so many people at the game, he shouldn't take it so lightly. The final score ended up being 11-7 for New York, but they had a 7-2 lead going into the second half. I had a four-point night, so I guess that sealed my spot on the Coasters. If my Coasters' team had played against my N.Y. Bauer team after the roster was set, I believe my Coasters team would've won on most nights, for sure. As for playing on quads, I was the only forward on the Coasters who had them, and our goalie, Neal Walsh, who Jim McGeough signed right after the game, wore them as well. I had to eat crow from all my Bauer teammates. They still tease me today that they kicked our ass. They pay no attention to me when I tell them that it wasn't the team that entered game one of RHI."

Vivona said that his chances of making the Coasters were slim at the time.

"McGeough was a hard-nosed guy; I think he was living in Montana," Vivona said. "He wanted to win every single game. For me, it was even more difficult because I wasn't one of 'his guys.' I was a roller hockey player from New York. He wanted to bring in as many ice hockey guys as he could, Canadian kids. I knew if I worked harder than anyone, I would make it hard for him to cut me. By the time it came time to cut me, it was too late."

When he made the Coasters' roster, Vivona remembered an interaction he had with coach McGeough.

"I'm the biggest [Wayne] Gretzky fan alive, [I've] been wearing 99 since I was 12," Vivona said. "McGeough says, 'Hey Vivona, what number do you want to wear?' I said, '99.' He gave me a little smile and touched my face, and said, 'I don't know, a good-looking American boy with no scars. I don't think the Canadian boys are going to like you wearing number 99.' I think he was trying to save me some beatings. He said, 'How about number 9?' I said 'OK.' "

CHAPTER 11

We Played that Game
on Adrenaline Itself

The rules that Ralph Backstrom put into place for Roller Hockey
International did the job as intended – most of the games were high scoring.
A 6-4 game was considered a defensive battle, and tallies of 13-5 and 16-8
were quite common. Another difference between the RHI game and the dull,
clutch-and-grab style of the National Hockey League at that time was the
extracurricular activities at pro roller hockey games.

In "Roller Hockey International at Mid-Season," an article in the October/
November 1993 issue of InLine magazine, I wrote that halftime exhibitions at
games "included such dubious crowd-pleasers as line dancing (to 'Achy Breaky
Heart'), a clogging exhibition (RHI President Dennis Murphy's grandchildren
participated) and a man throwing Frisbees to a dog named 'Soaring Sam.' (The
real crowd-pleasers – not surprising when you consider the rampant
testosterone in the stands – were skimpily outfitted cheerleaders such as the
Anaheim Bullfrogs' 'Polliwogs.')"

It's hard to know which Bullfrog had the first fan club, but there's no doubt
that Savo Mitrovic, Mike Butters and Victor Gervais had their constituencies.
In "Aloha from Anaheim" in the August/ September 1995 issue of InLine
Hockey News, IHC intern Kelly Howard explained the Gervais' groupies'
genesis: "Grass skirts, painted faces and tropical fruits. Sounds like a day in
the life of a Club Med vacation junkie, doesn't it? Well, it's actually just a few
of the madcap characteristics of the Anaheim Bullfrogs' 'Coconuts' – a group
of fun-loving hockey fanatics who just might be responsible for the current
resurgence of the Village People song YMCA. The Coconuts, nine guys
ranging in age from 16 to 22, are all Orange County natives who became fans
of Bullfrogs' star forward Victor Gervais due to technical difficulties at the
Pond. 'It was one of the first events held at the Pond,' explains head Coconut

Paul Smith. 'The sound system was so bad that we could only understand one name, and that was Victor Gervais. So we started cheering, and then he started scoring.' The group started out during RHI's 1993 regular season making signs and cheering for Gervais."

The Coconuts' next move was to paint their faces. It wasn't until the following year, when they were trying to figure out a way to make it onto the Pond's scoreboard video screen that the Coconuts truly came into their own and earned their name.

As Howard explained, the Coconuts tried to come up with the wildest ideas they could: "Then one member suggested they dress up in coconut bras and grass skirts, and things escalated from there. It went from a nightly dance in the stands with an Anaheim Polliwogs cheerleader to occasional free tickets to, eventually, a half-time show. The Bullfrogs suggested the use of the song YMCA, but the Coconuts took it to a new level with the addition of a country-western line dance called the Spanish Reggae. The Coconuts perform strictly for fun and a few free tickets. Their main goal is to get more people to come out to the games and to have fun. While they're open to new recruits, the group has only one rule – you have to carve your own coconuts."

Savo Mitrovic was one of the fan favorites on the team, partly for his unique way of celebrating when he scored a goal. His shtick was to skate down the middle of the rink, making several large hops along the way.

"I just figured we were frogs, you know, so I just ended up hopping," Mitrovic said. "When I was in college at the University of New Hampshire, I scored my first goal against Harvard in my first year and was so excited that I started spinning on my knees. I did that every single time I scored, for four years. You can't spin on your knees on inlines, so I figured I'd hop."

Another crowd pleaser at RHI games was the league's aggressive style of play, which included checking and violent collisions at open court and along the boards. The hits occasionally led to fisticuffs.

Though considered Neanderthal by many, fighting has always been a part of ice hockey and it didn't disappear in RHI. While the league didn't condone pugilism – a penalty shot was awarded when there was an instigator or a third man into a fight – there were plenty of fights – and even the occasional bench-clearing brawl.

"There has to be an instigator, but it seems we get two willing parties in most of the fights," deadpanned RHI spokesman Steve Pona at the time.

An early season incident during a game in New Haven, Connecticut, between the hometown Coasters and the visiting St. Louis Vipers, illustrated Pona's statement well.

"The game got frickin' chippy and *out of control,*" said, Berkley Hoagland. "Mugger [Coaster's coach Jim McGeough] brought in some heavy hitter guys from the East Coast League who were just fighters, Darren Houghton and this other dude [Rob McCaig]. He was a big defenseman, and he just loved to chuck 'em."

In an incident covered by the Associated Press and the Los Angeles Times, someone on the Vipers told the African-American Hoagland, "Why don't you go play basketball?"

"I frickin' lost it," Hoagland said. "I threw my stinkin' helmet off and I am trying to go after whoever I can. And meanwhile, Bernie Federko, I thought, was the one that said it to me. So I'm trying to get to this guy."

There's an adage that there's no such thing as bad publicity, but it would be hard to expect Bernie Federko to agree with it.

"Maybe somebody said, 'Go play basketball,' but it sure as hell wasn't me," Federko told the New Haven Register. "I have two different businesses, and I do hockey commentary in St. Louis, and if you think I'm stupid enough to make a racial comment... I'm not that dumb."

Federko called Hoagland two days later and forcefully denied making the statement.

"I had to believe him," Hoagland said. "That wasn't something he wanted to start his career on. He'd just signed this contract with St. Louis for doing the [St. Louis Blues] commentating and being on TV and stuff; that would not have been cool, you know?"

Jimmy Vivona, Hoagland's teammate, later defended Federko.

"I don't think Federko said it," Vivona said. "I think another player on the Vipers said it during the brawl. Bernie Federko was a classy guy; he actually sent me the tape of the game, in which I scored a goal."

"I know who it was," said St. Louis Vipers' forward Scott Rupp years later. "It was first attributed to Bernie, and it was not Bernie. I won't say who it was, but it was not a player. It was someone on our bench, because later that night, he told me that he said it. I said, 'As a man, you've got to step up to the plate. You're the one that said it. Bernie should not be accused. You should take Bernie off the hook.' He never stepped forward."

Later that weekend, tempers erupted again between the two teams at a hotel in New Haven.

"Robbie McCaig was a big kid, and he loved to scrap," Jimmy Vivona said. "He wanted to fight anybody, anytime. McCaig was having an argument with a monster by the name of Ken Ford of the St. Louis Vipers – he was as big as Lou Ferrigno. Ken punched Rob McCaig, and then, without a moment of hesitation, Berkley sucker-punched Ken, and rolled around the lobby with this animal, until it got broken up. We gave Ford some big kicks as he was getting up. Two minutes later, Ford came back to the lobby with the whole Vipers team in tow."

Vivona said that Vipers' coach made sure that cooler heads prevailed.

"It started to get pretty heated words-wise, but before anything could go crazy, Bernie Federko got downstairs and got in the middle of it before things really escalated," Vivona said. "It could have been nasty. I give Bernie Federko a lot of credit; he's a very classy guy."

Vivona, the quad-skating Connecticut Coaster who had given up his beloved number 99 on the advice of his coach, well remembered his first action in RHI.

"It was our first game; I still have the Ticketron tickets my aunt had saved," Vivona said. "Saturday, July 10, 1993. I took the opening draw. We played the Florida Hammerheads and we beat them, 10-9. Jim McGeough was Mario Lemieux's linemate in his first NHL season. He was the player/coach like Reggie Dunlop in 'Slapshot.' It was an electric night."

Vivona remembered being "jittery and raring to go." His assignment that night was to stop Don Martin, the best player on the Hammerheads and the league's seventh-leading scorer that season. "Seeing my jersey hanging up in the locker room before the game was a big thrill," Vivona said. "I thought, 'I'm actually getting paid to play hockey." We had a lot of guys who were really eager and ready to go. We could all say we played that game on adrenaline itself."

One of Vivona's opponents on the Hammerheads recalled that night as well.

"I get the chills talking about it," Joe Tamburino said. "It was definitely an amazing experience. My parents knew I was one of the better guys locally, but they didn't know when I went down there what would come out of it. When I told them I'd signed a contract, my father couldn't believe it; he was real excited. All I thought about was coming to Connecticut and having my parents and my brother and sister there to see me play in an arena where the Hartford Whalers used to play."

When the Hammerheads were introduced to the fans in Connecticut, Tamburino's mother was overcome with emotion.

"We came out in warmups and my mom was crying," Tamburino said. "It was very emotional. I was pumped. My grandparents were there, and aunts and uncles and 28 cousins and a ton of my friends. There was a write up in the local paper, and they mentioned the 'Long Island native' playing pro roller hockey. It's hard to explain. For a lot of the guys who were drafted, the AHL players playing pro ice, adapting to that atmosphere wasn't a huge adjustment for them. They were acclimated to it. Here I am coming into this new world of RHI playing pro hockey at 19, and sometimes the excitement took over. At times it felt a little overwhelming. I remember being so motivated just to make the team and to make those games in Connecticut so my family could see me play."

Ice hockey players can experience chippy ice and the rare indoor fog, but it's unlikely that they dealt with as many obstacles as RHI players had to overcome on a nightly basis in the first few years, including greasy concrete floors, slippery plastic surfaces and heat.

"It was so tiring," San Diego's Mike Duffey remembered. "It was four 12-minute periods, with fighting and full checking on concrete or plastic. In the Sports Arena the first year, they had a rodeo the night before a game, and the surface was slippery with forklift grease and dirt. It was such craziness to go out there and try to play four 12-minute periods. We'd skate so much that we'd have to change our skates at halftime because we had sweat through our skates. The sweat would go through the rivet holes of the skates from ice hockey, because you'd put a roller chassis on it. You'd be so sweaty that you had to change your skates at halftime, otherwise, you'd be slipping everywhere – that's how much you were sweating."

Players couldn't squirt water on their heads anywhere near the plastic surface to cool off, and goalies couldn't chance spilling any liquid in their goal crease, but that apparently didn't keep the occasional coach from surreptitiously spraying a bit of water in front of the opposing team's penalty box when the referees weren't looking.

Opponents of the Anaheim Bullfrogs that season probably wished they could have watered down the entire surface, because the Bullfrogs [13 wins and one overtime loss] were virtually unstoppable. Their closest Buss Division rival, the Los Angeles Blades, ended up nine points behind the Bullfrogs in the regular-season standings. The Vancouver VooDoo, playing in the King Division, were the league's highest-scoring team with 160 goals, and also had the league's second-best record, at 11-2-1. In the Murphy Division, the Toronto Planets [10-4-0] narrowly squeezed by the St. Louis Vipers [9-3-1] for first place. It seemed that every team beat up on the Florida Hammerheads and Utah RollerBees, the league doormats with identical 2-11-1 records.

VooDoo forward Mike Kennedy, the player that had given Stephane Desjardins the charley horse in game one of RHI's inaugural tour, scored 26 points in 11 games for Vancouver. Those numbers were eclipsed, however, by the VooDoo's Jose Charbonneau, who led the league in scoring with 25 goals and 43 assists for 68 points. Doug Lawrence of the Oakland Skates finished second in league scoring, with 60 points. Charbonneau's teammates Ryan Harrison and Todd Esselmont were no slouches, either, with Harrison tying Daniel Shank of the San Diego Barracudas for third place in regular-season scoring with 59 points, and Esselmont just two points back with 57.

The Calgary Rad'z regular-season record of 8-6-0 was solid, but Rad'z goalie Doug Dadswell pulled off something spectacular in the high-octane, offense-first RHI game that can never be repeated. Dadswell had played 28

National League Hockey games as a goaltender for the Calgary Flames in the late 1980s, but he'll probably be best remembered for earning a shutout in a regulation-length RHI game that season. He did it on July 13, 1993, in a 9-0 win against the Portland Rage. He made 38 saves, and though Portland (4-10-0 on the season) was not the team it would become in 1994 when it got to the finals against the Buffalo Stampede, the Rage did boast such snipers as Brad Harrison and Brent Fleetwood.

In "Lonely Goalie," an article by Mark Madden in the April 1996 issue of InLine Hockey News, three years after his feat, Dadswell said that he was surprised that no other goaltender had performed a shutout: "I can't believe no one else has one," said Dadswell, 32, who quit pro hockey after that first RHI season. "But we outplayed them pretty well, and I was on the ball. They had eight or 10 really decent scoring opportunities." One of Dadswell's teammates told him, "I bet no one else will ever get one," and it was a prescient prediction. In the six summers that RHI existed, no goaltender ever matched his accomplishment, and he apparently set a mark that can never be matched, as the league no longer exists.

One of the best games of the year was a divisional matchup between the Anaheim Bullfrogs and Los Angeles Blades at the Great Western Forum. The Bullfrogs had defeated the Blades in all three previous meetings between the two teams, and the Blades were out for revenge. Prime Ticket televised the game, and Anaheim fans made up a large portion of the crowd of 6,016. In a back-and-forth game, the Bullfrogs took the early lead, scoring three goals on four shots, but the Blades' Mike Callahan tied the game at 6-6 with just 3:38 remaining.

Both teams had great chances to win the game in regulation, but Bill Horn (Bullfrogs) and Mike O'Hara (Blades) both came up with big saves in net. When Anaheim's Brad McCaughey hit the crossbar on a breakaway with just 24 seconds to go, it became apparent that the game would go to a shootout.

In an article in the December/January 1994 issue of Street Hockey magazine, I wrote: "After a five-minute break, Anaheim's Devin Edgerton lined up at center 'ice' for the first of five one-on-one shots each team would receive... After 18 overtime shots, the game was still tied! Mike Butters provided a little comic relief, at least for L.A. fans, when he shot a weak flubber right at O'Hara, before Mike Ross, playing in his first game for L.A., ended Anaheim's unbeaten streak. His shot hit Horn's pads and rolled into the net. The crowd went wild as a swarm of Blades' players jumped over the boards to congratulate Ross. O'Hara, exhausted but smiling, lay on his back in front of the L.A. goal. After three tries, the Blades had finally beaten the Bullfrogs."

Dr. David Greenberg, the team physician for the Toronto Planets, had his own selection for game and player of the year.

"We had a game one night – you have to remember that they're playing their home games at Varsity Arena, this historical barn… right on the campus of the University of Toronto, with no air conditioning," Greenberg said. "Honest to God, it was 1,000 degrees, and Manny Legace played this game that had to be… besides from maybe Tony Esposito in game two of the 1972 Canada/Russia Summit series… the best game I've ever seen a goalie play in my life. I don't think he gave up a rebound all night. I can't begin to tell you how amazing it was. The fact that he went on to win a Stanley Cup [with the Detroit Red Wings in 2001/2002] was no surprise to me whatsoever. He was just phenomenal. We come into the dressing room in between halves and he's drinking Cokes, trying to get rehydrated. I said, 'Dude, this is a diuretic and it's loaded with caffeine. This is not what you should be drinking.' He said, 'This is what I always drink.' Those plastic pucks bounce like crazy, but he got in front of everything. It was as great a performance as I'd ever seen in my life, by any goalie, anywhere."

Perhaps the most surprising team of all in 1993 was the Oakland Skates. Skates' forward Daryn Goodwin remembered that the team promoted RHI anywhere and anyway they could, including introducing the players on the first base line at an Oakland A's game.

The Skates went 5-9-0 during the regular season and snuck into the playoffs because they had three more goals on the season than the San Diego Barracudas, who had an identical 5-9-0 record. No one expected the Skates to do much damage in the playoffs.

"There were some good teams," said Anaheim's Bob McKillop. "San Diego had Max Middendorf and Daniel Shank. Larry Floyd was a great player, too. As the season wore on, though we only played 14 games, it got tougher. Teams realized that they had to go and find ice hockey players. The second time we played San Diego it wasn't even close to the same. Word had gotten out, especially on the West Coast. Oakland really beefed up, and the other teams started beefing up, too. We had to win some tough games. There were many nights when we said, 'It's time to play, boys!' It wasn't like we walked through the whole league."

CHAPTER 12

The Brotherhood

As I wrote in "RHI Championship Finals: The Anaheim Bullfrogs leap over the competition," an article in the December/January 1994 issue of Street Hockey magazine:

"Raise the roof, give a standing ovation, do the wave and don't forget to boo the refs. Tip your Anaheim Bullfrogs' cap to Roller Hockey International's inaugural season – one of thrills, spills and body checks. Forwards crashed the net, defensemen crunched forwards and goalies took enough shots to stave off rabies. Between overtime shootouts and penalty shots, there was barely time to take a breath."

The league's first season was successful in many ways. It *completed* its first season, for one thing. Many attempted professional sports leagues don't survive beyond the grandiose planning stages. The Bullfrogs' beautiful venue of the Anaheim Arena and strong attendance numbers went a long way toward giving RHI a measure of credibility that first season. Roller Hockey International's founders must have breathed a collective sigh of relief that its flagship franchise had made it to the playoffs and beyond, rather than, say, a finals matchup between the Connecticut Coasters and the Utah RollerBees. Fortunately, the RollerBees' dismal regular-season record precluded the league's worst-drawing team from making the playoffs. While the Coasters *did* make the playoffs, they played an away game in Anaheim in front of 5,493 fans – perhaps twice the amount of their biggest regular-season crowd at New Haven's Veterans Memorial Coliseum. And probably better yet for all involved... they lost.

On August 24, 1993, as the Coasters prepared to play the Bullfrogs in that game, the team stood in the tunnel awaiting player introductions, and both Coasters' goalie Michael Cox and forward Jimmy Vivona wore quad skates. A Bullfrogs' fan noticed Vivona's weather-beaten and taped-up skates. Bouncing a crumpled-up dollar bill off of Vivona's helmet, the fan yelled, "Hey Vivona! Go buy yourself a new pair of skates!" The fan's entire section – and most of Vivona's teammates – had a great laugh.

"If he'd thrown a fifty, I would've put it in my glove and taken it with me to the bench," Vivona said.

The Bullfrogs handily defeated the Coasters in the one-game, sudden-death playoff game, 15-8, with Anaheim's Joe Cook scoring the winning goal. Both teams played aggressively – Anaheim's Mike Butters was kicked out of the game with a 10-minute misconduct penalty. One of Connecticut's best players, TJ Shantz, was carried off after tearing ligaments in his leg.

In another first-round matchup, the Los Angeles Blades took on the Toronto Planets, who had gone 10-4 and finished first in the Murphy Division. Unfortunately for the Planets, they had to play their first (and last) playoff game without goalie Manny Legace, RHI's regular-season MVP. Legace, who led the league in wins (10), saves (495), and save percentage (.881), had left the team early to play for the Canadian National Team at the Men's World Ice Hockey Championships. It was after Toronto went up 3-0 in the first period that the Planets really started to miss their ace goaltender, as the Blades scored six unanswered goals, the final one by Ralph Barahona, to take a 6-3 lead. Toronto scored two goals in the last five minutes of the game, but couldn't completely close the gap, and the Blades moved on with a 6-5 victory. Penalties hurt the Planets; they received 18 minutes to the Blades' 8. Just 2,713 fans attended the game at the Great Western Forum.

"We went out to L.A. for our playoff game, and for a lot of us, it was our first trip out to California," said Planets' forward Christian Skoryna. "We were kind of awestruck by L.A., the lifestyle and the beaches. I think it was more of a vacation to us than a playoff game. We were out at Venice Beach, wearing our skates, and we didn't even know we should be changing our wheels regularly. We were so in the dark with that sort of stuff. California was way far ahead in terms of the technology, the skates and the wheels."

Skoryna said that the Planets were surprised at the pre-game skate to see Blades' players with metal chassis and brand-new wheels. "We had sand falling out of our wheels because we had been skating on Venice Beach for two days,"

Skoryna said. "I had never changed my wheels the entire year. We were at a big disadvantage as far as that goes. It was an eye opener."

Other first-round matchups pitted the Calgary Rad'z against the Vancouver VooDoo and the Oakland Skates against the St. Louis Vipers.

Though Vancouver coach Dave "Tiger" Williams suited up for the VooDoo, and his team was ahead 7-6 with two minutes to go in the game, Calgary upset Vancouver in the match up of King Division rivals when the Rad'z tied the game and then went ahead for good when Todd Forsyth scored a nail-in-the-coffin goal. The game was played at the Pacific National Exhibition Agrodome in Vancouver in front of 7,069 fans. Despite having had three of the league's top-five scorers in the regular season, the VooDoo didn't get the goaltending they'd hoped for and bowed out in the first round.

The Oakland Skates squeaked into the playoffs despite having won only five regular-season games, and skated as the visiting team in each playoff round as a result. It seemed that the Vipers would squeeze the life out of the Skates, but it was the Vipers (9-4-1 in the regular season) who ended up getting snake bit. The Skates' goalie Brian Flatt held the Vipers scoreless until the middle of the third quarter, while his team built a 5-0 lead. St. Louis scored three goals in 84 seconds to cut into the Skates' lead, but Oakland's Brian Shantz scored just one minute later and Oakland held on to win, 7-5. The Vipers were led by Perry Turnbull, who had two goals and an assist in front of the hometown crowd of 3,115 stunned and saddened fans.

In their second-round playoff game, Calgary hosted the Skates in front of 5,824 fans at the Saddledome. Paced by the strong performance of RHI regular-season goal leader Sylvain Naud, the Skates continued their improbable playoff streak. Naud scored a hat trick and added two assists as the Skates defeated the Rad'z, 8-5. In the penalty-filled game, the Skates were assessed 28 minutes, the Rad'z 26.

On August 31 at 7:30 p.m., Anaheim took on their division rival, the Los Angeles Blades, in a second-round playoff game. Because of their stellar regular-season record, the Bullfrogs played all of their playoff games at the Anaheim Arena. The Bullfrogs hopped to a 4-0 lead early in the first quarter, and Bob McKillop set an RHI playoff record by scoring six goals in the game.

His teammate Brad McCaughey scored two goals and had three assists, and by halftime, Anaheim led 6-0. While the Blades scored four goals in the second half, Anaheim potted seven, for a final score of 13-4. The Blades, who had played all their home games on a Sport Court surface, never seemed to get comfortable on Anaheim's bare concrete floor.

For the championship series, the Skates took a short flight down to Anaheim to meet the waiting Bullfrogs for a two-game series on September 2 and 3. If one team won both games, the series would be over. But if the teams split the two games, it would come down to one of RHI's most interesting and controversial specialties – a 12-minute minigame. RHI Commissioner Ralph Backstrom had put the rule into place for various reasons: To have all the games in one city to keep down travel costs; to have the championship finish at a reasonable hour for the fans and for television; and for the inherent drama one 12-minute game would create, with all the prize money and championship trophy on the line.

As the two teams did their pre-game skate around the Pond's concrete floor, the Bullfrogs must have felt supremely confident. After all, they'd defeated the Skates four straight times during the regular season, and the Skates were coming into the game with a losing regular-season record.

Both teams circled with the puck cautiously in the opening period, gauging each other's strength and looking for a sure opening to the net. The game was played "playoff style," with an emphasis on defense and checking. Anaheim drew first blood – and the only goal of the first period – when Barry Potomski took a pass from Savo Mitrovic and buried it behind Skates' goaltender Brian Flatt. The Bullfrogs threw caution to the wind in the second period, however, building a 5-1 lead by halftime, and the 7,837-strong crowd was delirious. However, Oakland scored three power play goals in the third quarter, including long-blond-haired Doug Lawrence's second tally of the game. With the Bullfrogs getting one third-quarter goal of their own, it was suddenly 6-5, and the game took on an entirely different complexion. That's when the Bullfrogs' Brad McCaughey took over, scoring one of the most spectacular goals of the RHI season. Diving with his stick fully extended in front of him, McCaughey deflected an errant breakaway pass over Flatt's shoulder and into the back of the Oakland net. Two other Bullfrogs scored before McCaughey scored his third goal of the game, providing him with a hat trick and the Bullfrogs with a 10-6 lead. The Skates scored once more to make the final score Anaheim 10, Oakland 7.

The second game of the series started out much the same way, and the score was just 1-1 after the first quarter. Several times, the Bullfrogs missed chances to score when their forwards went too close to the net and were unable to convert rebounds that bounced into the slot. The teams each traded a pair of goals in the second quarter before Anaheim scored three straight goals in just one minute and 34 seconds to build a 6-3 lead. Both teams scored once in the waning moments of the half to go to their locker rooms with the Bullfrogs leading 7-4. In RHI's high-scoring game, a three-goal lead wasn't much of a cushion, but there was no way the Bullfrogs were going to let the Skates back into the game. In the second half, there were only two goals, both by Anaheim. The Bullfrogs won the game, 9-4, and the inaugural Roller Hockey International Championship.

Roller Hockey magazine's playoff Most Valuable Player, Bob McKillop, scored the final Anaheim goal, and as soon as the final buzzer sounded, the celebration was on. The Bullfrogs swarmed goalie Rob Laurie, then paraded the RHI championship trophy around the rink, as each player hefted the gleaming golden cup above their heads before 8,809 screaming fans. Oakland scored over half their goals during the series on the power play, and despite the loss, Skates' coach Garry Unger said he was proud of his team. "These boys have a lot of heart. We played some tough [playoff] games against St. Louis and Calgary, as well as the last game against San Diego that put us in the playoffs. We can play pretty well against any team. Anaheim just had too much depth."

The Bullfrogs had capped their nearly undefeated regular season by sweeping four playoff games. The scene on the Bullfrogs' rink after the game was pandemonium. I had raced down from my perch in the press box high above the rink before the final whistle, camera in hand, to get some shots of the celebration. One of my favorite photographs was of Kevin Kerr, the Bullfrogs' captain, raising the championship cup over his head, smiling widely, with one front tooth missing. (That photograph was later made into a Roller Hockey magazine cover shot and a player trading card, but the original transparency went missing, and to my great disappointment, was never found.) I also took some shots of Bob "Killer" McKillop, RHI's playoff MVP. McKillop said his fearsome nickname came not from his skills as a pugilist, but because when he hits a puck, or a baseball, or golf ball, "I don't get cheated."

During the regular season, McKillop scored 15 goals and added 8 assists for 23 points. In the playoffs, he topped all scorers with 9 goals, and added 4 assists.

After the awards were handed out, including the second-place trophy to the Oakland Skates, the Bullfrogs skated around the rink with their sticks held high to honor their fans. A few minutes later, the scene in the Bullfrogs' locker room was as raucous as the Skates' locker room was quiet.

"What a celebration night that was," McKillop said. "Champagne was flowing everywhere. Then we took the cup to the National Sports Bar and Grill and a couple other places. That whole night was unbelievable."

Trophy Follies

The National Hockey League's Stanley Cup is the oldest professional sports trophy, and the stories surrounding it are legendary. (It was once drop-kicked into Ontario Canada's Rideau Canal.) So perhaps it's not surprising that the RHI championship trophy that the Bullfrogs received has a unique story of its own. One of the places the cup traveled to that night was Legends, a bar in Long Beach. At some point, the Bullfrogs' players had learned that coaches McSorley and Sonier were getting players' shares from the playoff prize purse, which lowered the amount of money that each player was to receive, and as the consumption of alcohol increased, so did their anger.

"The very first damage to the cup came when it got accidentally stuck up into a ceiling fan," Bullfrogs' goaltender Rob Laurie said, who was with a group of teammates at Legends.

After that, it was open season on the trophy. Players would raise the trophy, knowing it would hit the ceiling fan, but pretending to be unaware. (The entire team was not there at that particular moment, and some players didn't hear the story until later.)

"The ceiling fan takes a chop out of it and creases it, and at that point it was gone," Laurie said.

Chipper Righter, the owner of a Newport Beach car dealership who had become a big fan and supporter of the Bullfrogs (and eventually became a sort of team VIP, even manning the gate on the bench at Bullfrogs' games), was also at Legends that night.

"We were celebrating, and some of the boys started smoking and dropping their ashes in the cup, some trash was going into the cup, and the boys were drinking and they were getting a little more pissed off," Righter said. "By the end of the night, the cup ended up on the floor with guys stomping it. So, on top of the wood block, you had this battered, creased, ball of a trophy."

A local television station was scheduled to do a segment about the Bullfrogs winning the city of Anaheim's first professional sports championship the following Monday morning, and the team needed the cup for the report. After the trophy was destroyed, Bullfrogs' players took up a collection and found a trophy shop owner who was willing to make a replica on short notice.

"I got a call about three in the morning, was told what had happened and I took a collection from the guys," Bullfrogs' enforcer Mike Butters said. "We got a trophy shop to make another trophy and replace it, so it wouldn't go missing. The guys were upset because of our playoff shares. I think we were going to get about nine grand a guy. We got our checks and… it was a lot less than what we thought it would be. It was five grand – $5,400, something like that. The guys were upset about it, and [we were told] that McSorley and Sonier took a players' share. The RHI cup in year two was not the RHI cup that was won in year one. That one ended up in a garbage can somewhere. It got demolished. We took it upon ourselves to fix it, to make it right, and that's what we did."

Just as the team closeness of the Bullfrogs helped them acquire a new trophy in time for the ceremony, their tightness as teammates was an element in their success on the rink that season. Some of that team bonding was the result of friendships they had made during their ice hockey careers, and some came from being pioneers together in a new professional sport. Victor Gervais, who led the Bullfrogs that season with 14 goals and 24 assists for 38 points, became a locker-room leader, despite a rather... um... shaky start. When Devin Edgerton arrived in Anaheim two days after the Bullfrogs' training camp had opened, Gervais picked him up at the airport, and the two began to catch up on old times at CC's, the pub in the Ramada Inn where the Bullfrogs stayed. Both players got sloshed, and at 6 a.m. the next morning, as the team walked by the hotel's outdoor Jacuzzi, they saw Edgerton passed out in the tub.

"Everybody's going, 'Who's the new guy?' " Gervais said. "I looked down and I said, 'That's Edgie.' So Edgie ends up missing his first practice. I go out on the floor and I'm skating around and Chris [McSorley] comes up to me goes, 'Vic, you've got to get off. You're still drunk.' He kicks me off and I'm trying to sneak back on, and he goes, 'You don't even have gloves. You forgot your gloves.' So I go into the locker room and I go, 'Has anyone got some gloves for the brotha?' They're like, 'Brotha?' From that day, we were called 'The Brotherhood.' "

"The practice was just terrible," Rob Laurie said. "Mike Butters is out there wearing plastic blades; he hadn't even gotten the real hockey Rollerblades yet. Chris McSorley just blew his whistle and stopped the whole practice and said, 'You guys aren't taking this seriously. We've got a new guy; he didn't even get here. Victor Gervais is so drunk, he can't even stand up.' And you hear Victor go, 'Scored a goal!' because he scored a goal in the scrimmage. And McSorley goes, 'Oh yeah? *Mike Butters* scored a goal.' So we just went at him the whole time he was here about 'The Brotherhood' – 'Anybody got any gloves for a brotha?' "

Each Bullfrog player, coach, team owner earned a shiny gold championship ring that summer that was festooned with diamonds and an emerald.

"It had 17 diamonds in the shape of the '0' that represented 0 regulation losses, and a [Bullfrogs'] green emerald for the one overtime loss we had," Mike Butters said.

But only the inner band of the players' rings bore the simple inscription: "The Brotherhood."

Some years later, Bullfrogs' forward Ken Murchison, who now runs a roller hockey rink in Corona, California, recalled a conversation he had with Tim Ryan, then the assistant GM of the Pond and currently the president of the Anaheim Ducks. Ryan told him that the first Ducks' coach, Ron Wilson, didn't like seeing the Bullfrogs' championship banner displayed in the Pond.

"Wilson was really upset and wanted that banner down from the rafters," Murchison said. "He wanted the Ducks to be the winners of Anaheim's first championship in the Pond."

The Mighty Ducks did win an NHL Stanley Cup championship in 2007, but the Bullfrogs will always carry the distinction of being the first professional sports team in Anaheim to win a title.

Bullfrogs' goaltender Rob Laurie would never forget what swirled through his mind when he skated with RHI's 1993 championship trophy the night the Bullfrogs won.

"It felt a little bit like we were making history," he said.

CHAPTER 13

That's the Secret, Boys: Aqua Net

After the Bullfrogs' victory, there wasn't much time for celebration. Instead, it was time for most of RHI's players to return to their ice hockey teams and for the lion's share of the team's staff members to look for new jobs.

"The Silvers didn't want to pay people through the off season, so everybody was let go," said Chris Palmer, who had been Bullfrogs' assistant general manager during the 1993 season. "I met with Dennis Murphy, and he offered me a position at the league office, kind of like an administrative assistant. When I was there, talks started heating up between RHI and David McLane's World Roller Hockey League down in Florida. We were all waiting to see what was going to happen. It took a while. I remember Dave coming in the office a few times, and they finally got a deal done. It was January of '94 when McLane came on board, and then you had [yet] another different personality [among RHI's founders]. I was scared, you know? I'm like, 'Who's this David McLane guy?' "

McLane, the longtime wrestling promoter who had morphed into a roller hockey impresario with his ESPN-televised WRHL, recognized that merging with RHI made good business sense. He felt that his marketing expertise would benefit RHI – and McLane *knew* that bringing in ESPN most definitely would. Although espn2 had taped the Bullfrogs' season opener in 1993, what McLane brought to the table was extensive television coverage of the blossoming league. Even better, ESPN paid for the production costs for all those games, something that is unheard of in today's sports broadcasting world.

"It was clear the two organizations would be better suited if they merged operations and combined the multi-owner arena operations with the marketing muscle we held with ESPN broadcasts," McLane said later.

In his autobiography, Dennis Murphy wrote that he knew that RHI would have to go through McLane if the league wanted ESPN to broadcast its games: "At the time, little did RHI team owners know one of the best moves in the growing RHI was about to happen. By making a deal with David McLane, RHI achieved what it needed to expand its marketing base with the broadcasting of its games on ESPN and the then upstart espn2 networks. RHI's leverage of having upwards of 24 markets in North America combined with ESPN and David's marketing knowledge created an instant credibility and success in terms of gaining national sponsors and licensees."

With McLane's move to RHI, the league quickly struck a multi-year deal with ESPN and espn2 to broadcast weekly games, playoff games, the July 9 All-Star Game and the 1994 league championship series. Additionally, espn2 would televise RHI's Game of the Week on the network's prime-time Monday slate, and ESPN would rebroadcast all of those games on a tape-delay basis in the fall.

"Running a roller hockey organization under one roof was great for me, because it resulted in allowing me to do what I do best," McLane said. "Sell the concept, bring in licensees and sponsors, and grow the brand of this new and growing sport."

McLane was named RHI's chief operating officer for RHI Promotions, the league's new marketing division. His focus would be on sponsorship acquisition, television contracts and special events.

Within a year of his hiring, RHI had signed deals with such national sponsors as Pepsi, Taco Bell and All-Sport athletic drink, as well as 20 licensees. The league's income from McLane's new division grew from "virtually non-existent to generating millions in revenues," Murphy wrote, adding that McLane's success in marketing the league put McLane on Murphy's short list to eventually replace him as league president.

"David knew what he was talking about when it came to promoting and marketing and television," Chris Palmer said. "He was the best. Without a television contract, you don't have a league, and some of the old-school roller hockey people – that was not what they believed. It was tough adjustment. People who didn't get that probably didn't like David, but David didn't care. He knew what was best for the league. David McLane really helped put the league on the map, and we wouldn't have gotten that ESPN deal without him."

RHI 1994 Tryout Camps, Draft & Pre-Season

Early in 1994, RHI held $100-per-player tryout camps in Atlanta (February 5-6) and Fullerton (February 19-20). "This is only for people who think they can make it," said RHI's Steve Pona. "This isn't for 'C' players."

The Fullerton camp was held at Stuart's Rollerworld, a facility owned by Stuart Silver, one of the owners of the Anaheim Bullfrogs. RHI Commissioner Ralph Backstrom was there to help evaluate players. According to Doug Jones, who was a referee at the camp, Backstrom was skating while carrying a clipboard and fell down. "He goes to take a turn, slides, and wipes out big time," Jones said. "So we blow the whistle and stop to help him, and he goes, 'Don't blow the bleeping whistle, I'm fine.' He gets up, goes off the rink and he goes in his bag, and he pulls out this big pink can and starts spraying it on his wheels. Play had already stopped, and we're all looking at Ralph Backstrom, former WHA and NHL player, who is spraying [something on] his wheels. Everybody's going, 'What the hell is he doing?' Ralph comes back on the rink goes in the same corner, makes the same turn, grips the floor, comes out of the turn full speed, and says, 'That's the secret, boys: Aqua Net.' "

Not long after the camp, the 1994 RHI draft took place on February 26 at the Los Angeles Airport Marriott. Covering the event for Roller Hockey magazine, I rubbed shoulders with and took photos of representatives from all the teams, including many famous former NHL players. In addition to those who had been involved in the league from the start – Vancouver VooDoo GM Dave "Tiger" Williams; Garry Unger, the coach of the Oakland Skates; St. Louis Vipers coaches Bernie Federko and Perry Turnbull; and RHI Commissioner Ralph Backstrom – a new crop of NHL-related personalities had been attracted to Roller Hockey International.

Former Philadelphia Flyers' tough guy Dave Schultz attended the draft as the coach and part owner of the newly formed Philadelphia Bulldogs. Yvan Cournoyer, the slick-skating, former Montreal Canadiens' star with 10 Stanley Cups to his credit, was the coach of the Montreal Roadrunners; the team sported his nickname. A former teammate of Cournoyer on the Canadiens, Terry Harper, was the general manager for the Sacramento River

Rats. Harper had played 1,066 NHL games with five teams.

Other former NHL players affiliated with RHI that attended the draft included New Jersey Rockin Rollers' General Manager Bobby Crawford, who had the proverbial "cup of coffee" [a few games] in the National Hockey League; Brent Callighen of the Toronto Planets, who once played on a line with Wayne Gretzky for the Edmonton Oilers; Bob Sirois, the owner of the Montreal Roadrunners, who played 286 NHL games, mostly with the Washington Capitals; Bob Kelly, a part owner of the Philadelphia Bulldogs and a former Philadelphia Flyers' teammate of Dave Shultz; Paul Messier, co-coach of the Tampa Bay Tritons and brother of NHL great Mark Messier; and Warren Young, a player/coach for the Pittsburgh Phantoms, who played 236 NHL games, mostly for the Pittsburgh Penguins.

With 24 teams participating in RHI's 1994 season, many new logos had to be created. The Connecticut Coasters and Utah RollerBees changed cities, and the Toronto Planets went on "hiatus." The Planets had hoped to find another venue to play in but never returned to the league, and most of the team's players ended up as Florida Hammerheads. The Connecticut Coasters became the Sacramento River Rats, and the Utah RollerBees became the Las Vegas Flash. The league's brand-new teams included the Atlanta Fire Ants, Buffalo Stampede, Chicago Cheetahs, Edmonton Sled Dogs, Minnesota Arctic Blast, Montreal Roadrunners, New England Stingers, New Jersey Rockin Rollers, Philadelphia Bulldogs, Phoenix Cobras, Pittsburgh Phantoms, San Jose Rhinos and Tampa Bay Tritons. Gone were the Buss, Murphy and King divisions. In their place was a two-conference (Eastern and Western) four-division (Atlantic, Central, Northwest and Pacific) arrangement.

Attractive "round-card girls" in hot pants carried signs announcing the number of each draft round written in dry-erase marker on a white board. Each team's representatives picked players that they hoped would bring them the 1994 RHI championship, but the draft was not without an element of fun – each team was also allowed to make one ceremonial "celebrity" draft pick. As I wrote in the June/ July '94 of Roller Hockey magazine, "The Calgary Rad'z grabbed Elvis Presley (probably so they could say: 'Elvis has left the building'), Chicago took Michael Jordan, Las Vegas nabbed Wayne Newton, New Jersey swiped Bruce Springsteen, Phoenix got Charles Barkley and Vancouver chose Tonya 'I Ain't No Role Model' Harding."

Established teams at the draft were each permitted to protect 14 players from their 1993 rosters. After that, all the teams drafted from a list that included the unprotected players and the cream of the crop of professional ice hockey's minor leagues. Many of those minor-league players never ended up on any RHI team's roster, however, and very few of the teams' final draft-choice lists looked anything like their 1994 opening-night rosters.

Western Conference, Pacific Division

In the new Western Conference, one of the major changes was in the coaching staff of the Anaheim Bullfrogs. Chris McSorley, who had guided the team to the 1993 championship, moved on to be part owner/GM and coach of the Buffalo Stampede. Grant Sonier, McSorley's assistant coach in '93, took over for the Bullfrogs, with help from player/coach Brad McCaughey. Anaheim protected the heart of its roster, including Joe Cook, Victor Gervais, Kevin Kerr, Rob Laurie, Savo Mitrovic and Darren Perkins.

Former NHL player Ken Morrow was the coach of the new Las Vegas Flash. Morrow was famous for being the first player to ever win an Olympic gold medal and an NHL Stanley Cup in one season. The Flash played in the Thomas and Mack Arena on the campus of the University of Las Vegas, Nevada, and drafted Kelly Dyer, the first female goalie to play in the Sunshine Hockey League.

In yet another connection to the National Hockey League, Bobby Hull Jr., son of former NHL and WHA star Bobby Hull, "The Golden Jet," became the new coach of the Los Angeles Blades. The Blades' 1993 coach, John Black, took over the helm of the Portland Rage. Returning to the Blades were Ralph Barahona, Steve Bogoyevac, Mike Callahan, brothers Mike Ross and Steve Ross, and Brett Kurtz. Goaltender Mike O'Hara was traded to the Phoenix Cobras for their first-round pick, which the Blades used to select forward Nick Vachon, one of the top scorers in the East Coast Hockey League and the son of the former L.A. Kings star goalie Rogie Vachon. Los Angeles also picked up goaltender Max Mikhailovsky from the Colonial Hockey League.

Garry Unger returned to Oakland to coach the Skates, and the team protected Shaun Clouston, Brian Flatt, Aldo Iaquinta, Doug Lawrence, Mark McCoy, Sylvain Naud and Chad Seibel. Stephane Desjardins, originally the Anaheim Bullfrogs' first draft choice prior to the 1993 season, played 16 games for the Skates in 1994.

Robbie Nichols coached the San Diego Barracudas, a second-year team. Few players whom the Barracudas protected or drafted actually played in 1994, but those who did included forward Larry Floyd, defenseman Marc Savard and goaltender Francis Ouellette. The Barracudas selected and kept Clark Donatelli and Barry Dreger from the IHL's San Diego Gulls, as well as top ECHL scorer Dan Gravelle. The Barracudas also selected Tony Szabo, but inexplicably let him get away. Szabo became the top scorer for the Atlanta Fire Ants in 1994.

Roy Sommer coached another new team, the San Jose Rhinos. The Rhinos were awarded the first pick overall and selected East Coast Hockey League All-Star Chris Foy of the Richmond Renegades in round one. The Rhinos also selected ECHL scoring standouts Darren Colbourne and Dennis Purdie. Doug Wilson, a former NHL defenseman for the Chicago Blackhawks and San Jose Sharks was a team co-owner.

Western Conference, Northwest Division

In the Western Conference's Northwest Division, Scott Atkinson coached the second-year Calgary Rad'z. The Rad'z had some *very* important NHL connections, including the team's number-one draft pick, Keith Gretzky, Wayne's younger brother, who had played for San Diego in the IHL in 1993. Glen Gretzky, another of Wayne's brothers, became the general manager of the Rad'z.

Don Depoe coached the Edmonton Sled Dogs, another new RHI team. The Dogs drafted Brian Shantz with their first pick, and then added Troy Hjertaas – both had played for the Oakland Skates in 1993. Gary Shuchuk of Los Angeles Kings, asked if he knew he'd been put on the protected list by the Sled Dogs, said, "Oh yeah, I knew that. But I can't play for them; I'm a co-owner of the Minnesota Arctic Blast." Lou Franceschetti, who had played 459

NHL games, coached the Phoenix Cobras. Phoenix protected several IHL players – none of whom joined the team. The Cobras' number-one draft pick was former Los Angeles Blades' goaltender Mike O'Hara, who did play 11 games for the Cobras.

The Portland Rage, another second-year team, hired John Black, 1993's Los Angeles Blades coach, and Black put together an almost completely new roster, except for three players – team owner Bill Conyard's son Tim, Dennis Holland and Greg Molnar. Portland selected Vadim Slivchenko, a top scorer in the ECHL, '94 ECHL All Star defenseman Sergei Berdnikov, and Gerry St. Cyr, a top-10 scorer in the Colonial Hockey League. Other players who would greatly help Portland in 1994 included Chris Valicevic, Brian Downey and Andy Rymsha.

The Sacramento River Rats, formerly the Connecticut Coasters, were coached by Jim McGeough, who had also led the Coasters. The River Rats filled their roster with a combination of returning RHI talent and college prospects. Returning players included Sean Cowan and Berkley Hoagland.

The returning Vancouver VooDoo, coached by Tiger Williams, protected RHI's 1993 leading scorer Jose "Joe" Charbonneau, but Charbonneau was fighting for a spot on the NHL's Vancouver Canucks and did not return to RHI. Vancouver also protected Ryan Harrison and Todd Esselmont, who were the number-four and-five scorers in RHI in 1994. Other players on Vancouver's protected list included Mike Kennedy and Shea Esselmont, both of whom played for the VooDoo in 1993.

Eastern Conference, Atlantic Division

In the Eastern Conference, the Chris McSorley-led Buffalo Stampede selected offensive-minded defensemen and an AHL scoring leader, none of whom played for the team. The Stampede also protected Manny Legace, who was RHI's leading goaltender in 1993, but he didn't play for the team, either. None of that seemed to bother the Stampede during the 1994 season, however, as would soon become apparent.

The Florida Hammerheads returned to RHI, albeit with a retread roster from the defunct Toronto Planets. Led by Dan Cameron, who coached the

Planets to a division title in 1993, the Hammerheads drafted and protected Christian Skoryna, the player who'd asked Bernie Federko who the hell he thought he was during a game back in 1993. The team would go through several coaching changes during a mostly forgettable 1994 campaign.

Another new RHI team, the Montreal Roadrunners, coached by team co-owner Yvan Cournoyer, selected several IHL All Stars, but only Stephane Charbonneau joined the league. The Roadrunners' number-one draft choice was Carl Boudreau, the CHL's top scorer.

The New Jersey Rockin Rollers, another new RHI team, were coached by former NHL player Nick Fotiu. New Jersey drafted several players from Team USA, including Lyle Wildgoose. They also selected Yves Heroux, who played for the San Diego Barracudas in 1993, and Manon Rheaume (acquired from the San Diego Barracudas), the first female goaltender to play in a professional ice hockey game.

One of the co-owners of the Philadelphia Bulldogs along with Dave Schultz and Mike Fox, a top replacement referee during the 17-day NHL official's strike in 1993, was Tony Danza, the television star of "Who's the Boss" and "Taxi." Danza would later appear on the David Letterman Show wearing a Philadelphia Bulldogs jersey.

Peter Esdale was a co-coach of the new Tampa Bay Tritons along with Paul Messier, NHL star Mark Messier's older brother. The team selected several IHL players who never ended up playing for the team. Even draft pick Nick Vitucci ended up going to the Buffalo Stampede. Those were not good signs, and the Tritons would have one mediocre season before disbanding.

Eastern Conference, Central Division

The Atlanta Fire Ants, owned by the same group as the International Hockey League's Knights, acquired Devin Edgerton from the Anaheim Bullfrogs in a deal that would allow Edgerton to play in both RHI and the IHL for the same owners. Edgerton would only play one game for the Fire Ants, although he would continue his ice hockey career for many years. Coached by John Paris, the only African-American coach in the league, the Fire Ants selected several IHL All Stars, but of those picks, only Jeff Madill played for the team.

Coached by Randy Boyd, the Chicago Cheetahs also selected many IHL players, though most decided not to play in RHI. The Cheetahs' selection of top AHL scorers was just as futile, though the team did pick up winger Cammi Granato. Granato had played on the U.S. national women's team and was the only female selected by an RHI team who was not a goalie. Although she practiced with the team, she did not play any RHI games. At the time she was drafted by the Cheetahs, Granato's brother Tony played for the NHL's Los Angeles Kings. The Cheetahs also had interesting jersey numbers – all of them were 70 and higher to honor a cheetah's top speed in the wild.

The new Minnesota Arctic Blast hired former NHL veteran (888 games) Dennis Maruk as coach. At the draft, the Blast chose solid ECHL goaltender Bill Pye and top scorer John Young; Jim Hau, the MVP of RHI's barnstorming tour of 1992; and Jay Moore, Reed Larson and Randy Skarda.

Barry Trotz and Paul Gardner were the co-coaches of another addition to RHI, the New England Stingers. The Stingers couldn't have known that one of their coaches, Trotz, would go on to have a stellar coaching career in the NHL with the Nashville Predators. New England selected many minor pro ice hockey players, including their top pick, Michel Picard, an AHL first team All-Star, but Picard chose not to play for the team. Neither did several other players the team picked. Perhaps that's why the Stingers, playing out of the Cumberland County Civic Center in Portland, Maine, would have a poor season and become the Ottawa Loggers in 1995.

Howard Baldwin, the owner of the NHL's Pittsburgh Penguins, bought RHI's new Pittsburgh Phantoms franchise and hired Rick Kehoe as coach. The Phantoms drafted ECHL standout Scott Burfoot and protected goalie Erin Whitten, who was the first female goaltender to record a win in professional hockey. But the Phantoms' most intriguing and famous player, by far, would turn out to be NHL Hall-of-Famer Bryan Trottier.

The St. Louis Vipers, back for a second year, were coached by eventual (2002) NHL Hall-of-Famer Bernie Federko and player-coach Perry Turnbull. The Vipers selected mostly ECHL and CHL standouts. Goaltender Matt DelGuidice was put on the team's protected list, mostly because his 2.97

average was tops in the ECHL, but DelGuidice ended up playing for the San Diego Barracudas. St. Louis also picked Brad Mullahy, who played in the 1994 ECHL All-Star Game and eventually played six games in 1994 for the New Jersey Rockin Rollers.

Perhaps all of the National Hockey League veterans affiliated with RHI helped some teams with their team promotions and ticket sales. Six weeks before the season began, Anaheim had sold more than 2,400 season tickets, up from 280 in '93; Montreal had sold over 2,000, and New Jersey was approaching the 3,000 season-seat mark.

"We're very confident; we're excited about the season coming up," Dennis Murphy said. "We think that we've got good new cities, a lot of enthusiasm, great owners and coaches. We think the future looks very bright."

CHAPTER 14

A Pyramid Scheme
and a Crucial Mistake

Roller Hockey International President Dennis Murphy blamed fear of potential National Hockey League competition for pushing RHI's leaders to expand their league from 12 to 24 teams for the 1994 season.

Cynics said that the league expanded so quickly because the founders were more interested in the incoming teams' franchise fees than they were afraid of the NHL creating a competing league. Whatever the case, RHI's rapid expansion set the stage for a complicated mishmash of teams departing the league, changing cities, or "going on hiatus," a handy phrase used by RHI's leadership to describe teams that, for the most part, would never return to the league.

Looking back, Jeanie Buss called the ill-advised expansion a "critical minor-league-era mistake." Doubling in size wasn't the major issue, however, Buss said. The problem was that many of the new team owners were underfinanced.

"To the people who bought in, it was like a gold mine," Buss said. "They were searching for a big hit, and they didn't necessarily have the funding. You weren't going to make money operating one of these teams, but a lot of people thought, 'Hey, if we double every year...' It's like a pyramid scheme, and that was a crucial mistake. There was absolutely no rush to expand the way we did, other than greed."

"There's no question that some owners came in with smoke and mirrors," said Rich Shillington, the owner of the San Jose Rhinos, one of RHI's expansion teams in 1994. "They didn't have any money. They thought they'd just get a franchise and then go find some friends who had money to back 'em, and that was a joke. They [RHI] hit the ground way too fast. It was simply human greed, that's all it was."

At the time, RHI's CEO Larry King was claiming a value of $20 million per team for an RHI franchise.

"Larry King was being a promoter," said Steve Pona, the director of RHI's supplier pool. "He was putting a bug in the ears of entrepreneurs: 'We're on to something. We're at the root of growth curve, invest with us now and you could see fairly substantial rewards.' It was a metaphor for wealth. In 1991, inline skate sales barely topped $1 million. By the time 1994 rolled around, inline skate sales topped $1 billion. It was the inauguration of a lifestyle. It was not just a fad. Larry's comments… were a strong forecast, they were confident, and they weren't out place. When you look at numbers on a macro scale, in three years, the industry grew from $1 million to $1 billion, so were Larry's comments really out of place? You're talking about a 2 percent piece of the pie."

Years later, Larry King explained it this way.

"Dennis is a great promoter, and he knows when you're starting something new like the American Basketball Association and the World Hockey Association, you either grow or die, there's no in between," King said. "Going from 12 to 24 was good for Alex Bellehumeur and it was good for Dennis and Larry to an extent. Dennis and Larry put their money into teams. We didn't get anything out of it; it allowed us to be foolish, I suppose, and be a team owner for a while. We did it, not for the money, although people can say we did it for the money… It's the way you grow a sport and the way you put a sport on the map."

King said that RHI had to be promoted heavily to survive.

"That's what Dennis was doing by going after doubling," King said. "It was actually the right idea. There was no limit of talent in hockey, that wasn't the limit. There was no limit of new fans to be brought in… The only natural limit was the number of rich guys that would support the activity until it caught on."

It's obvious in hindsight that Buss and Shillington were right, because many of the expansion owners *were* cash poor. And King and Pona were right, too – the inline skate industry at the time *was* booming. Perhaps the real question was, could RHI's leadership take that momentum and channel it to the league's benefit?

In "Chasing the Dream: RHI's 24 Teams Pursue Roller Hockey's Ultimate Prize," an article in the August/September 1994 issue of Roller Hockey magazine, I wrote: "Smash! Crash! Kapow! Do not change channels! This is not the new Batman movie, this is Roller Hockey International, and it has come to an epsn2 broadcast near you. All season long, 'The Deuce' is covering RHI's second season, and the cable channel's Monday Night Roller Hockey program has already seen its share of crunching body checks, acrobatic goals and on-the-spot interviews."

A game that probably should have been televised but wasn't featured Sacramento River Rats' goaltender Rick Plester playing the national anthem on his guitar before a home game. In a serendipitous coincidence, Plester did it on August 17, 1994, the 25th anniversary of Jimi Hendrix's performance of "The Star Spangled Banner" at Woodstock in the summer of 1969.

"I did it in full gear in middle of the rink," Plester said. "It was so loud, I could have played 'O Canada' and they wouldn't have known. The crowd was crazy. I've done concerts for people in large venues for rock and roll, but it was absolutely crazy."

Plester had difficulty focusing on the game after his bravura performance.

"I let in a couple of quick goals, and then I calmed down, and it was a close game after that," Plester said. "After the game, the fans lined up for autographs. I signed for like two hours, and when the place finally shut down, people were still banging on the glass and screaming as I was walking out, trying to get autographs. I felt like I was Elvis or something."

Mike Butters, who had played for Anaheim in 1993, was traded to the Montreal Roadrunners for the 1994 season. Traveling home from a bus trip, he and some teammates opened a window at the back of the bus and broke out some cigars. Yvan Cournoyer, the team's coach, demanded to know where the smoke was coming from, and Butters walked up to the front of the bus to explain and to apologize. Cournoyer told Butters that he loved cigars, but his wife wouldn't let him smoke them anymore.

"I said, 'Yvan, no one's going to know," Butters said. "'Why don't you have a cigar?' So I got to smoke a cigar with my hero, Yvan Cournoyer. At the year-end banquet, it's a tradition that everyone gets up and gives a speech. I'm one of the last guys to go up, I've done my speech, and I'm smoking a cigar, and Yvan's wife comes over to me and she says, 'Oh, I see you with that cigar. You know, Yvan used to smoke cigars, but he doesn't smoke them anymore ever since we've been married.' He's standing behind her and he looks at me with a million-dollar smile, like we've got something over on his wife. It was the greatest moment – a little secret with my childhood idol."

Cournoyer amazed Butters with his skillful stickhandling, many years after he'd retired from professional hockey. One day at practice, Cournoyer was describing to Butters how he could switch hands and shoot.

"As he's explaining it, he goes and grabs a puck in the corner, and he does it," Butters said. "He skates out – the whole team's watching – and as he looks like he's going to shoot left, he switches hands, shoots right, and rips it, top shelf. Yvan was in his 60s, probably, and he was still able to do that. It was just amazing."

Christian Lalonde, who played for the Anaheim Bullfrogs in 1993 and 1994, fondly recalled one of his 1994 teammates.

"Yuri Krivokhija was a funny Russian guy," Lalonde said. "He wanted to be an American. He would wear a New York Yankees hat and chew tobacco. I don't think he knew you had to take it out after a while, and so he said, 'This is making me sick.' Every time we'd go out, he'd order a White Russian. One time we went to the cash machine and he couldn't get any money. He said, 'The machine, Christian, help me. No money, no money.' I don't think he had a concept of money management. I told him, 'You don't have any more money in your account.' "

Making money was behind the Chicago Cheetahs' attempt to grow the team's attendance by hiring a public relations firm. The firm had intriguing, if not dangerous, connections.

"We hired this PR firm that was tied in with the mob," said Jerry Weber, the Cheetahs' director of operations. "They didn't tell us that they were tied into the mob, but I was invited to a luncheon at the Marriott near the airport, and I met this fine gentleman who was 6'4", very lean, very trim looking, soft spoken. We had a wonderful conversation about helping us and all, and he never told us who he was with. When we left, my associate said, 'You know who that was?' and I said, 'No,' and he said, 'He's the head of the mob.' I said, 'You're joking. He's a class act.' "

Weber said he didn't give it another thought, until he attended a dinner that the firm hosted at a local steak house.

"I was sitting across from a very handsome Italian guy, and he said, 'We'd like to work with you. Anybody owe you any money?' " Weber recalled. "I said, 'Yeah, there's a guy out in Mt. Prospect that owes us some money.' He said, 'OK, what's the guy's name,' and I gave him the guy's name. Two days later, the guy in Mt. Prospect calls me and says, 'Call 'em off, call 'em off, I'll give ya what I owe ya.' So, I thought, that was nice. And these guys owned a bunch of restaurants, so we could eat there, players could eat there, use it to entertain, no cost. That was great. And then they'd help us advertise, they had some places they had control over that would publicize it, so attendance started to pick up, and I got a call from them and they said, 'Who's making your merchandise,' and I said 'There's this guy.' And they said, 'We want to do it.' So I split it between the two."

Besides some rather sketchy team owners and dubious hangers-on, RHI also had to deal with venues that often had attendance issues, no air conditioning, slippery concrete floors… or all of the above. Despite having one of the league's premier facilities, if not the very best, even the Anaheim Pond ran into an occasional hitch.

According to Chris Kincaid, the Bullfrogs' equipment manager, the team still played on the concrete subsurface in 1994, and there was to be an ice hockey camp at the Pond starting the following day at the Pond.

"Somebody got the idea, 'Hey, let's turn on the compressors now, ahead of time, keep the floor nice and cold, and we're already a step ahead, so once the roller hockey game's over, we can start making ice,' " Kincaid said. Unfortunately, when the team staff mopped the floor, condensation created frost. Once the compressors were turned off, water formed on the floor as the frost melted. The game was delayed for nearly two hours.

Tim Ryan, then the assistant general manager of the Anaheim Pond (and current GM of the same facility, now called Honda Center), remembered that night well.

"Charlie Simmer was a friend of mine who played for the [NHL's] Los Angeles Kings on the Triple Crown Line," Ryan said. "He was doing color commentary for the Bullfrogs, and I get a call at home and he says, 'I think we've got a problem.' All of a sudden, we didn't know if we were going to play the game. I came back into work and we gave everybody in attendance – and I didn't know there were 10,000 people – free sodas and popcorn. I think it wounded up costing us $30,000 or $40,000 dollars."

Christian Skoryna was playing for the Florida Hammerheads against the Tampa Bay Tritons in 1994 when he got himself and the league some unintended press coverage. The Hammerheads had a solid lead before penalty calls turned the game around.

"The ref had just blown one call after another, and he just kept giving them power plays," Skoryna said. "The next thing you know, we're down 7-6. Our coach was just losing it. He goes, 'Skoryna, go put one in our net.' I turned around to look at him to see if he was serious, and he's like, 'Yeah, go put one in our net.' So, we pull our goalie, I win the draw straight back and shelf it in my own net. There were probably 6,000 to 7,000 people there, and you could have heard a pin drop in the place. I don't know what to do, so I just stick my hand up in the air, like I had just won the Stanley Cup. Everyone started booing and throwing shit at us. They put it in USA Today: 'Player and coach get suspended.'"

Skoryna also remembered playing against the Pittsburgh Phantoms. Former NHL star Bryan Trottier played home games for the Phantoms, and he was dominating Skoryna in the faceoff circle the entire game.

"I was like, 'Hey Trots, why don't you let a kid win a draw once in a while?'" Skoryna said. "So, we both put our sticks down, they dropped the puck, and Trottier didn't even move his stick. I won it straight back and he goes, 'Don't ever say I didn't do anything for ya.' He was totally laid back out there. He obviously had nothing to prove. He was just trying to build some interest in the game and have some fun, and I think he did that the best way he could."

Craig Minervini, who did play-by-play for the league's ESPN broadcasts, will never forget one Phantoms' home game at the Igloo in Pittsburgh in 1994.

"We did a game there were they still opened the [retractable] roof," Minervini said. "The press box is all the way to the top of that building. They opened the roof, literally, within 30 seconds of the drop of the puck. We got a wind blast and a giant ESPN banner blows over our heads, literally over our heads, and we're not saying anything, and the director says 'Talk! Say something!' We start to talk, but we can't even see – the ESPN banner is over our heads. Stuff was flying around, and our mics were all messed up."

Goaltender Mark Cavallin was playing in net for the Oakland Skates at the Great Western Forum against the Los Angeles Blades on June 14, 1994. The date of the game didn't mean much in terms of Roller Hockey International, but it was huge in the National Hockey League, as the New York Rangers were playing the Vancouver Canucks in Game 7 of the Stanley Cup Finals.

"There weren't many people in the stands, and during our game, they were showing a live feed of Game 7 on the Jumbotron," Cavallin said. "I couldn't help watching the Jumbotron while the play was in the far end, and I could see both benches looking up most of the time instead of watching our own game."

Some players who read an article in Roller Hockey magazine that season called "Chasing the Cup" asked, "What *is* the name of the cup we're chasing?" At the time, RHI had been looking for a company to sponsor the name of the championship trophy, something that would bring in more dollars to the league's coffers. That allowed me to riff on the topic in the magazine's following issue: "We implore RHI to forget this idea. Do we really need a 'Ross Dress for Less' Cup? A 'Minute Lube' Cup? A 'Sure Deodorant' Cup? The NHL succeeded for the past 75 years without selling the Stanley Cup to the highest bidder; RHI can, too. How about naming it the Murphy Cup, the Backstrom Cup, or the King Cup, after one of the league's founders?"

And that's what they did. The RHI championship trophy became the Murphy Cup.

The Minnesota Arctic Blast rocketed to RHI's best regular-season record in 1994, largely because they had four of the league's top seven goal scorers in John Young (#1), Randy Skarda (#2), John Hanson (#6) and Tim Hanus (#7). Young had 79 points in 22 games, while assist leader Randy Skarda had 59 assists and 77 points in 21 games. The Blast ran up the score against the

Atlanta Fire Ants in one game, a 23-3 shellacking that broke the Vancouver VooDoo's 1993 single-game scoring record of 18. Minnesota was also a part of the league's record for most goals scored by both teams in one game (29) when they defeated the Chicago Cheetahs 18-11 on August 9. Arctic Blast coach Dennis Maruk was named RHI's Eastern Conference Coach of the Year for leading his team to the Central Division championship.

The Blast edged out the Los Angeles Blades for the best regular-season record by one point, winning 18 games, losing three in regulation, and having one overtime loss for 37 points. The Blades, who went 18-4-0 for 36 points, were led by goaltender Max Mikhailovsky. The "Big M from Moscow" was RHI's leading goaltender during the regular season, with a goals-against-average of 5.60 and a record of 15 wins and three losses. Named both the league's Koho MVP of the Year and RHI Goalie of the Year, Mikhailovsky was offered a tryout by the Los Angeles Kings even before the RHI season was over. His coach, Bobby Hull, Jr., was named the league's Western Conference Coach of the Year.

In one game, however, the Blades nearly joined the Portland Rage to become the second RHI team ever to be shutout. In Anaheim's 7-1 opening night victory over their archrival, Bullfrogs' goaltender Rob Laurie missed getting RHI's second-ever shutout by 3 minutes, 53 seconds. That was how much time remained when L.A.'s Brett Kurtz scored L.A.'s only goal. On July 2, Laurie set a league record with 64 saves against the San Diego Barracudas.

Another goaltender to make big news in 1994 was Manon Rheaume. On June 20, in a game televised by espn2, Rheaume, "the first lady of ice hockey," became the first lady of roller hockey when she was brought in to replace Daniel Berthiaume after the Buffalo Stampede took a 6-1 lead over the New Jersey Rockin Rollers. Rheaume got the Rockin Rollers within two goals (7-5) before Buffalo put the game away.

Stampede coach Chris McSorley, who had won the RHI championship with the Anaheim Bullfrogs in 1993, saw his unbeaten streak as a coach in RHI end at 22 games when the Stampede lost after winning their first four games of the season. The Stampede ended the regular season with a 15-3-4 record, good for 34 points, putting them behind the Central Division Arctic

Blast's 37 points and the Pacific Division Blades' 36. The Vancouver VooDoo, the best team in the Northwest Division, finished 15-6-1 for 31 points.

The Pittsburgh Phantoms finished second to the Arctic Blast in the Central Division with a 13-9-0 record and made the playoffs, but a winning record wouldn't be enough to keep them in the league for a second season.

Fred Hetzel, a fan of the Steel City team, sent InLine Hockey News one of my favorite freelance submissions, published as "So Long, Phantoms" in the August/September 1995 issue's "Politically InCorrect" column. Hetzel wrote about how he stood and applauded on opening night in 1994 when Bryan Trottier's name was announced, and how he knew it wasn't his father's game of hockey when he saw the blonde ponytail sticking out from behind goalie Erin Whitten's helmet: "With lights dimmed, and Andrew Lloyd Weber's music playing, a local inline skating instructor, dressed as the team's Phantom mascot, was lowered from within the scoreboard to the Sport Court surface below. With arms spread and cape flapping in the wind, the Phantom took several strides on her inline skates before unceremoniously falling to the ground. And so, the season had begun."

Hetzel mentioned the Phantoms' effort to engage those who came to games and to build a fan base. The team gave fans questionnaires, had a "meet-the-team" session, and went the extra mile to cement their fans' loyalty. After a game on July 3, fans were invited to stay after to watch fireworks through the partially retracted dome of the Civic Arena.

"As fans jockeyed for the best seats from which to watch, a handful of Phantoms' players came back out from the locker room – some skating, others walking – to watch with us from the playing surface," Hetzel wrote. "They clapped as we clapped, they cheered as we cheered. We celebrated – together."

But soon, the fans heard rumblings, and then an announcement that the Phantoms would not be back for a second year.

"We found out that a sport that we thought belonged to us, didn't," Hetzel wrote. "Much like the mascot before the first home game, the Phantoms have fallen."

CHAPTER 15

That Guy's Face is So Flat He Could Bite a Wall

If Roller Hockey International's founders were thrilled with the 13,000-plus fans at the Anaheim Bullfrogs' home opener in 1993, they must have been delirious at the sellout crowd of 16,150 fans who attended RHI's inaugural All-Star Game in Vancouver on July 9, 1994. The largest crowd in league history squeezed standing-room only into the Pacific Coliseum, home of the National Hockey League's Canucks, to see RHI's Eastern Conference All-Stars face the very best players in the Western Conference.

Vancouver VooDoo owner Mike King organized the game, bringing in VooDoo sponsors Coca-Cola and McDonald's. Tiger Williams, coach of the Vancouver VooDoo, and Garry Unger, coach of the Oakland Skates, shared the coaching duties for the Western Conference All Stars. Despite coaching the Anaheim Bullfrogs in the Western Conference, Grant Sonier reunited with former Bullfrogs' coach Chris McSorley to coach the Eastern Conference team. Each of the 24 RHI teams was represented by at least one player. Rob Laurie, one of the two goalies for the Western Conference, recalled that the players on the two teams bet on the game... and that one team went home hungry.

"Chris McSorley and Tiger Williams had a little bit of a rift from their playing days," Laurie said. "They were both fighting for a spot as the tough guy on, I think, the Los Angeles Kings during Chris' playing days. Anyway, there was a little bit of animosity between the two of them. At the Vancouver All-Star Game, Chris was coach, and he arranged a little side bet. Everybody bet their meal money. Whatever team wins, you get the other team's meal money."

Laurie, who had played for McSorley on the Bullfrogs the previous season, said that McSorley had encouraged the Eastern Conference All-Stars by telling them, "Hey guys, we gotta beat Tiger! That guy's face is so flat, he could bite a wall."

Before the game could start, however, 1993 VooDoo star Joe Charbonneau was presented with the 1993 RHI scoring champion's trophy for his 25 goals and 43 assists during the 1993 season. Because of his stellar play, Charbonneau got another shot with the Canucks, whom he'd played 13 games for back in 1988-89. Charbonneau made the NHL club in the fall of 1993, in large part because of his high level of fitness after his stint in RHI. He had played another 30 games for the Canucks in 1993-94.

"The VooDoo did an incredible job of promoting the All-Star game," said RHI's Steve Pona. "They had moved to the big arena, and the game was live on ESPN. The walkup crowd was huge and the game sold out."

A problem cropped up on the facility's Sport Court, however, after a pre-game skate that was open to the public.

"There were over 300 people on the floor at all times, and they were all skating in the same direction for over two hours," Pona said. "Little by little, the floor started to shift and crawl up the boards. Before we knew it, the floor had gaps as much as three feet wide in the corners, while the other three feet was crawling up the opposite walls. We were live on ESPN in less than an hour. We used a table saw, hand saws and just about every other tool to pull the floor apart and fill the gaps as best we could. The teams skated around us during warm ups and we were still working through the national anthems, but just as the referees were ready to drop the puck and the red light went off to signal the game was on the air, we placed the last piece to make the floor playable... like it was scripted."

With the surface problem solved, a surprisingly hard-checking game ensued. The score was tied at one after the first quarter when Manon Rheaume of the New Jersey Rockin Rollers rushed into the arena straight from a hockey collectible card trading show. Rheaume had flown from New York to Minnesota in the morning, participated in the card show and arrived just after the first quarter. She was scheduled to play in the second quarter against Kelly Dyer of the Pittsburgh Phantoms, so time was tight.

"Nobody else was available to warm her up, so it fell to me," Pona said. "We went to the tunnel outside of the locker room, found a net and a few pucks. We did the usual – shoot at the pads, shoot at the blocker, shoot at the glove, shoot low, shoot high, etc., so she could get loose. Maybe she was nervous, because I was *not* peppering her, but she was having a very hard time stopping anything unless it hit her. What I choose to think is that I was shooting so slow that it would be like a major league ballplayer hitting a high school pitcher... too slow! We'll never know."

In the second quarter, the teams traded the lead four times, with the West scoring two goals in the last three minutes against Rheaume, and the Western Conference went into the half with a 5-4 lead. In the third quarter, the Eastern All-Stars exploded for four unanswered goals as Bill Pye of the Minnesota Arctic Blast allowed just one goal in the third and fourth quarters. Real Godin of the Montreal Roadrunners led the East with two goals and an assist (and suffered a broken nose) as the Eastern Conference All-Stars won the game going away, 11-6. Former NHL great Bryan Trottier of the Pittsburgh Phantoms had two assists for the East, and best of all, McSorley's team got a free lunch.

The 1994 "Dream Match" in Japan

Roller Hockey International had impressive plans for expansion into Japan and Europe from the very beginning, as evidenced by the word "International" in the league's name. To help build interest in the game among the Japanese, RHI produced a special exhibition game in the spring of 1994 between Team USA and Team Canada at Tokyo's Yuyogi Park as a way to kick off the league's hoped-for 1995 expansion into Japan.

Team USA's roster included goalies Mike O'Hara and Rob Laurie, defenders Rob Hyrtsak, Rik Wilson and Steve Ross, and forwards Mark Ashlee, Myles Hart, Brad McCaughey, Mike Callahan, Bob McKillop, Brett Kurtz, Steve Bogoyevac, Shaun Clouston and Ryan Fujita. Chris McSorley and Grant Sonier teamed up as coaches for the American squad.

Team Canada included goalies Manny Legace and Francis Ouellette, defensemen Mike Butters and Tim Conyard, and forwards Scott Frizzell, Ryan Harrison, Todd Esselmont, Dean Dorchak, Savo Mitrovic, Stephane

Desjardins, Brent Fleetwood, Scott Fukami, Sylvain Naud, Chad Onishenko and player/coach Tiger Williams. Robbie Nichols was the assistant coach.

The two teams enjoyed themselves right out of the gate.

"On the flight there, we drank all the alcohol on the 747," said Stephane Desjardins. "They had to give us the duty-free alcohol. By the time we got there, I went to my hotel room, I passed out, I woke up and went outside and I forgot I was in Japan."

The next day at practice, run by Tiger Williams, a local television channel wanted a player to say a few things in Japanese for a commercial. Tiger decided that there would be a shootout, and whoever won the shootout got to do the spot. Desjardins picked up a puck, skated down the rink toward the goalie, and wham!

"The next thing you know, I get hit in the back of the leg with a hard slap shot," Desjardins said. "I went down. I turn around and it's Tiger Williams saying, 'What the bleep are you doing? I go first.' I ended up winning the shootout, and I did the commercial."

The "Dream Match" was taped by Fuji Television for national broadcast in Japan, on May 6, 1994. Team USA defeated Team Canada 7-5 in front of almost 6,000 fans at Tokyo's Yoyogi Park Arena. The game was part of a larger event called the Live UFO Festival.

"I can remember when we scored a goal, there was no music," RHI Commissioner Ralph Backstrom said. "So I asked them, 'When there's a timeout, could you play music to keep the atmosphere going?' They played the same song over and over. I told them, 'Can't you mix the music up?' But I couldn't communicate with them."

The league's founders hoped that the game would also lead to an eight-team league called RHI-Japan. The league was to be run by RHI Chairman Alex Bellehumeur, along with Japanese businessmen Ichiro Roy Fujita and Gunji Odaka. Bellehumeur and Fujita had spent the two previous years working on the proposed Japanese division of RHI.

"Gunji Odaka was the head of Dentsu, then the world's largest advertising agency," Steve Pona said. "Odaka was to be the president of RHI Japan as its principal investor, and he had the influence and connections to make it roll."

At the time, RHI Commissioner Ralph Backstrom said that the league hoped to "truly be international, with a rotating world championships, say between North America, Japan, Australia and Europe, and have rotating championship series on different continents on a year-to-year basis."

RHI Chairman Alex Bellehumeur and Ichiro Roy Fujita echoed Backstrom's enthusiasm.

"Japan right now is beginning its surge in the recognition and love of inline roller hockey," Bellehumeur said. "We feel our timing is absolutely perfect." Bellehumeur hoped that RHI would make sports history by becoming of the few truly international sports leagues.

"There is no doubt about it; RHI will become an international league," Fujita said. "I feel in a few years the league will be all around the world."

With RHI-Japan's wheels now set in motion, Roller Hockey International's founders anticipated forming a five-conference international league as early as 1996, with two of those conferences in North America, the Japan Conference in Asia, a European Conference, and an Australian Conference.

Heady plans, indeed, for a league that had just doubled the amount of its franchises from 12 to 24. Unfortunately, a series of natural and man-made disasters rocked Japan in 1995, derailing RHI's plans. First, the 7.2 magnitude Kobe earthquake struck on January 17. On March 25, a release of poison sarin gas in Japan's subway system shocked the country. The biggest obstacle to RHI's hopes for a professional inline hockey league in Japan, however, might have been the U.S. dollar's plunge in value against the yen in the first quarter of the year. The devalued dollar meant RHI's money was worth less, making it that much more difficult for the league to fulfill its expansion plans in Asia.

"There are a number of reasons why that great opportunity did not move forward," said Alex Bellehumeur. "I've always regretted that, really, because it was really a slam dunk. We had all the right people in line, and the Japanese just loved the game."

RHI 1994 Post-Season

If Chris McSorley's Anaheim Bullfrogs had won RHI's first title by putting together a team of minor-league ice hockey stars, then every other team in the league in 1994 was forewarned and had the same opportunity to stock their teams in the second season. As a result, McSorley's success with the Buffalo Stampede in the 1994 playoffs simply cemented his status as RHI's preeminent coach. After rolling to a 15-3-4 regular-season record, "McSorley's Mob" dispatched the New Jersey Rockin Rollers in two straight games, and then did the same thing to the Montreal Roadrunners to earn a berth in the conference finals against the Minnesota Arctic Blast. (The Roadrunners had defeated the Philadelphia Bulldogs in round one, overcoming a game-one controversy in which Bulldogs' coach Dave Schultz protested the result, complaining that water had been sprayed on Philadelphia's side of the penalty box.)

The Arctic Blast earned the right to play against the Stampede by defeating the Atlanta Fire Ants in the first round and dispatching the Pittsburgh Phantoms in round two. The Phantoms had defeated the Chicago Cheetahs in the first round after losing the first game in a shootout. In game two they annihilated the Cheetahs 23-5 and then squeaked past Chicago 2-1 in a shootout following game three's scoreless 12-minute minigame. The Phantoms' 23 goals in game two set an RHI playoff record.

In the conference finals, the Stampede flew to Minnesota for game one to meet the Arctic Blast, the league's top regular-season team (18-3-1). The Blast won that game, 8-7, forcing the Stampede to defeat them twice back in Buffalo. The Stampede was up to the task, winning game two, 11-6, and the minigame tiebreaker, 5-1, to claim the conference title.

In the Western Conference, the Pacific Division Los Angeles Blades were supremely positive about their chances, confident in their 18-4-0 regular-season record and in goaltender Max Mikhailovsky, the winner of RHI's Most Valuable Player award. The Blades swept the San Diego Barracudas in round one of the playoffs and looked forward to playing the Anaheim Bullfrogs in round two. The Bullfrogs dispatched the San Jose Rhinos in round one, but had been stymied by Mikhailovsky during the regular season – Mikhailovsky had made 97 saves in two previous regular-season games against the Bullfrogs. Unfortunately for the Blades, Mikhailovsky proved human in the playoffs. Anaheim swept the Blades in two hard-fought battles, 9-6 and 9-8, knocking the Blades out of the playoffs for the second year in a row.

"Max was a phenomenal goalie for us the entire year," said Blades' defenseman Steve Wilson. "He stood on his head. Unfortunately, that game just came at the wrong time. I wish it would have happened a little earlier in the season, when the game didn't really count as much, but it just kind of happened at that crucial time. That's roller hockey. It's about peaking at the right time and being ready when the crucial game is on the line."

In Northwest Division first-round matchups, the fourth-place Portland Rage stunned the division-winning Vancouver VooDoo and the Calgary Rad'z bested the Phoenix Cobras, setting up a Rage/Rad'z matchup in the second round. Portland knocked off Rad'z in a series-deciding minigame, 2-1, which set up a matchup between Anaheim's stellar goaltending (Rob Laurie was undefeated in seven career playoff starts) and Portland's firepower. Coming into the series, Rage forwards Andy Rymsha and Brian Downey were the top two playoff scorers with 19 and 17 points, respectively. The Rage also had Gerry St. Cyr, who had potted a league-high 42 goals (adding 31 assists) during the regular season, and defenseman Chris Valicevic, who had scored 75 points. Add to that the all-Russian line of Sergei Berdnikov, Vadim Slivchenko, Andrei Bachkerov and Mikhail Zakharov, and Portland's high-scoring offense proved too much for the Bullfrogs. Portland won game one at the Memorial Coliseum in Portland 10-7 and won game two 11-7.

"I was really impressed with Portland's power play," said Anaheim defenseman Joe Cook. "Basically, we were beaten by a team with one great line. The Russian players are good, but the line with Rymsha, St. Cyr, Downey and Valicevic was what beat us."

The stage was now set for Roller Hockey International's second championship final, between the Portland Rage and the Buffalo Stampede. The Rage, a team that had started the season with just three wins in its first 11 games, had turned its season around after acquiring goaltender Lance Carlsen. Carlsen finished the regular season as RHI's number-three goalie, with a 6.58 goals-against average. Portland's combination of finesse and high scoring, backstopped by solid goaltending, seemed to be a sure recipe for success in the finals.

Buffalo, on the other hand, was a team that seemed to rely on brawn and bad behavior. The Stampede had racked up 749 minutes in penalties during the regular season, 100 penalty minutes more than any other team, and 226 minutes more than Portland. On the other hand, the Stampede had also led the league in short-handed goals, with 19, and boasted a secret weapon – John Vecchiarelli. The long-haired Vecchiarelli led the Stampede with 32 goals and 33 assists during the regular season, and was the only player on the team to crack the top-20 in league scoring, but it was in the playoffs that Vecchiarelli really turned it on. Against Minnesota in the Eastern Conference finals the previous week, Vecchiarelli had scored five goals in game one, four in game two, and three in the series-deciding minigame.

That was just a warm up.

In the first game of the championship series in Portland on August 31, Vecchiarelli, a native of Toronto, Ontario, scored *seven* goals and added three assists, setting a league record for points in a playoff game, as the Stampede defeated the Rage, 11-8. Vecchiarelli had almost single-handedly defeated the Rage in that game, scoring shorthanded, on the power play, from in close, from a distance, and every which way but loose.

The teams then flew back to Buffalo for game two on September 1 and, if necessary, a minigame that same night to crown the league champions. News of Vecchiarelli's feats had obviously reached Buffalo, because one sign in the stands read: "John Vecchiarelli – One Man Wrecking Crew." Portland was aware of him, too, and would mark him very closely in the second game.

I was fortunate enough to attend game two in Buffalo, along with Roller Hockey magazine's associate publisher Robert Dean and some hardware – a trophy that Robert would present to the playoff MVP. I remember thinking that the Stampede's home, the Memorial Auditorium, popularly known as the "Aud," looked old, and it was – it had opened on October 14, 1940, and would close just two years later. But what it lacked in amenities was more than made up for with a kind of working-class charm and 14,175 screaming fans. Two of those fans held up a sign with a drawing of TV cartoon characters Beavis and Butthead that read, "The Stampede on ESPN is cool," and "Yeah, those guys rule." Also attending was "Crazy" Claude Scott, a comedic trumpet player whose shtick to pump up the crowd included blowing a two-note " wolf whistle" at pretty women and leading humorous chants directed at the referees.

Backing off the Stampede immediately, the Portland Rage silenced the large home-town crowd in the first half, racing out to a 6-1 lead midway through the second quarter. Buffalo's Jay Neal and Vecchiarelli each scored to make it 6-3 at halftime, but that didn't stop Chris McSorley from lighting into his players at halftime.

"Let's just say we had a little pow wow and got these guys pointed in the right direction," McSorley said. "I knew we had the horses if we just woke these guys up, so I had to kick the bed frame to get these guys out of bed and on the way."

After the break, Chris Bergeron scored to make it 6-4, but when he received a five-minute major penalty for high sticking, giving Portland an automatic penalty shot *and* five minutes to score as many goals as possible on the power play, it seemed that the momentum would switch over to the Rage. Surely Portland's high-powered offense would reopen the gap and give the Rage a commanding lead. Instead, Stampede goaltender Nick Vitucci saved Gerry St. Cyr's penalty shot, much to the delight of the roaring crowd, and Alex Hicks scored a shorthanded goal to make it 6-5. The decibel level in the building was abruptly cut short when Andy Rymsha finally scored what would be Portland's only goal on the major power play, making the score 7-5. That's when Vitucci, who had played in all of Buffalo's 22 regular-season games, slammed the door shut on the Rage. Then Jason Cirone scored for Buffalo to make it 7-6, and Portland appeared to crumble. Dave Lemay tied it at 7-7 on a Stampede power play with just 3:25 left in the fourth quarter and six seconds remaining with the man advantage.

To complete the comeback for Buffalo, Jay Neal battled for the puck in the corner and threw the puck into the slot. That's where teammate John Hendry fired a high, hard shot that beat Portland goalie Lance Carlsen, making it 8-7 with just 1:27 left. The building actually seemed to rock a little in the ensuing tumult. Still, the game was not over, and Portland put on a furious effort to tie the score with just seconds left. Vitucci and the rest of the Stampede stood tall, however, and when the final buzzer sounded, the Stampede's celebration was on.

"It seems we play well with our backs against the wall," Vitucci said after the game in the Stampede's champagne-soaked dressing room. "We were under the gun all year. If we have a big six- or seven-goal lead, we always let teams back in the game, and if we're back four or five goals, we always seem to rise to the occasion."

Portland coach John Black expressed disappointment that his team seemed to change its attacking style after the first half, which kept the Stampede on their heels and pressure off the Rage in the defensive zone.

"As the game progressed, they really started taking it to us, and rather than getting back into the attack mode, we started getting on our own heels and never seemed to recover from it," Black said. "We started to play more of a defensive game, and that's not us."

Black added that Portland's failed power play was the turning point in the game. "That was unfortunate," Black said. "A tremendous amount of credit has to go to Vitucci. We hit the post a couple of times, we had some great opportunities, but he just came up big. Vecchiarelli might be MVP, but Vitucci stopped us time and time again."

Gerry St. Cyr, one of Portland's big guns, broke down the finals loss years later, saying that the Rage's Russian line failed in the clutch.

"On paper, we probably weren't one of the top two teams in the league, but the way that we played, we very easily could have won the whole thing," St. Cyr said. "We were a couple shots away from doing that. Through the playoffs we played great, did everything that we needed to do, and when it came down to the finals, we honestly had basically one line kind of go to work that game, and didn't get any help from the other line when it counted the most in the championship game."

St. Cyr led Portland's offense in the playoffs, scoring 36 points on 18 goals and 18 assists.

Immediately after the game, Robert Dean awarded Roller Hockey magazine's playoff MVP trophy to John Vecchiarelli, the playoff's "one-man wrecking crew" for his 23 goals and 17 assists in nine games, one of which was a 12-minute minigame. Portland had cut his production down to a goal and an assist in the final game, but Vecchiarelli's teammates certainly picked up the slack. Stampede captain Alex Hicks was presented with the Murphy Cup.

With Buffalo's win, Chris McSorley had his second RHI championship in a row. Each Stampede player earned $13,720 for winning the championship. Not a bad summer gig. Not bad at all.

CHAPTER 16

Teammates, Tough Guys and Toughest Opponents

One of the best aspects of team sports is camaraderie and shared experience. On true teams, players stand up for each other through thick and thin. On the tightest teams, that solidarity extends from the team owner on down through the coaches, administrators and staff. And while compliments for opposing players were probably rare while Roller Hockey International was still in existence, years later, players who participated in the league were open in their admiration – sometimes still tinged with a bit of animosity or fear – for their competitors in RHI.

Some, like Craig Coxe, Mike Butters, Darren Langdon, Troy Crowder and Sasha Lakovic, were best known as fighters and enforcers; others were just relentless in going for the puck or incredibly annoying as agitators who tried to take opponents off their game in any way possible.

Gerry St. Cyr recalled being drafted by the Portland Rage for the 1994 season, along with two of his ice hockey buddies, Andy Rymsha and Brian Downey. After first wondering, "What the hell's roller hockey?" St. Cyr figured it would be a nice two-week vacation, at the very least.

"It took me a while to pick up the game, to stop, the whole works," the native of North Vancouver, British Colombia said. "But after a month of going at it every day, and learning how to play the game, I just absolutely fell in love with it. The best thing about the game of roller hockey was actually learning the game."

St. Cyr said he couldn't stop, crashed, twisted his ankle and wondered, "What the hell am I doing on bloody wheels?" But after learning how to play the game, he was hooked.

"I loved the whole aspect of the game," St. Cyr said. "It's the same thing as ice hockey, but it's totally different. I fell out of ice hockey and into inline and never looked back. Pro ice was a lot more like a business. Inline was a business, but it was a little more laid back than the normal ice-hockey life."

On road trips, St. Cyr and his closest teammates had a favorite diversion.

"We used to bring a board game on the road and play Risk," St. Cyr said. "We used to gamble, and there would be five of us, and it would always be the same five that would play. We would literally get off the plane and get to the hotel, check in, go up to the room, set up the game, and play till game time. When the game was over, we'd bring case of beer back to the room and get right back at it and finish the game. We would wager on it."

They'd even bet on whose hockey bag would be first off the belt in baggage claim. If they were on a bus, they'd tape a Wheel of Fortune on the bus tire with an arrow on the inside, and then sell numbers on the bus to see whose number came up. When the bus stopped at its final destination, the players would get out, see where the arrow pointed, and if it was at 20, whoever put two bucks on 20 would win the pot.

In hotel rooms, the players would call each other on the phone and make bets.

"Andy Rymsha and I were pretty tight together while we played," St. Cyr said. "The World Cup [soccer] was on, and we were in Calgary. I'll never forget picking up the phone and calling Andy, and saying, 'You watching the game?' He'd say, 'Of course I am.' I said, 'Well, I got 20 bucks. The next throw-in is by Croatia.' He's like, 'OK, well, I'll pick the other team.' "

"I was very lucky to play with some good guys that were close friends of mine in Portland and New Jersey," St. Cyr said. "We kinda stuck together for a few years. With Rymsha and Downey and Valicevic, when we were playing together, the four of us were probably the best line in hockey. Everyone had a job on that line, and everyone did it, and nobody was selfish. If one guy was getting all the goals and the other guy was doing more of the defensive side, there was no bitching or complaining. I don't think I've ever played with better linemates."

Christian Skoryna, who played for the Florida Hammerheads in 1994, had a teammate he'll never forget.

"We had this little Czech guy, Roman Hubalek," Skoryna said. "They

[Czechs] speak English with a thick accent which I just find hilarious; they could be talking about what they had for breakfast and I'd be cracking up. So we're playing in the Montreal Forum for Miami and they're singing the national anthem and I turn around and Hubalek's got tears running down his face. I'm like, 'Hubalek, what's wrong?' And in his little Czech accent, he's like, 'All of my life I dream of playing in the Forum, and now here I am!' I just pissed my pants laughing. It was awesome."

Skoryna also played with Tony Szabo in 1999 with the St. Louis Vipers.

"He's a guy that really impressed me, because when we picked him up, you don't know how a former star is going to react to your team chemistry," Skoryna said. "It can go one way or another, and one way is going to be a cancer… but Szabo went the other way and he accepted a little less of an offensive role, and he didn't demand that he dominate power play minutes. Whatever Perry [Turnbull] asked of him, he did, and he was amazing as far as camaraderie. He was probably the missing piece of the puzzle, the last equation that pushed us over the edge to that championship."

Szabo was a star in the league in the early years, but then "he fell off the map for a few years." Skoryna said. "I attribute 100 percent of that to those V-Form skates. Szabo's whole game was his quickness and his shot, and as soon as he became the front and face of V-Form, his quickness was completely gone, which made it impossible for him to really take advantage of his shot."

Skoryna made an impact with his play, as well.

"Christian was a helluva player," said Scott Rupp, who played with St. Louis in 1993 and 1994 and followed the team as a fan in later years. "He wasn't a guy you ever wanted to hit, because if you miss him, then you're done. He had great hands, great moves and could score. He understood the game. What a great player."

Bullfrogs' forward Savo Mitrovic raved about teammate Victor Gervais' mad skills.

"Victor is probably one of the most elusive players I played with, probably one of the most enjoyable linemates I ever had," said Mitrovic. "He was somebody that could certainly break a game just by thinking his way through it. That was something that Victor did very, very well. He was methodical.

He wasn't the fastest skater, but he could go north and south and east and west better than anybody else could. Some of the guys can go forwards and backwards, but he went east and west better than anybody. That's what made Victor very elusive. He would come at you at full speed and then he would make a right turn and continue going right at that same speed. He was certainly one of the best players that have played that game, absolutely."

Joe Bonvie, who played goal for the San Jose Rhinos in 1996, roomed with Rhinos' veteran Ken Blum.

"He and his girlfriend decided it would be funny to take the rookie down to the beach," Bonvie said. "I'd never really been exposed to California. I soon realized that a lot of people were looking at me and I realized I was on a nude beach, and just about everybody was a guy. They took me there because they thought it would be kind of a culture shock, which it was."

San Jose's Mark Woolf remembered how close the Rhinos became after training camp every season.

"We kind of had had a rule in our dressing room, leave your attitudes at the door; we're here to play and have fun for the summer," Woolf said. "We really didn't have any guys that were too worried about, 'Oh, I need more ice time,' or 'I want to score this goal or that goal,' it just kind of happened. We found a lot of good mixes within our group, whether it was be the power play or shorthanded situations or even-strength situations."

Living together in one place made all the difference.

"Everybody had great chemistry because we lived in the same apartment complex," Woolf said. "The pool, the wives, the barbecue and the beers and stuff. It's not like nowadays where guys are spread out all over a city where it's tough to get everybody together anymore."

Living together enabled the team to gel together quickly.

"Every year Roy [Sommer] gave us about four or five days off. in between games right in the middle of the season, and we rented a couple of big houses in Lake Tahoe," Woolf said. "We let the partiers live in one house and people that liked to hike and do different things in another house, so everybody wasn't disturbed. It was beautiful time; we'd always go to the Truckee River, and we'd take everybody and put 'em in the rafts with some beer and take the four-hour cruise down the Truckee River. A lot of us guys were from Canada and had never experienced that kind of thing, and it was awesome."

Just because teams hung out together, it didn't mean that they always agreed with each other. Dave Cairns, coach of the Vancouver VooDoo, recalled sitting around with six or seven players at the hotel bar after a game in Sacramento.

"Tiger Williams and Craig Coxe get into *the* best debate of hockey fights that you can ever imagine," Cairns said. "Craig Coxe is saying it's better to fight as a gentleman and lose than to fight dirty and win. And Tiger's saying to Craig Coxe, 'You're bleeping crazy. You've got an advantage over somebody? You take advantage of that and you win the fight. That's your job. You're getting paid to win fights.' Craig would say, 'I would rather fight and lose, and drop the gloves and fight man to man and fight him this way...' It went on and on. These guys are going back and forth, and *they're* getting heated. Craig Coxe – that year – had two or three of the greatest hockey fights in history. Coxe is sitting there telling Tiger, 'No, fight him like a man,'" Cairns said, with a measure of awe and disbelief in his voice. Fortunately for the hotel bar and its furniture, the debate did not become physical.

You've probably seen the television ads with Chuck Norris that go, "Where tough meets classy." In Sasha Lakovic's case, the line would read, "Where tough meets skillful."

"Sasha Lakovic was in San Jose when I first played against him," said CJ Yoder, recalling one of the toughest players of RHI's 1997 season. "It was in the playoffs, and he lined up across from me. He's standing there just kind of looking at me. I look down, and his forearms were about the size of my thighs. I'm like, 'I shouldn't be out here with this guy.' He got room, just because of who he was, but he hit the brakes where some guys could only circle and stuff like that. He would stop and he would go and he could skate. He could wheel. I remember I hit the brakes with him one time and picked his pocket, and started going the other way. I put one on net that was directed wide. I went in the corner, and I just saw him out of the corner of my eye... he was just truckin'. I don't think I've ever pulled a chute quicker in my life. I hit the brakes like, 'You can have that puck.' He went slamming into the boards. He could have killed me."

One former NHL enforcer played four games for the Los Angeles Blades in 1995. Chris Nelson remembered him well, despite his short stint with the team.

"Troy Crowder was a tough guy with New Jersey Devils," Nelson said. "Everybody looked at Troy Crowder like a big fighter, so they tried to coax him into taking a penalty. This one guy was sticking Troy in the corner and spearing him and slashing him, trying to get Troy to take a cheap penalty. Right before the second period on a line change, Troy got back on, and the guy was coming back off when Troy was going out. Troy, as quick as I've ever seen it, elbowed this kid so hard in the face and broke his nose… it was so quick that no one saw it but me. And this kid was laid out. I was like, 'Wow.' That's when you know you don't want to mess with the tough guys."

Sometimes, toughness comes with a touch of crazy.

"This guy is absolutely out of his mind," Berkley Hoagland thought when coach Jim McGeough brought Link Gaetz to the Sacramento River Rats in 1994, two years after he'd been released by the NHL's San Jose Sharks.

"He was absolutely out of control," Hoagland said. "You couldn't even talk to him. We had this van, we all lived in this apartment complex, and [goaltender] Rick Plester would go around and pick everybody up in the morning for practice. We had a bunch of Russian guys who liked to play their Russian music on the way to the hockey rink for practice. Every time Link needed a ride, no matter who was sitting in front, it was unspoken, when Link came out, you would just get out of that front seat. Because if you didn't, he would pull you through the window and he'd kill ya. So the Russian kid got out and went and sat in the back and Link sits in the front, and the frickin' CD starts playing and he almost tore a hole in the CD player. He took the frickin' CD, and sputtered, 'What the bleep is this friggin' bullshit?' and threw the CD out the window. Oh, my god. We were *rolling*."

Hoagland also told a story about Gaetz's dysfunctional relationship with his roommate on the River Rats.

"Link was rooming with our backup goalie," Hoagland said. "He had to clean Link's room, and he had to do all this stuff, because Link said, 'If you don't do it, I'm going to kill ya.' So this dude pissed Link off or something, so the whole practice, Link was taking shots and trying to hit him in the head and was trying to kill the dude. The next thing you know, Link is running after this dude, and the guy took off, and skated, in his hockey gear, down the street. He took off, and he didn't come back. We played three games without a backup goalie, because the dude was terrified of Link."

According to Hoagland, when the River Rats went to San Jose for a game against the Rhinos, it was apparent that Gaetz was a local legend.

"He looked like Boss Hogg from the Dukes of Hazard," Hoagland said. "He had the cowboy hat on, he had a full suit, and he had on a bolo tie and big old cowboy boots. When the bus pulled into the San Jose rink, everyone was saying 'Welcome back, Link. We missed ya!' Oh, my god. He thought he was in heaven… it was unbelievable. They ate Link up. They loved him to death. And that team was trying to go after him and trying to get him all going… Link flipped out. He tore our locker room to shreds, took the team van, and went missing for three days."

When Gaetz brought the team van back, all the windows were broken out.

"Mugger let him go after that," Hoagland said. "He was like, 'This guy's sick. This guy's out of control.' He had to let him go. He couldn't even get through a game without trying to kill someone. He would literally try to kill someone. Nobody would fight him. Nobody would even go near him. So that was even more frustrating to him, because nobody would even go near him."

A player didn't have to be known for fisticuffs to gain respect from his opponents, however.

"Probably the most difficult opponent that I ever played against, and I battled him on a lot of different fronts, was Gerry St. Cyr," said Anaheim Bullfrogs star defenseman Joe Cook. "I hated playing against him. He was big, strong and mean. I played against him when he was on Team Canada and I was on Team USA. He was the whole package. He could hit, he could fight, he could score. He was an ox. He was hard to get off the puck, probably the most difficult to play against. I couldn't stand it."

"Gerry St. Cyr, I thought, was the biggest asshole on the floor," said St. Louis Vipers' star CJ Yoder. "But now I know him off the floor and he's a great guy. I still don't want to play against him on the floor, you know what I mean? I've never taken a whack harder than when Gerry St. Cyr whacked me in RHI my first year. I didn't know who he was, and I've taken my share of whacks. I pick his pocket and I'm in all alone, and he just turned and two-handed me across the thigh *so* hard. I'm like, 'I've gotta work through this, I've gotta work through this.' I'm in the Kiel Center, I'm in all alone, but I was hurting. I didn't score. I go off the rink with a big charley horse. I'll never forget that, because I know I picked his pocket and he just wheeled around, stick and all."

Los Angeles Blades' defenseman Mike Doers also had a St. Cyr story.

"One time I was clearing the puck out of the zone and I took a two-handed swipe at the puck, almost like a golf swing, and my stick went up and hit Gerry, and he started bleeding," Doers said. And Gerry just turned around and said, 'Who did that?' The play stopped, and we're all looking around, and I'm, 'Oh, geez. Oh, shit. I'm going to get beat up. Gerry's going to beat me up.' So I kinda raised my hand and said, 'I did it, Gerry. Sorry.' And he's like, 'That's OK. We'll let you go on this one.' I saw him afterwards and he said, 'Hey, it's no problem.' "

Doug Lawrence, a long-blond-haired forward who played for five RHI teams during his career, was another tough player to go up against.

"Doug was a competitor," said Anaheim's Joe Cook. "He played hard. I don't want to say he played the game dirty. He just played the game the right way, the way I teach the game, with grit and battle hard. Doug Lawrence was absolutely an agitator. He was the guy with the shirt off in the warm ups; he was all show."

Both Cook and CJ Yoder said that Mark Woolf of the San Jose Rhinos was a challenge to compete against. Woolf was known for his shot and for his ability to quarterback the power play.

"Woolfy was tough," Joe Cook said about San Jose's star forward. "Same kind of player as Gerry St. Cyr, but he wasn't as fast or as strong. Woolfy was tough to play against, no question. He had an absolute cannon."

Scorers who gave defensemen like Cook fits included Doug Ast of the Vancouver VooDoo and Bill Lund of the Minnesota Arctic Blast. "Doug Ast was a helluva player," Cook said. "He was an incredibly strong guy. Lund was really good."

"Good" is an understatement of the highest degree, sort of like saying Paris Hilton is a bit of a publicity hound. Lund had 85 goals, 140 assists and 225 points in 95 RHI games. In comparison, Ast had 116 goals, 95 assists 221 points in just 72 games. Talk about piling up the points.

Chris Valicevic, who played for the Portland Rage, New Jersey Rockin Rollers and Sacramento River Rats, was singled out for high praise from someone who should know. "Chris Valicevic was the best player I think I've seen on another team," said ESPN color man Jim Fox, a 10-year National Hockey League veteran with the Los Angeles Kings.

Mike Duffey of the San Diego Barracudas, who played both with and against him in RHI, praised Daniel Shank. "He was awesome. He was a total team guy, but some people didn't like him. I don't know why. I liked Dan Shank… until I had to cover him."

Mike Duffey impressed Victor Gervais of the Anaheim Bullfrogs, though Gervais couldn't recall his name years later.

"They had someone from San Diego who was always all over me, pestering me," Victor Gervais said. "I can't remember his name. [It was Duffey.] From San Jose, it was always Garry Gulash," Gervais said. "He was just all over me. He *abused* me."

CHAPTER 17

The Whole Puck Fiasco

Why is the disk used in ice and inline hockey called a "puck," anyway?

The word's origins have become hazy with the passage of time – according to The Oxford English Dictionary, it may have originated "from the Scottish Gaelic *puc*, meaning to poke, punch or deliver a blow" in the game of hurling. When it comes to Roller Hockey International's puck, however, it somehow seems more reasonable to think of the "Puck" character in Shakespeare's play "A Midsummer Night's Dream." Based on a figure in ancient English mythology, Puck, states the Encyclopedia Britannica, personifies the trickster, "a combination of opposites – including a malicious destroyer and childlike prankster."

As mentioned in Chapter 5, the puck that was created specifically for Roller Hockey International, which should have been a financial boost and major promotional tool, became an object of controversy and a daily distraction at all levels of the league. Emotions still run high when many people from the league speak about the puck.

For RHI to even get off the ground, it had to reinvent the puck, as existing pucks would not stand up to the abuse of amateur play, let alone professional games in front of paying audiences and television coverage. One plastic puck of the period was filled with rice and would occasionally bust open. Imagine the headaches of cleaning up hard white rice on a Sport Court floor in the middle of a game with cameras running and it's easy to see why the league needed a puck it could count on. But the seemingly simple process of creating a puck for the league was complex, controversial – and extremely confusing.

Originally, and this may come as a surprise to many fans of RHI, the league didn't even plan to play with a puck. Murphy and Bellehumeur had traveled to Canada to get ideas for the league. When they returned, they told Paul Chapey, whom they had hired as a consultant, that Roller Hockey

International would play outdoors… with a ball.

"That's the worst thing you can do," Chapey told them. "You can have Mylec [a company that made low-end plastic bladed hockey sticks and shin pads] as sponsor. You don't need equipment to play roller hockey with a ball. You're just wrong. You've got to use a puck and play inside."

Because Chapey had the highest level of roller hockey expertise within 100 miles, Murphy and Bellehumeur became convinced that the league had to play with a puck and asked Chapey to do testing on prototypes. As Murphy was in charge of the league's organization, with Larry King taking care of legal issues and Ralph Backstrom running all hockey operations, Murphy asked Bellehumeur to design an official puck for Roller Hockey International.

This is where things begin to get complicated.

"Another big issue was the puck and what style it should follow," Dennis Murphy wrote in his autobiography. "Over the years, Alex had been tinkering with new inventive ideas and considered himself to be an 'inventor' of new products. Along with my son-in-law, Guy Haarlammert and his partner John Newman, they spent hours looking at existing hockey pucks and then coming up with their new version."

Murphy's description of the process was simplified and inaccurate in some details. The name of Guy Haarlammert's partner was John Nehmens, and Haarlammert's company created the metal molds that were used to form the puck. Haarlammert and Nehmens also spent many hours testing the product. Many more people were involved, if not in *inventing* the puck, then in testing it, taking prototypes from one engineer to another, or helping in the process in some way. Some felt that their contributions to the creation of the eventual RHI puck were belittled or ignored and that they were not given the credit they were due. Additional people who had a hand in at least moving the league's puck from its initial concept to eventual appearance at RHI games included Anno Willison, Daryn Goodwin, Jeff Buma, Dan Kotler, RHI Commissioner Ralph Backstrom, Steve Pona and Matt Dovin (the son of Jerry Dovin, Bellehumeur's accountant).

According to Willison, one key design feature that would become a part of the puck was inspired by a trip he and Matt Dovin took to a tire store. The metal rim inside a tire had aerodynamic cutouts. Willison claims that he and Dovin mentioned that to Bellehumeur, and that the concept was utilized in RHI's puck design.

Bellehumeur also claimed credit for coming up with the idea for the cutouts.

"The other thing that I created with the puck were the windows – as you know, there's an opening in the center – the windows provided a cushion, so that when you hit it, it would spring and the space would accelerate it," Bellehumeur said. "Rather than being a solid lump of polymer, it had that opening for two reasons: Number one, it acted like a spring, and secondly, it prevented it from frisbeeing. Because of the openings, it had a straight, true line of action."

The animosity over the puck that still exists to this day is somewhat breathtaking. Former RHI CEO Larry King contradicts Bellehumeur's contention that he invented the puck.

"He didn't invent it," King said. "It was invented by Matt Dovin, who came up with the idea of putting holes in it."

Of course, it was more complicated than that, but King and Bellehumeur never saw eye to eye on much, if anything.

(What's especially ironic about the RHI puck story is that a similar controversy erupted in the American Basketball Association – another league that RHI co-founder Dennis Murphy helped bring into existence – over the ABA's red, white and blue basketball. The league failed to patent its basketball's distinctive design, so the ABA earned nothing from the approximately 30 million tri-color basketballs that were eventually sold to consumers.)

Paul Chapey said that the puck that Bellehumeur eventually patented along with Haarlammert and Nehmens had already existed, in a way. Call it an old-school puck.

"We would use type 33 or 35 3M electrical tape and glue thumbtacks into the top and bottom," Chapey said. "It wouldn't roll, it would stay flat, and the thumbtacks would make it slide really well on the wood floor. Alex got it molded and was named inventor of the puck. It was my roll of Type 88 Scotch electrical tape with thumb tacks, converted by Alex Bellehumeur to make it pretty and a product. That's all the puck ever was. The funny thing, though, is the tape with thumb tacks always worked better."

Perhaps, but like a rice-filled puck, a roll of tape spiked with thumbtacks certainly wouldn't have been an appropriate puck for Roller Hockey International. One of the first attempted improvements to the puck was replacing the thumbtacks with beveled metal studs, and then replacing the roll of tape with a pliable polymer to keep it from getting brittle in cold weather.

"In the meantime, there had to be a patent recorded," Bellehumeur said. "Without a patent being recorded, then there's no protection. So I went to the league – at that point Larry [King] was involved – and I tried to get the league to pay for the patent, which was several thousand dollars, and the cost of the molds. They were not interested. They wanted nothing to do with it. They wouldn't do it, so I went and did it myself and proceeded to put the patent in my name."

Dennis Murphy does not recall this particular discussion about the puck patent.

"I cannot honestly say that that's a fact," Murphy said. "I can't remember him coming to Larry and I and asking for that. He was in charge of properties and we kind of let him run properties, but as far as the money stuff, I don't know."

Murphy said that it wouldn't have made sense for him to refuse to pay for the puck's patent.

"No, I don't recall saying that," Murphy said. "Especially if my son-in-law was involved. Why would I do that? Logically, why?"

Larry King also denied Bellehumeur's version of events.

"I'm with Dennis," King said. "No such conversation ever took place."

Bellehumeur contended that it was critical to only put someone's name on a patent if they had an "inventive involvement" in the patented product, otherwise, a challenge to the patent could be made and the patent voided.

"I made an arrangement with Guy and John that if they were to take the risk of putting together the molds and producing a prototype or prototypes, then they would receive a certain percentage of the proceeds and they would receive the first monies out, which was a pretty large sum, repaying them for the mold," Bellehumeur said. "They agreed to do so. That was the only way we could get the mold done at that point, because, like I said, the league would not come to the table with the funds, nor share the cost."

Larry King scoffed at Bellehumeur's contention that King and Murphy's names couldn't be put on the patent because they didn't have "inventive involvement."

"The company should have been on the thing," King said. "It should have been Roller Hockey International."

King said that if someone worked for a company, say IBM, and created a patentable product while on the company clock, the patent is owned by IBM.

"If it's done on their time, it doesn't go on the individual, it goes on the company," King said.

(Several years later, another conflict arose when Guy Haarlammert and John Nehmens stopped receiving payments for the mold that they'd created for the league's puck. They blamed Alex Bellehumeur, but Bellehumeur claimed he had turned over the rights to the puck to the league at that point and that it was RHI's leadership that stopped paying Haarlammert and Nehmens. As Bellehumeur had a contract proving he no longer owned the puck, Dennis Murphy had to support Bellehumeur's contention. Unfortunately, this caused a painful rift between Murphy and his son-in-law, Haarlammert, making the topic a difficult one for Murphy to discuss. Nearly 20 years later, Haarlammert ignored repeated requests to discuss the puck for this book.)

Joe Cook of the Anaheim Bullfrogs came to Bellehumeur's defense years later.

"I have an incredible amount of respect for Alex," Cook said. "I think Alex is a visionary. If he doesn't agree with what you're saying, he'll tell you. You may not like what you're hearing, but at least you know where he stands. Whether Alex was supposed to put the puck in his name... I don't know, but I think he deserves a lot more respect than he gets from people for what he has done for the game. When he puts his mind to something he works through, he gets to the end. I don't like these guys who come up with these grand ideas and let them drop. He works at it. He churns, he churns, he churns."

Bellehumeur later alienated many other people in the industry by aggressively protecting the puck's patent.

"Since 1993, I have spent over a quarter million dollars protecting the integrity of the puck's patent – none of which came from RHI or anyone else," Bellehumeur said. "Literally dozens of patent infringers had to be taken to task, otherwise, the SpeedPuck's patent would be of no value. Not a pleasant task, but it comes with filing patents."

One of the early puck designs used were rolls of electrical tape rigged up with rivets that Anno Willison purchased at a building materials store.

"The only problem was that the metal runners would wear down real quick, because back then, we were playing on concrete – we didn't have the plastic flooring as we do nowadays," Bellehumeur said. "So it really just ground the hell out of the metal."

After much thought and testing, nylon runners replaced the metal studs. Unfortunately, the runners had a propensity to come out upon impact with sticks, goalposts and boards. Bellehumeur said that after the runners were redesigned, that problem was solved.

"The nylon runners worked really well," Bellehumeur said. "That was the heart and soul of the puck."

According to Bellehumeur, RHI was using "a reasonable facsimile of a puck" during RHI's inaugural tour in 1992, but "it had not been perfected at that point in time." By the end of that tour, at the final event in Las Vegas, Nevada, Bellehumeur, King and Murphy met with representatives of Karhu USA, a hockey equipment company whose brands included Koho, Jofa, Titan and Canadien. The league needed a company to market the puck, and Karhu was intrigued by RHI's potential.

David Smallwood, vice president of sales with Karhu at the time, remembered meeting in Las Vegas and being shown the proposed RHI puck.

"John Pagotto and I flew out to see what it was all about and to have our first meeting with Larry, Dennis and Alex, at the last USA/Canada game at the Santa Fe Casino in Las Vegas," Smallwood said. "Shortly thereafter, we were able to pull together not only a licensing deal that allowed us to produce the official stick for Roller Hockey International, but also... to purchase the worldwide rights to what became the Jofa SpeedPuck, which was the official puck of Roller Hockey International. I saw the original prototype with thumbtacks shoved in to show the way the runners were going to work. The whole concept was something that moved better on a synthetic or a Sport Court surface and didn't roll and didn't bounce. We quickly saw that this puck and some of its patented features had accomplished that and allowed it to play like an ice hockey puck on ice."

Karhu agreed to become the exclusive worldwide distributor of the league's new official game puck, placing it under its Jofa brand. Jofa had the international marketing rights to sell the puck, and RHI got royalties from those sales.

It was "an unheard of deal on a brand-new product in a brand-new sport that they would have exclusive marketing rights of the puck, provided that they paid us $50,000 up front, for the rights," Bellehumeur said.

Since the Jofa SpeedPuck that RHI used in 1993 often broke or had the runners pop out, in 1994, RHI came out with an improved SpeedPuck with wider spokes, better runners and a stronger base material.

Dan Kotler, who had moved his Utah Rollerbees to Nevada to become the Las Vegas Flash, recalled a meeting where he was asked if his company, Sport Court, could design an improved puck for the league.

"They showed me the puck that they were gonna have made," Kotler said. "It was going to cost them about three or four dollars to have it made. I laughed and said, 'Give me that puck. I'll take it to my plant and I'll make that puck for you and I guarantee you I can make it for less than a buck.' So, I took it back, I gave it to my tool-and-die shop, and we made the puck and I was selling it to the league for 80 cents or something like that."

Kotler's modifications were utilized in RHI's second version of the Jofa SpeedPuck, as well as the thicker Jofa SpeedPuck Pro in 1995.

Kotler said that he became very angry when he learned how much Bellehumeur was earning from the puck, and that's when his company stopped making the SpeedPuck Pro for RHI.

"I just said, 'I don't want to make it anymore. I'm done,' " Kotler said.

"Without Dan, RHI never would have gotten the puck in play in 1994," recalled Steve Pona, who initially came to RHI as an administrator in the league office in early 1993, when the puck that eventually became the official RHI puck was being refined and improved. "He did make it affordable for Karhu. He did accommodate Alex and the league when it came time to make improvements to the product... and helped Alex to make the SpeedPuck Pro. In addition to his ownership of the Rollerbees, Flash and Sport Court, he was a key cog in the process of creating the puck and delivering a quality product to Karhu. But he had a greater interest than just the puck and his teams. As roller hockey grew, demand for his floors grew. As his floors grew, so did his product line. He did a great job of leveraging one element into the next."

Players liked the second version of the Jofa SpeedPuck but still complained that it was too light (3.6 to 3.75 ounces) compared to the heavier (6 ounce) vulcanized rubber pucks they were used to playing with on ice, and goalies couldn't 'feel' shots to predict or control rebounds. Defensemen and forwards also grumbled that when they took wrist shots, the runners lifted the body of the puck off the playing surface, causing the puck to flip.

"The runners were obviously necessary, though," Pona said. "The runner material was a highly wound nylon that delivered significantly less resistance than the material used in the body of the puck. So, players just had to make an adjustment."

In 1995, Jofa marketed the thicker and heavier SpeedPuck Pro, but it never made it into an RHI game.

"Alex and I were convinced that after many months of testing, the SpeedPuck Pro would make a glorious entry into the pro game in 1995," Pona said. "But the response from the street was loud and clear. They wanted to play with the same puck as the pros – the original."

Over the years, many people would say that the league might have survived longer if the income from the puck had gone to Roller Hockey International instead of Alex Bellehumeur, but Bellehumeur claims that was a misconception. Bellehumeur said that the entire $50,000 advance went into RHI's coffers, and that while he did earn a substantial 20 percent of the revenue from RHI's shares of the profits from the puck, out of that he paid Guy Haarlammert and John Nehmens for cost of the molds and a percentage of the proceeds. "I turned every dime of that over to the league," Bellehumeur said. "In addition to that, the league made literally hundreds of thousands of dollars off that puck over the years, which was used to keep the league in operation – especially during the first few years. I provided the league the exclusive use of the invention and agreed to receive a very small percentage of the income. I have 13 patents; the puck invention was not just a fluke."

Bellehumeur also paid Paul Chapey for his contributions to the league's puck. Bellehumeur and Chapey later had a falling out over the size of the payments that Chapey received, those payments eventually stopped, and the two men nearly came to blows at Bellehumeur's house over it. Bellehumeur said that he tried to contact Chapey to resume payments "in a manner we could each agree on," but that Chapey didn't acknowledge Bellehumeur's attempts to reach him.

"Paul was very helpful," Bellehumeur said later. "I had very strong words for him. If someone does good work, I don't care what your feelings are. I have a lot of respect for him. I feel badly that I got so angry at him. Some people forget [such blow ups], some don't."

Despite his falling out with Bellehumeur, Chapey said later that "the puck wouldn't have gotten done without Alex" working so hard to push the process forward.

The income from the puck over the years was definitely substantial. The May 1997 issue of InLine Hockey News stated that 300,000 Jofa SpeedPucks were sold in 1996 alone. Between April 19, 1992 and August 14, 1995 [according to records that I was shown during an interview at Bellehumeur's home], revenue to RHI from the Jofa SpeedPuck was a total of $1,082,977.48, with Bellehumeur's share coming to $211,016.01.

Vancouver VooDoo owner Mike King recalled that while he did hear a lot about the infighting over the patent, he wasn't intimately involved with those discussions.

"The thing I remember from an owner's perspective is there was always this promise from the league that there would be royalties coming back to the individual teams, and I don't think that a nickel ever came our way," King said.

"I have always felt that this issue caused the largest, deepest and most irreparable fracture in the RHI partnership and team owners," Pona said. "It's ironic, but the puck really is the enigma of RHI; the league couldn't have been formed without the Jofa SpeedPuck, but the RHI partnership (and the league) was torn apart due to numerous puck disputes. I look back at that time and just shake my head, because in my heart, I know many of the disagreements between the partners were caused by the puck. I could see how important this four-ounce PVC biscuit was to all of us. But I could not believe that they would allow their egos and greed to disrupt a league that many felt had a real chance for long-term survival. In hindsight, it's easy to see that they cut off their noses to spite their face."

"The puck was a whole 'nother disaster, for sure," said Chris Palmer, who worked in RHI's offices at the time. "I remember that there was a lot of yelling and all sorts of brawling in the office. That was one of the main reasons why that trio of ownership just did not work. Everyone was out kind of for their own thing. That was the whole puck fiasco. That was not good. Lots of arguments, lots of yelling, and that was just how that office ran."

The two sides of RHI's puck ended up resembling the "two-faced" nature of Shakespeare's Puck – a destructive trickster, indeed.

CHAPTER 18

We Want the Chick!

One of the most intriguing things about Roller Hockey International was its inclusion of women as media directors, general managers, team owners – and players. That's probably not surprising, considering that Larry King, the league's CEO, had once been married to tennis legend Billie Jean King, and with her, had co-founded World Team Tennis, the Women's Sports Foundation, and Women's Sports + Fitness magazine in 1974. The magazines and the foundation were created with the idea of bringing more women into the world of sports – as executives as well as athletes. Dennis Murphy was a WTT co-founder, and Jerry Buss, who later became the owner of the NBA's Los Angeles Lakers and the NHL's Los Angeles Kings, first jumped into professional sports when he bought the league's Los Angeles Strings. The Strings were also where Buss's daughter Jeanie Buss learned her first lessons in professional sports.

Most professional team sports are played purely by men or by women, not both, largely because of size and strength differences. Many women – Babe Didrikson Zaharias, Annika Sorenstam and Danica Patrick among them – have made their mark in non-body-contact professional sports. But there has never been a woman who has played a regular-season game at the highest levels of professional sports in the National Football League, the National Basketball Association, Major League Baseball or the National Hockey League. While Manon Rheaume was the first woman to play in a professional ice hockey game on September 23, 1992, for the Tampa Bay Lightning, making seven saves on nine shots, it was during the NHL exhibition season. Three months later, on December 13, Rheaume played in a regular-season game in the minor professional leagues, when she replaced David Littman as the starting goalie in a game for the Atlanta Knights of the International Hockey League.

Rheaume, who was born in Lac Beauport, Quebec, on February 24, 1972, played in her first professional roller hockey game in 1994. That year, originally chosen by the San Diego Barracudas, she was traded to the New Jersey Rockin Rollers for a first-round draft pick. Rheaume played four games for New Jersey in 1994, winning one on July 12 against another female goalie, Erin Whitten of the Pittsburgh Phantoms. Rheaume stopped 24 shots, allowing just two goals in the second half during a 10-7 home victory. It was the first matchup between female goaltenders in Roller Hockey International and Rheaume's first RHI victory.

Whitten played three games for the Pittsburgh Phantoms in 1994 and one game for the Oakland Skates in 1995. A third woman played in RHI games, goaltender Kelly Dyer, though it is unclear from the historical record how many games she played, or what her record was. Dyer had begun playing ice hockey as an 11 year old against boys in her neighborhood in Foxboro, Massachusetts. In high school, she played with such future NHL players as Tom Barasso, Bob Sweeney and Jeff Norton. She was passed over by some colleges for being "too aggressive."

Rheaume also participated in RHI's 1994 All-Star Game. The same year, Harper Collins published Rheaume's autobiography, "Manon: Alone in Front of the Net."

In 1995, while she was still with Rockin Rollers, a wheel manufacturer named Kryptonics made a poster with Manon in net, wearing goalie gear but no helmet. The caption read: "Women have dealt with offensive men for over 5 million years. Why should hockey be any different?"

Though RHI Stats (http://rhistats.tripod.com) credited Rheaume with playing one 1995 game for the Rockin Rollers, no game statistics are given. In February 1996, the Rockin Rollers traded Rheaume to the Ottawa Loggers for two draft picks. That season, RHI Stats recorded Rheaume as playing a half a game for the Loggers, allowing five goals while making 13 saves in 24 minutes.

In June 1996, Rheaume was traded again, this time from Ottawa to the Sacramento River Rats. There she got some playing time, appearing in four games, allowing 27 goals and making 100 saves for a 0.779 save percentage. Rheaume won two games and lost one. On July 3, in her first game as a River

Rat, Rheaume defeated the San Diego Barracudas, 12-10. She stopped 21 of 31 shots and had two assists. It was the first time a male goaltender had lost an RHI game to a woman. Rheaume later beat the San Jose Rhinos.

"We lost," said Rhinos' backup goalie Mario Sousa. "I will never forget. We went into the locker room and Jay Murphy was beet red. He told all the guys, 'This will be some kind of story, when I get older and I have kids, and I gotta tell my kids that we lost to a chick.'"

Cammi Granato, the younger sister of Tony Granato, a former NHL player and head coach, had a tryout with RHI's Chicago Cheetahs in 1995, but she was a forward, unlike Rheaume, Dyer and Erin Whitten. (Three years later, Granato won a gold medal as the captain of the U.S. women's ice hockey team at the 1998 Winter Olympics in Nagano, Japan, while Rheaume led Team Canada to the silver medal.)

Although RHI was a niche sport, Rheaume and Whitten and Dyer did achieve something singular – making it to the pros in a men's league. The lady players had a lot to contend with. For instance, Manon Rheaume had to put on her gear in a private locker room and had no roommate when the team traveled, thus missing some of the camaraderie that goes with team sports. She also got tired of defending her decision to play against men and sometimes being treated as a sideshow. In one home game in which the New Jersey Rockin Rollers starting goalie Daniel Berthiaume had given up several goals, the crowd began chanting, "We want the chick! We want the chick!"

When I interviewed Rheaume in August 1994, she said that she received more than 100 fan letters per week.

"I have some people help me to send back some stuff to them," Rheaume said. "That's why I do card shows during the summer, because I have a chance to meet the fans, talk to them and sign stuff for them."

I asked her about her hopes of possibly playing in the National Hockey League one day, and I hit a nerve.

"I'm really sick about the NHL," she said. "I never said I'm going to make the NHL. Before you make the NHL you need to play a lot of ice hockey in the American League, and I'm not there yet. I just want to improve myself and see how far I can go. I like to work hard and train. I told myself I'm going to see how far I can go after that."

Cammi Granato, who'd been chosen by the Chicago Cheetahs as their first draft choice for the 1995 season, did not play after all. Granato and her family decided the risks of participating in RHI's hard-hitting game were just too high. Unlike Rheaume, Dyer and Whitten, whose goalie equipment and rules against goaltender interference provided more protection, Granato would have been faced with potential checks by some of RHI's 200-pound defenseman.

Though she never played in a game, Cammi Granato did practice with the team.

And while it's true that Erin Whitten didn't play many games in Pittsburgh, as there were two male goaltenders on the depth chart in front of her, she appreciated the opportunities she did get.

"I played the third period during some games, the last period during others," Whitten said. "It wasn't a publicity stunt. I had a blast in Pittsburgh. I was single, and I was able to go out and hang out and be 'one of the boys,' in a sense. At that time, it was when the O.J. Simpson occurrence was going on. I remember all of us sitting there and watching O.J. driving away on television."

Whitten recalled one Phantoms' practice when the team's home rink, Mellon Arena, was booked for another event.

"We skated at an outdoor rink, it was about 90 degrees, and a lot of the guys had gone out the night before," Whitten said. "I think that the head coach, Rick Kehoe, knew. It was a Sport Court rink outside of Pittsburgh. We had lost our last game, and he put trash cans out and it was all about skating – no pucks; we just skated. There were a few sick individuals. I remember thinking that it was so hot, and the smells on the rink were awful."

Women who made major contributions to RHI as owners and general managers included Larry King's second wife, Nancy King, who had been the media director for the league before becoming president of the Sacramento River Rats. Other important women included L.A. Blades' owner Jeanie Buss, Florida Hammerheads' owner Julia Neal, Oakland Skates' co-owner Gail Bettinelli, Buffalo Wings' co-owner Dr. Frances Edmonston and Phoenix Cobras' General Manager Madeleine Simon.

In the August/September 1995 issue of InLine Hockey News, OJ Callahan wrote an article called "Trailblazers," on the women of RHI.

Simon, the Phoenix Cobras' GM in 1994 and 1995, told Callahan that although she had run into "old school" attitude from some of RHI's hierarchy, the league did show a relative openness to women, and deserved credit for it.

"If there's any chance for a female to have a position of authority and to get respect, RHI presents those opportunities," Simon said. "I am especially proud of how the RHI rule book states 'his or her' when referring to players."

Gail Bettinelli, one of the owners of the Oakland Skates, found herself on the wrong side of the respect equation at an Oakland Skates' team party in 1994. Stephane Desjardins, new to the team, badly wanted to score some goals. So when Garry Unger, the Skates' coach, told him, "If you push her in the pool, you'll play on the power play tomorrow night," Desjardins didn't hesitate.

"There she goes, down in the drink," Desjardins said. "She was wearing a dress, I think. I thought she was going to send me home."

The next night, Desjardins was ready for his time on the power play, but Unger wouldn't put him in.

"I'm screaming at him," Desjardins said. "That's Garry Unger. He's a legend, the Iron Man. He's like, 'Desjardins, you'd better shut up, because you're going to be on the plane home so bleeping fast.' So, I didn't get no power play time. I was so pissed. Are you kidding me? I almost got sent home before the game."

Nancy King, RHI's director of public relations, also spoke to OJ Callahan for his article.

"Many times, Dennis [Murphy] and I would hash out the details on the number of teams, the number of players, etc., before ever approaching Larry. I was part of a team, never feeling separated because I was a woman," King said. King added that having female players like Rheaume and Whitten brought a unique flavor to RHI, increasing the number of fans – and publicity. "It's key to the success of a new league," King said. "Manon Rheaume alone generated coverage in USA Today, MTV, ESPN and more. In that respect, it's very, very important to the league."

Later, King told me that she used the contacts she'd made working for

World Team Tennis to promote Roller Hockey International.

"I was working on the Women's Tennis Association from 1984 to 1990," King said. "And then Larry and I married and I still had a lot of tennis contacts, so I was using a lot of those media contacts. We got the first article in USA Today about roller hockey. Nobody knew what it was at that point."

King's role was to make sure that RHI's teams filed their game stories and worked to get game stories published in their local markets. Some teams were more successful than others.

"Anaheim was good, and the New Jersey Rockin Rollers did a good job," King said. "Owner E. Burke Ross did a nice job on promotion and PR. The teams that had worked in sports did better jobs, because they kind of knew what to do. And Jeanie Buss's team, of course, did well."

Teams that could afford to promote themselves did very well; conversely, teams that had fewer financial resources struggled.

King said that her contacts in the media helped give RHI decent national press initially, but when teams didn't draw enough fans, much of that media attention fell away.

"I think we were lucky because the sport was so new, and there was so much excitement about it on the ground level in terms of the kids playing, and it just caught like wildfire, initially," King said. "You saw rinks just start popping up all over. So you figured, 'OK, this is going to go.' But we just couldn't get the spectatorship out of it. They were willing to give us a little boost to jump-start us, but then we had to draw. We weren't drawing. It grew too big too fast."

Jeanie Buss generated some rather unique coverage – or un-coverage – for Roller Hockey International when she posed in the May 1995 issue of Playboy.

Los Angeles Times' columnist Robin Abcarian expressed puzzlement at Buss's decision to shed her clothes for the men's magazine. She couldn't understand why Buss, who owned the Los Angeles Blades and was a member of the board of directors for the Los Angeles Lakers, would bare all. Abcarian used amateur psychology to deduce Buss's logic, arguing that the clothes came off for a variety of reasons – to gain attention and approval, to be provocative, or to show her independence. All those reasons had merit, but I like to think that Abcarian's final suggestion might have been closest to the mark – that it would help promote the sport and the Blades. After all, one Canadian player Buss recruited to play for the Blades decided to join the team after she sent him a copy of the issue. Attracting players to the team was only one part of the equation, however.

"The fans were the most important thing," said Jeanie Buss in an interview years later. "It impressed me so much that there were people that wanted to pay for this product and had a passion for it, and would come to every game. It mattered to them, every win and loss. They loved our players."

The fans' passion inspired the Blades to bring the players out after home games to sit at tables and sign autographs – even if it took two hours to get through the long lines of spectators.

"I remember that we had one player who complained about it," Buss said. "He was like, 'I really don't want to have to do that.' It was like a hassle for him to have to sign autographs. That made me crazy, because, who are you to say that? I said, 'OK, if you don't want to do it, that's fine. But I'm going to take your name off your jersey, and I'm going to take you out of the media guide and the program so that our fans won't know who you are. They won't want your autograph because they won't know your name.' He backed off that real quick."

According to league co-founder Dennis Murphy, "If we didn't have Jeanie [Buss], we probably wouldn't have had the league."

"Jeanie lived and ate and breathed RHI," said Bob McKillop, who had played for Buss's Los Angeles Blades in 1996. "She loved that thing so much. She put every single thing she could into that league. It was her child from conception. She treated us wonderfully, and she deserved a lot better fate for what she put into that league. She's extremely smart, and she promoted the league through herself. She was the vice president of the L.A. Lakers. She didn't have to do that, but it didn't matter – the league was her thing; it was everything to her. That league was what it was because of Jeanie Buss."

CHAPTER 19

Beep, Beep, and So Long, Charlie

One attractive element of Roller Hockey International, from a hockey fan's standpoint, was its many connections to former National Hockey League stars. They added glamour and excitement to the league. Heck, back in the late 1960s, I had collected hockey cards of players like Ralph Backstrom, Terry Harper, Yvan Cournoyer and Garry Unger, all of whom became involved in RHI. Backstrom, the NHL's Rookie of the Year in 1959, was RHI's commissioner. Harper, who had played 1,066 NHL games for five different teams, winning five Stanley Cups with Montreal Canadiens, became the general manager of the Sacramento River Rats. Cournoyer, who coached the Montreal Roadrunners in 1994 and 1995, had won 10 Stanley Cups with the Montreal Canadiens, second only to Henri Richard among NHL players. Unger, as mentioned earlier, set a longstanding consecutive-game record, coached the Oakland Skates for several seasons.

Younger former NHL players also lent their names and fame to RHI. Jim McGeough, who had played 57 NHL games in the early '80s, played for 1993 Connecticut Coasters, 1994 Sacramento River Rats, 1995 Oklahoma Coyotes, and one game for the St. Louis Vipers in 1997. Perry Turnbull, who played in 608 NHL games with St. Louis Blues, Montreal Canadiens and Winnipeg Jets, took to inline skates for the St. Louis Vipers in 1993 and 1994, and he later coached the team. Dave "Tiger" Williams, a veteran of 962 NHL games for five teams, played one game for the Vancouver VooDoo in 1993 and was the team's GM and coach thereafter. Dave Schultz, who became infamous as an enforcer for the NHL's Philadelphia Flyers, was a co-owner of the Philadelphia Bulldogs in 1994. In 1995, the Detroit Motor City Mustangs, owned by Dino Ciccarelli and Shawn Burr of the Detroit Red Wings, were coached by Marty Howe, the son of the NHL's "Mr. Hockey," Gordie Howe of the Detroit Red Wings. Dennis Maruk, who coached the Minnesota Blue Ox to a record of 13-11-0 in

1995, scored nearly a point a game in 888 NHL games for four different teams.

While I did my best to keep a professional journalist's demeanor around some of my ice hockey heroes, I won't deny that it was a thrill to be on speaking terms with many of them. Even Bobby "The Golden Jet" Hull was connected to the league, if only through his son, Bobby Hull, Jr., who coached the Los Angeles Blades in 1994 and 1995. If my favorite player from my youth, Dave Keon of the Toronto Maple Leafs, had been involved in the league, I would have felt I'd died and gone to heaven.

Walt Poddubny, Bryan Trottier and Rik Wilson also laced up inline skates and played in RHI games. Poddubny scored 47 points in 19 games for the Las Vegas Flash in 1994 and another 17 points as a player/coach for the Orlando Rollergators in 10 games the following season. Poddubny, who died March 21, 2009, played 468 NHL games in 11 seasons, scoring 184 goals and 238 assists for 422 points. Trottier, a six-time Stanley Cup champion who had scored 523 goals and 901 assists during his NHL career, played home games for the Pittsburgh Phantoms in 1994.

The first time Trottier played competitive inline hockey, it was during a pre-season scrimmage with the Phantoms, and he had two goals and three assists. During the 1994 season, Trottier, wearing the same number 19 he wore in the NHL, played nine games for the Phantoms. He scored nine goals and had 13 assists for 22 points, and represented the Phantoms at the inaugural RHI All-Star Game in Vancouver.

New York Rangers' captain and Tampa Bay Tritons' owner Mark Messier brought the Stanley Cup to Expo Hall in Tampa Bay's Expo Hall on June 22 for a game against the Florida Hammerheads.

Christian Skoryna remembered that night well.

"Tampa Bay was our cross-state rival," Skoryna said. "We always had good games with them, despite being terrible against everybody else. We went out to party afterwards, and I found myself shuffling into some club at about three in the morning. I was just obliterated, so I went and sat down on a couch. I look over, and I'm sitting beside Mark Messier, and the Stanley Cup is between us. It was completely by accident, and I was like, 'Wow.' I got someone to snap a picture. I still have that picture of Messier and I on a couch with the Cup between us."

"I liked Mark Messier, the way he handled himself and presented himself," said Colin Baustad, who played for the Tritons in their one and only year in RHI. "It was a family-run hockey team. The whole family was so professional in their attitude in the way they carried themselves and in the expectations that they had of us. They taught us how to be high-performance athletes."

Bobby Hull, a former NHL and World Hockey Association star, attended a game his son, Bobby Hull Jr., coached for the Los Angeles Blades on July 23, 1994. The senior Hull was very impressed and said he found the game as exciting as ice hockey.

The following evening, the elder Hull was a ceremonial Blades' coach at the Los Angeles Blades-Edmonton Sled Dogs game alongside his other son, NHL sniper Brett Hull of the St. Louis Blues. Brett must have been extremely envious of the space and time that Roller Hockey International's players had to utilize – at the time, the National Hockey League's game was a dreary mix of dump-and-chase, clutch-and-grab hockey that slowed down the pace and handcuffed the game's stars. While on the Blades' bench, Hull was probably dreaming about all the goals he could score if the NHL emulated RHI's wide-open style of play.

Perry Turnbull, a teammate of Federko's on the St. Louis Blues, played 26 games for RHI's St. Louis Vipers in 1993 and 1994 and scored 57 points – adding 116 penalty minutes. I later asked Turnbull if any of his old NHL colleagues ever laughed at him or made jokes about him being involved with roller hockey.

"If they did laugh at me, it was under their breath," Turnbull said.

Yvan Cournoyer, who had played 968 games for the NHL's Montreal Canadiens, coached RHI's Montreal Roadrunners in 1994 and 1995. In the October 1994 issue of InLine magazine, Cournoyer explained how the Roadrunners dealt with one of the most critical elements of inline skating – stopping. He exhorted his players to keep rolling.

"It's a little harder to stop quickly in roller hockey, and it is a far more wide-open game with the four-on-four format," Cournoyer said. "So why stop at all? I want my guys moving and harder to catch – just like the roadrunner bird.

Beep, beep, and so long, Charlie."

Garry Unger was an important part of RHI, and not just because he coached the Oakland Skates or because of his consecutive-games streak in the NHL. Unger followed Chris McSorley's lead by bringing to the Skates most of the roster from his Central Hockey League ice hockey team, the Tulsa Oilers. That was probably why the Skates had played the Anaheim Bullfrogs in RHI's 1993 championship final rather than one of the RHI teams that had depended upon rosters composed of roller hockey players lacking rough-and-tumble ice hockey experience.

Nick Fotiu and Ken Morrow were two other NHL veterans moonlighting in RHI. Fotiu, who coached the New Jersey Rockin Rollers in 1993, suited up for two games, scoring no points and gathering just six penalty minutes. That was very uncharacteristic, considering that Fotiu had accumulated 1,362 penalty minutes in his 646-game NHL career.

Other players who had a short stint in the NHL *before* coming to Roller Hockey International included Ralph Barahona, Daniel Berthiaume, Max Middendorf, Jeff Rohlicek and Daniel Shank.

Of those players, Shank was the most successful in RHI. He scored a journeyman-like 27 points in 77 NHL games for the Detroit Red Wings and the Hartford Whalers, was a star in RHI. He compiled 325 points and 302 penalty minutes in 94 games for four different teams – the San Diego Barracudas (1993), Phoenix Cobras (1994), Anaheim Bullfrogs (1995), and the Orlando Jackals (1996 and 1997). His chippy play earned him respect and enmity, both on *and* off the floor.

A Two-Way Street

While many former National Hockey League stars were involved in Roller Hockey International, numerous RHI players moved the other direction and had a stint in "The Show," the National Hockey League.

Though he'd played 22 NHL games in the 1998-99 season, Jose "Joe" Charbonneau got another shot at the big league after a stunningly successful RHI season in 1993 with the Vancouver VooDoo in which he led the league in scoring, with 25 goals and 43 assists for 68 points in 14 games. Playing in RHI did wonders for his physical fitness, which along with his scoring championship, helped Charbonneau earn a spot on the NHL's Vancouver Canucks after RHI's 1993 season.

One of Roller Hockey International's most successful alums was Glen Metropolit, who played for the Long Island Jawz in 1996. He scored 32 goals and had 39 assists in 28 games, and played another six games for the Anaheim Bullfrogs and New Jersey Rockin Rollers in 1997. Metropolit followed up his RHI stint by playing 407 NHL games for several teams, with his most productive season coming for the Boston Bruins in 2007-08, when he had 11 goals and 22 assists in 82 games. In 2009-10, Metropolit had 16 goals and 13 assists in 69 games for the Montreal Canadiens, despite missing much of the late season with a shoulder separation. In the playoffs, Metropolit and the Habs, who had finished eighth overall in the Eastern Conference, had a stunning run. They shocked the first-place Washington Capitals and then eliminated the defending champion Pittsburgh Penguins, both in seven-game series, before falling in the Eastern Conference championship to the Philadelphia Flyers.

Several other RHI players had longer NHL careers, including goaltender Manny Legace, who led the Toronto Planets to the RHI playoffs in 1993. At the time of this writing, Legace had played more than 365 NHL games over 11 seasons and had won a Stanley Cup with the Detroit Red Wings in 2002. Unfortunately, his name was misspelled on the Cup as "Legece."

"Manny Legace was unforgettable," said Christian Skoryna, Legace's teammate on the Toronto Planets in 1993. "He won league MVP that year. Facing 60 shots a game, he'd bag 58 of them. He was the true MVP of that league by far. And that's the only year he ever played in RHI; he was obviously on to bigger and better things."

Skoryna said that he'd never played with a better player, saying that Legace was supremely focused, recognizing what it would take to get to the next level.

"Where we'd all be listening to music and hanging out and joking around before the game in the dressing room, Manny was just in a zone from the time he came to the rink," Skoryna said. "When it came time to work, he was all business, and he took that focus into the rink with him. I took those lessons from him away from roller hockey as to what it takes to become a consummate professional."

Darren Langdon, who played for the Anaheim Bullfrogs in 1994, skated in 521 NHL games with the New York Rangers, Carolina Hurricanes, Vancouver Canucks, Montreal Canadiens and New Jersey Devils. Langdon may have not scored many points in those games – just 16 goals and 23 assists for 39 points – but that was not his role. Instead, Langdon stood up for his teammates and fought the NHL's toughest brawlers while accumulating 1,251 penalty minutes. Los Angeles Blades' backup goaltender Brad Sholl remembered a 1994 game against Langdon and the Bullfrogs in Anaheim.

"There was some physical play along the boards right in front of our bench, and some guys were jawing and yapping at Darren; they didn't know who he was," Sholl said. Anaheim coach Grant Sonier looked over at our bench and at [Chris] Nelson and said, 'Nelly! You better tell those guys who he is.' The very next year, Langdon was a rookie for the New York Rangers, and I saw him get into a fight with someone on the Kings. Oh, my gosh. I'm glad that no one [on our team] did anything."

During the 1993/94 and 1994/95 seasons, Alex Hicks played ice hockey for Chris McSorley in Toledo and Las Vegas, and joined him again with the Buffalo Stampede in the summer of 1994. Signed by the Mighty Ducks in 1995, Hicks had two goals and an assist and was named the number-one star in his very first NHL game.

Other RHI players who made it to it to the NHL included Harry York, Mike Kennedy, Barry Potomski and Sasha Lakovic. Potomski, who played for the Anaheim Bullfrogs in 1993, got a taste of the NHL with the Los Angeles Kings, scoring two goals and accumulating 30 penalty minutes in his first six NHL games. Rob Laurie and Victor Gervais, Potomski's teammates with the Bullfrogs in 1993, remembered Potomski's nightly run to Del Taco in the team van.

"You'd be in your room and you'd just hear, 'Vrooomm! Screeeeechhhh! Vrooomm! Screeeeechhhh!'" Laurie said.

"He was pounding on the gas or he was going around the corners on two tires." "Every night, around 1 or 2 o'clock in the morning, we'd hear this screeching of brakes and it would be Barry Potomski in this 15-passenger van, going around the Ramada, trying to break his time from the night before," Gervais said. (Potomski passed away on May 24, 2011, after collapsing at Lifestyle Family Fitness in his hometown of Windsor, Ontario.)

Sasha Lakovic played in 56 RHI games between 1993 and 1997, scoring 100 points and adding 311 penalty minutes for the Vancouver VooDoo, Oakland Skates and San Jose Rhinos. He later played in 37 NHL games for the Calgary Flames and New Jersey Devils. He also played for the Philadelphia Sting of Major League Roller Hockey in 1998, during RHI's hiatus season.

Nicknamed the "Pit Bull," Lakovic recalled a stunt during the 1993 season with the Vancouver VooDoo.

"The first time I came out on the floor, we had my buddy's Pit Bull wearing my jersey, and I came out and wrestled the jersey off him," Lakovic said. "After putting the jersey on, I came on and skated around and hit the glass like I was making a body check. The glass in the Fairgrounds here was so thick that I smashed my elbow pretty good – but I broke the glass. I smashed the glass and had a big bump on my elbow for the rest of the game."

CHAPTER 20

We're the Guys with
the Picks and Shovels

During a ceremony in December 1994, RHI President Dennis Murphy was inducted into the Anaheim Sports Hall of Fame. Murphy's reward was well deserved, and it was one of the few highlights for RHI's leadership in the following year. For if the 1994 season had been one of rapid expansion, the 1995 edition was marked by contraction and conflict, much of it related to that expansion. At the time, it was incredibly difficult to get accurate information about league's plans for the upcoming season because so many conflicting statements had come from the league between September 1994 and February 1995. It was announced that the Buffalo Stampede would not return because of a mutual lawsuit with RHI, ostensibly over nonpayment of league dues, but they eventually did; that the Florida Hammerheads would move to Quebec, but they didn't, and folded; and that the Las Vegas Flash and Calgary Rad'z were still in the league, and they weren't. The franchise changes alone were mind boggling.

Besides the Hammerheads, Flash and Rad'z, other teams that left the league between the end of the 1994 season and the beginning of the 1995 season included the Atlanta Fire Ants, Edmonton Sled Dogs, New England Stingers, Pittsburgh Phantoms, Portland Rage and Tampa Bay Tritons. The Stingers and Tritons took "hiatus" status, though they never returned to the league. The Minnesota Blue Ox replaced the Minnesota Arctic Blast, the Sled Dogs became the Orlando RollerGators, and the Fire Ants became the Oklahoma City Coyotes. Two new teams were added – the Detroit Motor City Mustangs and the Ottawa Loggers. Once the shuffling had ended and the smoke had cleared, RHI would field 19 franchises in 1995 instead of 24.

Additionally, the Phoenix Cobras, owned by Anaheim Bullfrogs' co-owner Stuart Silver and a business partner, were in Chapter 11. Richard Shillington, the owner of the San Jose Rhinos, was said to have lost $480,000 during the 1994 season.

There *was* much discord behind the scenes, and the league leadership was trying to do damage control. That was hard to do, however.

"They had split offices," said Anaheim GM Bob Elder. "Nobody was in one office. Dennis was in Orange County, Larry was in Grass Valley and Alex had a home office. Today's market may be easier because of teleconferencing and you can put your meetings up on TV, but back then, conference calls were a bitch. A better idea would have been to put everything in one place."

RHI's Chief Operating Officer David McLane had his own office near the Great Western Forum in Inglewood, at one point, as well.

In addition to dealing with the changes at the top and communication issues, RHI's leadership had to fight a rearguard action with some unhappy franchise owners. Pittsburgh Phantoms' owner Howard Baldwin had hoped that the National Hockey League would buy RHI, and complained that he had paid large franchise fees to RHI for little in return. There were also rumors of an East Coast/West Coast split in RHI, with East Coast team owners making noises about creating their own league to compete with RHI. On March 20, 1995, RHI's new president, Jerry Diamond, announced that Baldwin and the Phantoms had left the league.

The league that was supposedly planning to go up against RHI was to be owned and televised by the Liberty Sports Network, which also owned Prime Sports and Sports Channel. Baldwin, who also owned of the NHL's Pittsburgh Penguins at the time, and Peter Jocketty, owner of Minnesota Arctic Blast, were to be limited partners. Months of news reports about this potential competitor to RHI followed, but it was all for naught, as Liberty Sports was eventually purchased by Fox Television, and the idea was shelved.

Baldwin was angry because RHI's 1994 expansion brought in many team owners who did not have stable financing.

In Mark Madden's "It's Like This" column in the April 1996 issue of InLine Hockey News, RHI CEO Larry King said that franchises had increased in price from $50,000 in 1993 to $300,000 in 1995. King justified the increase. "We've spent $35 million to get to where we are," King said. "We're pioneers.

We're the guys with the picks and the shovels. We built the market."

Unfortunately, few RHI team owners had the combination of deep pockets and patience to survive over the long haul. Keeping track of the teams that departed and arrived since the league had started was like trying to remember everyone's names at a party where half the people are identical twins.

At the same time that factions were battling it out inside Roller Hockey International, the sport was booming and the league had incredible potential. At the Super Show, the world's largest sporting goods trade show held each year in Atlanta. Liz Dolan, Nike's vice president of marketing, commented on the incredible growth of off-ice hockey: "The future just showed up and it's wearing a hockey mask."

In 1994, the Anaheim Bullfrogs sold more than $500,000 in merchandise, including $301,000 worth of jerseys, $27,000 in pogs, $101,000 in hats and $81,000 in T-shirts. The Vancouver VooDoo sold about $350,000 worth of team merchandise in 1994, including 2,237 jerseys, some of which ended up in Jamaica.

"A member of a Jamaican roller hockey team saw our logo in the 1994 RHI program and phoned us," said Mike King, the president of the Vancouver VooDoo, at the time. "Now the whole team in Jamaica is wearing Vancouver VooDoo jerseys."

RHI's overall attendance numbers had been climbing as well, from 25,000 spectators during the U.S./Canada tour in 1992 to 400,000 fans in 1993 to 1,300,000 in 1994.

"I think we'll have between 1.7 million to 2 million spectators in 1995," said Larry King.

Two surveys, published in the June 1995 issues of InLine Retailer and Roller Hockey magazine, stated that roller hockey was America's fastest-growing sport. According to a sports participation study conducted by American Sports Data for the Sporting Goods Manufacturer's Association, roller hockey grew 58.3 percent from 1993 to 1994, for a total of 3.7 million participants. In the second survey, by the National Sporting Goods Association, the number of participants 7 and older nationwide grew from about 1.5 million to about 2.2 million, a 50.3 percent increase.

Inline hockey's popularity had not gone unnoticed by the National Hockey League. In the June 1995 issue of InLine Retailer & Industry News, the NHL's COO Rick Dudley said, "Roller hockey broadens the access to the game of hockey to more people. ... Picture a pyramid at the top of which is the NHL and the game on ice, the middle is roller hockey and the bottom is street hockey – that's how we view the world of hockey. At the lowest barrier of entry is a kid with sneakers and a stick and a ball. This is the basis for the rationale behind the Nike/NHL Street program, which is a program with Nike where we're giving sticks and nets to boys and girls clubs and YMCAs and encouraging them to make street hockey part of their curriculum."

Dudley said that the NHL viewed roller hockey as a complement to ice hockey and "a great marketing tool." He touted the NHL Breakout Tour, originally designed for amateur players, as a potential opportunity for professional players to "compete on a weekly basis or league-type format. It's the natural extension of the roller hockey explosion that we see out there right now."

Even better, on March 27, 1995, Roller Hockey International announced a combined partnership and television package for the upcoming season in which Pepsi Cola, Taco Bell and All-Sport would promote their product lines in RHI's markets and sponsor ESPN's airing of 18 games, including a Monday night game of the week on espn2.

For many people, it seemed as if the sky was the limit for the sport of inline hockey and RHI.

1995 Regular Season

The third RHI draft was held on February 17 in Los Angeles, and notable picks included the Chicago Cheetahs' choice of Cammi Granato and the Detroit Mustangs' selection of NHL legend Gordie "Mr. Hockey" Howe. While it was obvious that Gordie Howe, 66 years old at the time, was not likely to play for the Mustangs, the pick certainly gained the league some media coverage.

Two months later, the league gained the kind of media attention it didn't want. Gerry St. Cyr, Chris Valicevic, Brian Downey and Andy Rymsha, the four-man unit behind Portland's run to the RHI championship finals in 1994, were traded to the New Jersey Rockin Rollers on April 7, 1995, just before the Rage went on hiatus. Mark Madden, a writer for the Pittsburgh Post-Gazette, slammed the shady trade in his column in the June/July 1995 issue of InLine Hockey News:

"Now I don't know if money discreetly changed hands. I don't know if someone in Portland owed someone in New Jersey a favor. I do know that the quartet of players involved were Portland's four best. I do know that it unfairly shook the competitive balance of the league."

As the 1995 season progressed, the Montreal Roadrunners raced to the top of the Eastern Conference's Atlantic Division, finishing with 15 wins, six losses and three shootout losses for 33 points. Guy Rouleau led the Roadrunners offensively with 37 goals and 46 assists for 83 points, while the team's goaltenders, Francois Gravel and Corrado Micalef, held opponents off the scoreboard in the offense-oriented league. Gravel went 8-3-2, Micalef 7-3-1. The Ottawa Loggers, a first-year team, finished second with a 14-9-1 record. The New Jersey Rockin Rollers (13-11-0), Philadelphia Bulldogs (12-10-2) and Orlando RollerGators (7-16-0) rounded out the division.

"Orlando was a mess," recalled RollerGators' defenseman Lance Brady. "I think we had seven skaters the first practice I was down there. We were practicing in a roller skating rink on wood. I felt I was back in high school trying to get a date with one of the roller girls. The head coach, Walt Poddubny, didn't know if he should coach or be a player coach. One game he would be on the first line, the next, he would be behind the bench."

Brady suffered a bad injury that season when he took a slap shot to the eye.

"I knew something was wrong as soon as I got hit," Brady said. "I almost puked right on the floor. I was rolling off the floor with help of one of my teammates, and it was like a black wall was rising over my left eye. Eventually, it just filled up with blood, as I had what is called a hyphema – a severely bruised eye. I remember being in the locker room waiting for the ambulance, looking in the mirror, I put a hand over my left eye – 'OK, I can see.' I put a hand over my right eye, 'Damn it, nothing. Completely blind.' "

Brady stayed in the hospital for about two weeks. Fortunately, the fluids that had built up in his eye drained, and he was able to return to the team – wearing a shield for the remainder of his RHI career.

"And because the cheap owner of the RollerGators had a $1,000 deductible on hospital visits, they tried to stick me with the bill," Brady said. "Man, those creditors are tough. It was two years that they tracked me down from city to city. I eventually found the contract that I signed with the team and sent the creditors off to the original owners of the RollerGators."

The Eastern Conference's Central Division was tight all season, with the St. Louis Vipers (13-7-2) edging out the Minnesota Blue Ox (13-11-0) and Detroit Motor City Mustangs (11-9-4) for first place by just two points. The Chicago Cheetahs (10-12-2) and Buffalo Stampede (10-13-0) occupied the last two spots in the division. Buffalo, the 1994 defending champion, had gone from first to worst and missed the playoffs. Tony Szabo led the Central Division's Detroit Motor City Mustangs to a third-place finish in a big way, scoring a Roller Hockey International record 50 goals in 24 games, breaking the previous record of 42 in 22 games set by Gerry St. Cyr of the Portland Rage in 1994. Szabo, a scoring machine, also had 32 assists and 82 total points, putting him third in regular-season scoring behind Oklahoma City's Doug Lawrence (23-68-91) and Guy Rouleau of Montreal (37-46-83).

In what was the league's most competitive division, the Vancouver VooDoo (13-10-1) and Sacramento River Rats (12-9-3) battled it out for first place in the Western Conference's Northwest Division. Each team had 27 points, but the VooDoo edged the River Rats on the basis of number of wins. Vancouver was paced by sharpshooting forwards Ryan Harrison (31 goals and 32 assists for 63 points) and Doug Ast (34 goals and 27 assists for 61 points). The chippy San Jose Rhinos finished third with 13-11-0 record and 819 penalty minutes, 166 more than New Jersey's 653. The Oakland Skates finished fourth in the league's smallest division (four teams) with a 10-10-4 record. Their 24 points were just three points off the pace set by the VooDoo and River Rats.

The Anaheim Bullfrogs ran away from the rest of the Western Conference's Pacific Division with an impressive 19-4-1 record, a whopping 13 points ahead of the second-place Phoenix Cobras (13-11-0). The San Diego Barracudas (12-11-1) finished third, one point behind the Cobras, followed by the 9-10-5

Los Angeles Blades and 7-17-0 Oklahoma Coyotes. Despite having Doug Lawrence setting league records for assists (68) and points (91), the Coyotes joined the Buffalo Stampede and Orlando RollerGators as the only three teams not to make the playoffs in 1995. Anaheim's 19 regular season wins set a league record, topping the record of 18 wins shared in 1994 by the Los Angeles Blades and Minnesota Arctic Blast in a 22-game season. The Bullfrogs' success helped vault coach Grant Sonier to the Western Conference Coach of the Year award. Bullfrogs' rookie Todd Wetzel deserved a lot of credit for the team's success, scoring a franchise-record 40 goals and adding 27 assists. Victor Gervais, with 23 goals and 55 assists for 78 points, led the Bullfrogs in scoring. Daniel Shank, acquired from the Phoenix Cobras in a preseason trade for Anaheim's popular Bobby McKillop, added 72 points on 24 goals and 48 assists.

Just two days before the playoffs started, Anaheim played the Barracudas at the San Diego Sports Arena in a meaningless regular-season game. Well, meaningless except for bragging rights. In a game that was tied 9-9, Barracudas' forward Mike Duffey scored the game winner on a rush with just 10 seconds to go. The game was televised by ESPN, and Jim Fox, who was doing color commentary, tried to interview Duffey on the bench.

"Jim Fox wanted to interview me, but I was in a psycho stage," Duffey said. "They used to call me Charles Manson. I said, 'I don't talk to nobody when I'm playing.' I just didn't recognize him at first. My teammates said, 'That was Jim Fox,' and I went, 'Oh, shit.' He was kind of pissed at me, so, after I got the winning goal, he said, 'Not known for speed, not known for scoring, Duffey scores the winning goal.' He hacked on me a little bit because I didn't interview with him. I have the tape. After the game, Oleg Yashin and Lev Berdichevsky, a couple Russian guys, came up to me and said, 'Hey, Duff. ESPN's waiting out in the hallway for ya for an interview.' I'm like, 'Oh, really?' And I went on up and there's nobody out there. They laughed and said, 'You stupid ass, you didn't fall for that one, did you?' The whole team said, 'You dumb shit.'"

Barracudas' GM Joe Noris remembered the game well.

"One of the greatest memories we had there was when we played against the Bullfrogs here in San Diego," Noris said. "It was a tremendous rivalry,

mostly between Dennis Murphy, our owner here, and the Silvers from
Anaheim, who had a magnificent team. I was sitting with Dennis Murphy a
couple of rows behind the Silvers, who had come down for the game. Late in
the game, and at just a perfect angle for all of us sitting there, Mike Duffey
came screaming down the right side and let a shot go that won the game for
us. The Silvers sank in their chairs, and Dennis became 8 feet tall. He was
smiling like mad and rubbing it in, and it was a very fun thing."

On July 15, RHI held its second All-Star Game at Missouri's Kiel Center,
the home of St. Louis Vipers. The game showcased the skills of Tony Szabo of
the Detroit Motor City Mustangs. Szabo scored five goals and paced the East
in a 14-12 win over the West. Named the game's MVP, Szabo won a check for
$1,500. Not bad for a night's work. Szabo very nearly missed the game – he'd
passed out from the heat in a Mustangs' home game the night before against
the Philadelphia Bulldogs.

St. Louis Vipers' coach Perry Turnbull said he was impressed by the skill
assembled for the All-Star Game. "If you could have had them play a more
physical game with that level of talent – boy, we could have a spectator
sport there."

After an incident during a VooDoo away game against the Sacramento
River Rats, Tiger Williams caught the sharp eye (and pen) of Mark Madden.
In Madden's "It's Like This" column in the October/November 1995 issue
of InLine Hockey News, he slammed Tiger harshly: "Dave 'Tiger' Williams
was lucky his NHL career occurred when it did. He debuted in 1974-75,
the heyday of goonery. He fought, slashed, speared and butt-ended his way
through 14 seasons and a record-setting 3,966 penalty minutes. Williams' era
was a time when acting like you belonged in a straitjacket made you colorful."

Madden then discussed a game on August 9 in Sacramento in which
Williams punched River Rats' Vadim Slivchenko, and as Arco Arena security
personnel walked Williams out of the building for his transgression, he
broke away and went into the stands after someone who poured a beer on
his head. Williams was arrested, faced misdemeanor assault charges, and
was suspended by RHI Commissioner Ralph Backstrom for three games.
In his column, and at a relatively safe distance away in Pittsburgh, Madden

demanded that Williams be suspended for life from coaching, banned from the league and forced to sell his interest in the VooDoo. I admired Madden's courage... while questioning his sanity.

Dave Cairns, who was coaching with Williams that night, said that Tiger was upset because Sacramento was fielding some Russian players whom he'd hoped to get to play for Vancouver.

"We get to the rink and you have to file your roster, so Tiger's got to take these guys off," Cairns said. "Well, we get to the rink, and the two guys are there for Sacramento."

After going out for a run in Sacramento's summer heat, Williams came back to the building in a rage and almost literally on fire.

"We'd never seen him so mad," Cairns said. "Not a player, not a coach, *nobody* spoke to Tiger. He sat at the end of the bench and he worked the gate. I was working the bench."

One of the Russian players, Vadim Slivchenko, skated past Vancouver's bench and said something to Williams, and the anger that Williams had been storing up all afternoon finally erupted.

"Tiger nearly tore the gate off to get at this guy, and I'm holding him, trying to hold Tiger back on our bench, because we'd never seen him like this," Cairns said. "This was like two-and-a-half hours of being in a rage at this point. This is a kind of two-for-one beer night in Sacramento; this is a drunk, rowdy crowd. And they noticed him trying to go after some of the Sacramento players; what do you think is going to happen?"

Both benches emptied, and when Williams climbed into the stands, he was followed by VooDoo enforcer Craig Coxe. Other players tried to, but couldn't get any traction with their skates on.

"Guys were literally going back to the bench, taking their skates off, and then climbing into the bleachers," Cairns said. "Tiger and I and Craig Coxe, we're just punching. I remember getting hit in the side of the head, and there's this guy running past me in the aisles, and I remember swinging, but mistiming it, and as I swung, I missed the guy, fell over two rows, and was being swarmed by everybody. Craig Coxe reached out and grabbed me by the back of my suit jacket, and pulled me and threw me back on my feet."

The incident was one of the season's low points and a black eye for the league. Fortunately, it was eclipsed by the ensuing RHI playoffs, which led to the exciting matchup between San Jose and Montreal in the championship finals.

CHAPTER 21

Maybe the Ghosts *Are* True

The 1995 Roller Hockey International playoffs contained some of the league's most exciting, exhilarating and historical games. Exciting and exhilarating because of the action and thrills throughout each playoff round, historical because the finals concluded in one of ice hockey's most legendary buildings, the Montreal Forum in Montreal. The arena was the home of the Canadiens, winners of more Stanley Cup championships than any other National Hockey League team.

In the first round of the Western Conference playoffs, the Anaheim Bullfrogs knocked off their hated rival, the Los Angeles Blades, after spotting the Blades the first game 10-8. The Bullfrogs roared back in game two, winning 9-1 before shutting out the Blades in a 12-minute minigame 3-0. Afterward, I noticed a sign in the Bullfrogs' locker room: "Winning is the name of the game. The more you win, the less you get fired."

The San Diego Barracudas were also forced to play a minigame after splitting the first two contests with the Sacramento River Rats, winning game one 11-7 and losing game two 7-5, before narrowly escaping in the minigame 3-2. The San Jose Rhinos made quick work of the Phoenix Cobras, winning 9-7 and 7-3, while the Vancouver VooDoo knocked off the Oakland Skates 7-4 and 10-4.

In the second round of the Western Conference, Anaheim continued its winning ways, first thrashing the Barracudas 10-3 and then holding them off in a close one, 9-7, while San Jose overcame the Vancouver VooDoo 9-3 and 6-5. That set up a conference final between the Bullfrogs, the top team during the regular season, and the Rhinos. The fireworks were about to start, as the two teams had little affection for each other. San Jose pounded the Bullfrogs flat at home in game one, winning 11-4 in a game marked by a bench-clearing brawl and 129 minutes in penalties. The Bullfrogs turned the tables in game two, however, bouncing back in Anaheim to dominate the Rhinos 9-4. That set up a minigame immediately afterward that lit a fuse.

Four minutes into the minigame, Jay Murphy drew blood first for the Rhinos, firing a long slapper past the Bullfrogs' goalie Rob Laurie. Daniel Shank tied it up within a minute, snapping a quick shot through the legs of San Jose goaltender Jon Gustafson. As the clock wound down, approaching one minute remaining, Bullfrogs' star forward Victor Gervais got tied up with the Rhinos' Garry Gulash along the boards as they fought for a loose puck. Battered by shoves and crosschecks, Gervais slashed at his nemesis in frustration. Naturally, that's what caught the attention of the referee, and Gervais was sent to the penalty box, much to the outrage of the hometown crowd.

With the man advantage, the Rhinos moved the puck quickly from man to man. If the Bullfrogs could just get out of the shorthanded situation unscathed, there was a potential sudden-death period to follow and another chance to keep their playoff run alive. But with just 41 seconds left in the minigame, Darren Colbourne took the wind out of the Bullfrogs' sails and infuriated Anaheim's 10,000-strong crowd by blasting a one-timer past Laurie. After time elapsed, soda cups, popcorn cartons, game programs and other debris rained down on the Sport Court as the angry Bullfrogs surrounded the referee and the Rhinos congratulated their goaltender. Gustafson had held the Bullfrogs' league-best power play to just one goal in 19 opportunities during the series.

Years later, the penalty still stung Gervais.

"That was the hardest day of my roller hockey career," Gervais said. "I must have stayed in the locker room for two hours, just crying. That's how upset I was. I knew if we'd have won that, we probably would have won the championship; we had the team. Unfortunately, I took a bad penalty."

Gervais said that it was a questionable call because Gulash had mugged him as much as he'd slashed Gulash, but he'd lost his composure.

"It was a really questionable call because we were battling; he hit me and I hit him back, but the ref just looked over and saw me," Gervais said. "It was retaliation, and I shouldn't have put myself in that position, anyway. I felt really bad for all the other guys on the team. They wanted to win that championship bad and they worked so hard all summer, and then one penalty cost us the whole championship."

None of Gervais' teammates blamed Gervais for the loss.

"Everybody's been in those shoes at some point; it's just the way it goes," said Bullfrogs' goalie Rob Laurie. "I don't think anybody holds it against Victor Gervais. That was just one of the things that happened. A shot went off the ref's ass and into the net – that's another thing that happened, you know? You've got to win despite those things, and sometimes because of those things. It's just the way it goes. All you can do is put yourself in a position to win… I've seen games in which maybe the best team that night didn't win, but it's who puts the puck in the net the most. There are a million things that can happen, and that's what makes the game interesting."

Every Eastern Conference first-round matchup was over in two games. The Montreal Roadrunners moved on by defeating the Chicago Cheetahs 12-3 and 9-8; the Philadelphia Bulldogs carved up the Ottawa Loggers 10-3 and 10-8; the St. Louis Vipers KO'd the Detroit Motor City Mustangs, 11-9 and 9-5; and the New Jersey Rockin Rollers ended the Minnesota Blue Ox's season, winning 9-7 and 8-5.

In round two's tightest series, home-court advantage may have been the difference. Philadelphia narrowly defeated Montreal at the Spectrum in overtime in game one 9-8, and Montreal returned the favor in game two at the Forum, winning a game that went to a shootout, 7-6. That set the stage for another minigame, in which the Roadrunners held off the Bulldogs 2-1.

The other second-round series also went to a minigame, though the scores weren't as close. The Vipers defeated the Rockin Rollers 11-5 in game one, New Jersey bounced back to win game two 5-3, and then St. Louis crushed the Rockin Rollers 5-1 in the minigame.

The Eastern Conference finals between the Montreal Roadrunners and St. Louis Vipers matched Montreal's league-leading defense (Roadrunners' goalies Corrado Micalef and Francois Gravel allowed only 133 goals in 24 regular-season games) and the Vipers' grit. St. Louis took game one at home, 7-3, sending the series back to Montreal for game two. Montreal evened the series with an 8-4 win, forcing a minigame, and Micalef backstopped them to a 1-0 shutout win. Real Godin scored the decisive goal for the Roadrunners after slicing through two Viper defenders and zipping a backhander past St. Louis goaltender Chris Rogles. The rough three-game series saw the referees dole out 211 penalty minutes, including nine 10-minute misconducts and three game misconducts.

The Championship Finals, Game One

Any bumps and bruises that the Roadrunners picked up in the St. Louis series had no chance to heal – the very next day, the Roadrunners flew to San Jose for game one of the Murphy Cup championship finals, which took place at the San Jose Arena the following evening. Tired and not knowing what to expect from playing their first Western Conference opponent, Montreal coach Yvan Cournoyer admitted a case of nerves.

"The day I don't get a little bit nervous before a big game, I'll be dead," Cournoyer said.

The Roadrunners didn't put up much of a fight in game one, playing without much passion or energy and losing 7-4. The Rhinos jumped on the Montreal squad early and didn't let up. When Montreal did close within two at 6-4, San Jose coach Roy Sommer took a timeout to settle his team down. The ploy worked, the Rhinos stayed out of the penalty box, and San Jose had a flight to Montreal and a 1-0 series lead. During the game, a Rhinos' fan had held a sign that read, "Roadrunners are Road Kill." Adding injury to insult, the Roadrunners lost speedy forward Real Godin to a hip pointer for all but a few shifts in the first half of game two.

After the game, Cournoyer said he was amazed at the number of mistakes his team made in game one, but that the Roadrunners would be better prepared for the Rhinos in game two. Roadrunners' goalie Corrado Micalef was confident about his team's chances, citing home-court advantage.

Micalef was not just blowing smoke. Montreal came out flying in game two in front of 11,412 screaming fans at the Forum. Wisely, the top section of the Forum had been curtained off, bringing the fans closer to the surface and concentrating the sound of the crowd. Perhaps attendance was boosted because the evening's contest would be the final championship ever held at the venerated Forum – it was to be mothballed the following March as the Canadiens were moving into the new Molson Centre. The next few hours gave those fans their money's worth and more.

Craig Minervini (play-by-play) and Jim Fox (color commentary) covered the game for ESPN's broadcast, and Fox said that Montreal would have to show some enthusiasm and fire or their season would soon be over.

"The Roadrunners came out with no emotion in game one," Fox said. "Expect that to be different here tonight at the Montreal Forum. The Roadrunners want to get back on track, and they want to provide some excitement for the fans in Montreal."

"It is said that the rhinoceros has a keen sense of smell," Minervini added. "I'll tell you what – the San Jose Rhinos can indeed smell a championship, and it is only 48 minutes away."

After a rousing version of "O Canada," and a ceremonial faceoff between team captains Andre Dore and Mark Woolf under the 24 Stanley Cup banners hanging from the rafters, the game – and the hitting – began. The Roadrunners started to throw their weight around, and the Rhinos responded in kind. Just 41 seconds into the game, Montreal's Brassard pushed Colin Foley into the Montreal net, with Foley very nearly smashing his head on the crossbar. Brassard's charging penalty gave San Jose's second-best playoff power play (successful at a 51 percent clip) a chance to give the Rhinos an early lead.

Mark Woolf carried the puck on the man-advantage, trying to set up teammate Darren Colbourne for his powerful one-timer. Colbourne led the league in power play goals during the regular season with 17, and had scored in every playoff game to that point. Montreal had apparently scouted San Jose well, however – goalie Micalef positioned himself smartly when the shots came in. While Montreal was shorthanded, Montreal's Eric Messier played aggressive defense on San Jose's Jay Murphy, knocking him down while avoiding taking a penalty. (Messier would go on to play 406 games in the NHL and win a Stanley Cup with the Colorado Avalanche in 2001.) The puck came to Woolf at the point just after the penalty to Brassard elapsed, and racing out of the penalty box, Brassard made a beeline toward Woolf, giving him a hard check just as Woolf launched a slapper at the Montreal net. Score! Though Woolf was knocked off balance and Brassard got in a good lick, the puck ended up behind Micalef and San Jose was on the board with a 1-0 lead.

San Jose defenseman Darren Wetherill took the next penalty, giving Montreal its first man-advantage against San Jose's playoff-best penalty killing unit.

The collisions along the boards and in open court were resounding and often borderline illegal. After Jay Murphy got into a shoving match after a faceoff with one of the Roadrunners, referee Mark Lachapelle, mic'd up by ESPN, took him aside and told him in no uncertain terms to knock it off or he'd get a misconduct penalty: "That's a guarantee." San Jose coach Roy Sommer had a few choice words for Murphy at the Rhino's bench, as well.

On the ensuing power play, Montreal's Guy Rouleau set up on his off wing to take advantage of his powerful slap shot, but it appeared that he and the other Roadrunners who were taking shots were trying to pick top corners on Gustafson, as many went wide or over the net. Before San Jose could kill the penalty, however, Carl Boudreau had a rebound of his own shot bounce right back to him. On Boudreau's second swipe, the puck squeezed between Gustafson's pads and rolled on its edge, just enough inside the goal line for Montreal to tie the game 1-1. ESPN camera's panned through the crowd and captured a group of grinning youngsters who looked like they were definitely enjoying the action.

"Montreal's doing it all here tonight; they're checking hard, they've got their spirit," Minervini said, noting that the difference between winning and finishing as runner up in the chase for the Murphy Cup was a cool $4,000 – the victors would take $8,000 a piece, the losers half that.

Not long after Boudreau's goal, Mike Taylor wrapped up and took down Rouleau, taking a holding penalty, and Montreal went back on the power play at the 6:30 mark of the first quarter. The Roadrunners swarmed the net, with Brassard and then Lacroix taking shot after shot that Gustafson kicked out successfully – until Boudreau pounced on yet another rebound and banged it home. Montreal had its first lead of the game, 2-1. San Jose lost an argument with the referee, claiming that Boudreau had cross-checked a San Jose defender to create the space he needed for his shot.

It didn't take the Rhinos long to come back, however.

Colbourne and Murphy came into the Montreal zone on a two-on-one and the puck bounced off Murphy's skate and into the corner. Colbourne beat Montreal's Brassard to the puck and whipped a shot – from the goal line – at Micalef. Somehow, seemingly against all rules of physics, the puck made its way past the stunned goaltender, and just like that, it was 2-2.

"That might be the sharpest-angle goal ever in RHI history," Minervini said, and Fox concurred.

"You hear about a shooter's touch in basketball a lot of times; well, Colbourne is a pure goal scorer," Fox said. "And he took a chance here. He says, 'the play's over, but I'm going to fire it at the net,' and he spun around, and it banks off the leg of the goaltender. You have to call that a bad goal if you're Montreal. Micalef, the goaltender was surprised; Colbourne, he knows what he's doing."

Colbourne's goal was the last of the first half, and the two teams went into their respective locker rooms knotted at 2-2.

In the second half, Montreal's Alain Savage missed a check on San Jose's Dennis Purdie but caught him knee-on-knee, and Purdie went down in pain. San Jose's trainers helped Purdie off the rink and to the dressing room, and the Rhinos went back on the power play with 10:10 remaining the third quarter. Colbourne and Woolf passed the puck back and forth until Colbourne got the shot he wanted – whipping a quick snap shot past Micalef and putting San Jose back on top, 3-2. It was Colbourne's second goal of the night.

The two teams traded goals for the rest of the period, and San Jose went into the fourth quarter with a 5-4 lead. All of Montreal's goals up to that point had been on the power play. With about eight-and-a-half minutes left in regulation, Montreal's Mario Doyon stuck out his leg and tripped San Jose's Colin Foley, an obvious penalty that the referees ignored. The Rhinos blew off the non-call and kept attacking the Montreal net, and Ken Blum gave San Jose a 6-4 lead at 8:09 by ripping a shot over Micalef's glove hand.

Jim Fox raced down to interview Mark Woolf on the San Jose bench. "Mark, we're getting down to the nitty gritty, under seven minutes," Fox said.

"You guys still confident here?"

"Oh yeah, definitely," Woolf replied. "You know, this building's all charged up. They've got great fans here in Montreal. You've gotta watch, you gotta stay composed; you gotta keep yourself between your man and the net. It's the most important part of the game; you gotta keep it tight and keep it honest here."

With seconds ticking away on the Roadrunners' season, Sylvain Beauchamp raced toward the Rhinos' net, made a pull-and-drag move that kept the puck away from the defender, and ripped off a quick shot, but Gustafson stayed with him all the way and made the save.

Minervini was already giving the MVP trophy to Gustafson when Montreal's Alain Savage blasted a shot from just inside the red line that sailed over Gustafson's left shoulder.

"Whoa!" Minervini exclaimed. "I just put the jinx on Jon Gustafson! He just gave up an 82-footer from Alain Savage. We'll see if it was deflected along the way. A rarity: a soft goal by Gustafson. And with 4:05 to go, don't count the Roadrunners out yet."

The home crowd cranked up the volume another notch.

San Jose's Colin Foley raced down the left side of the rink and passed the puck to Ken Blum just after crossing the red line, but Blum mishandled the puck, which squirted to Beauchamp. Beauchamp chipped a quick pass to Martin Lacroix, sending him off on a breakaway, and Lacroix's shot with 2:02 remaining in regulation snuck under Gustafson's arm. The game was tied, 6-6, and when ESPN cameras cut to the San Jose bench, Rhinos' coach Roy Sommer wore a stone-faced, thousand-mile stare. His team had given up a two-goal lead and its stranglehold on the Murphy Cup in just two minutes and three seconds.

Neither team was able to score another goal in regulation, so game two was followed by a sudden-death overtime period. If Montreal scored, they'd buy themselves another lease on life and play a 12-minute minigame. If San Jose scored, the championship was theirs.

Game-Two Overtime

Sometimes during sudden-death scenarios, both teams circle each other cautiously, feeling each other out. Not this time. Eric Messier took down the Rhinos' Colin Foley, and Brian Goudie returned the favor, knocking Lacroix into the San Jose net after a rush.

"I don't expect any power-play situations, short of a mauling on a breakaway," said Minervini, who noted that Dennis Purdie, who'd been knocked out of game two with a knee injury, had returned to the San Jose bench.

Montreal had the first scoring chance of the period after Brassard threw a shot at the net, but Gustafson knocked it down and threw his big glove down on the rebound. Micalef made the next save, on Darren Colbourne, and Gustafson matched it with a game-saving glove save on a high shot by Rouleau.

The back-and-forth action continued with alternating rushes by San Jose and Montreal. When Rouleau got open in front of the Rhinos' net, Lacroix tried to send him a pass for a clear breakaway, but Garry Gulash made a desperation sweep check to knock the puck away.

San Jose's Ken Blum apparently scored the game-winning goal, but it was called back when the referees determined that Blum had received an offsides pass. Montreal's Christian Lariviere had broken his stick trying to slow Blum's momentum on the play. At that point, 2:41 remained in the sudden-death period.

"Lariviere gets away with a check," Fox said. "He broke his stick right into the midsection of one of the Rhinos and Roy Sommer cannot believe it. The last two minutes have been chance at one end, chance at the other. Any goal right now will end this."

That goal didn't take long. After Montreal and San Jose traded chances, the Roadrunners turned the puck up the other way. Savage skated around Foley along the boards, cut into the slot, holding the puck on his backhand with one hand on his stick, and then switched to his forehand. Gustafson dove out to poke check the puck, fully extended, but missed. Savage's momentum took him parallel to and away from the net, and he waited to fire the puck until he was right at the lower edge of the face off circle to Gustafson's right. Savage's shot squeezed just inside the post on the short side, and the little Montreal-born forward did a funny little dance in celebration.

Minervini echoed the excitement of the crowd: "Whoa! Score! This series is going to a minigame! Montreal wins game two, 7-6. Do not go away. We're not done yet!"

Minigame Starts

Now, in a sense, everything started over. With Montreal's 7-6 win in game two, the series was tied 1-1. Whoever won the 12-minute minigame would win the series… that is, *if* someone won. If the minigame ended in a tie, a five-minute sudden-death period would follow. If *that* remained scoreless, a shootout would follow. One got the sense that the Montreal fans would be happy to stay all night… as long as it was *their* team that emerged victorious.

Again, neither team played it safe, and came at each other in force, checking hard, attacking each other's net hard and giving no quarter. The referee appeared to swallow his whistle, content to let the teams fight it out at even strength, barring a felony infraction.

Montreal got the best chances early, with San Jose's Wetherill stopping a three-on-one Roadrunners' rush and Savage being held off the scoreboard when the San Jose net was knocked off its line.

Montreal held a nearly two-to-one edge in faceoffs during the evening, and the Roadrunners drew first blood after a faceoff win in the San Jose zone. Once Montreal controlled the puck, Andre Brassard took a shot and then followed up the rebound, poking it between Gustafson's legs for a 1-0 lead with 8:43 left on the clock.

"Montreal has scored the last four goals of the evening," Minervini announced shortly after the goal. "All of a sudden, how things have changed. Montreal is now 8 minutes and 22 seconds away from the RHI championship."

San Jose responded with a rush led by Mark Woolf, who threw the puck at the net. His teammate Blaine Moore tipped and redirected the shot, and the puck bounced off the post and crossbar, but refused to go into the net. The play continued to go back and forth as much of the crowd stood, anxiously awaiting the next Roadrunners' goal and hoping against hope that San Jose wouldn't score.

The Rhinos disappointed thousands when Darren Colbourne picked up the rebound of a shot by Wetherill and scored with 6:32 left to tie it, 1-1.

The continuous action prompted Minervini to exclaim, "You get the idea that guys like Ralph Backstrom and Dennis Murphy and Alex Bellehumeur had just this in mind when they dreamed up Roller Hockey International about four years ago. And what a dream it's been. Last year, over 13,000 took in the championship game in Buffalo; tonight, in hockey-starved Montreal, 11,412 Canadians are out to cheer on the Roadrunners."

With just over 90 seconds remaining in the minigame, San Jose pressed hard, putting a flurry of shots on Micalef, but the former National Hockey League goaltender [123 games for the Detroit Red Wings] stood tall, and even shoved his glove in Mark Woolf's face after a net-front scrum. Montreal's Boudreaux and Brassard had good chances in front of the San Jose goal, but Gustafson held firm. Tackles and cross checks and slashes were ignored by the referee as the two teams fought it out with the clock ticking down. With 12 seconds left, San Jose's Wetherill got one final slap shot away, which bounced off the end boards and landed next to Micalef, but Brassard cleared the puck around the boards and out of the zone. A siren signaled the end of the minigame as Rouleau skated behind the San Jose net, a helmetless Jay Murphy matching him stride for stride. The 12-minute "game three" was over, the scored tied, 1-1.

Next up was another sudden-death period, but this time, for both teams. Finally, there *would* be a final goal and a conclusion.

Five-Minute Sudden Death

Just before the five-minute period began, it became obvious that fatigue was a factor – Rhinos' goalie Jon Gustafson was shown bent over at the San Jose bench, exhausted and soaked in sweat. Still, both Micalef and Gustafson continued to trade saves, and Fox marveled at the tight checking with 3:26 left in sudden death.

"Wow. The man-on-man coverage is fierce," Fox said. "There's not an inch to move on that floor to try to set up for a shot. Neither team is backing down an inch. Even if you're nowhere near the puck, you're going to be picked up."

"I'm not sure if San Jose respected Montreal after a pretty shoddy outing in game one, but no doubt there is mutual respect at this point," Minervini added.

After that exchange, three Rhinos fought for the puck in the corner to the right of Gustafson against a lone Montreal player, Martin Lacroix. Taylor took the loose puck up on his backhand, wheeled and turned the play up the rink. Rouleau chased him along the right boards, turned him around and almost stole the puck, but both players overskated it. Ken Blum picked up the loose puck just inside the Montreal zone.

"Blum's got the puck… Blum shoots, he scores!" Minervini shouted. "San Jose wins! The San Jose Rhinos have done it. They have come back… and won it in sudden death!"

Corrado Micalef lay collapsed on his back in his crease as Taylor and Blum hugged in celebration and crashed to the floor. Roy Sommer climbed to the top of the boards at the San Jose bench to receive a bear hug and a lift to the rink surface by Gary Gulash. Gulash then raced, screaming with joy, down the rink to join the pile up, while Sommer ran down the court, pumping both fists and then jamming his game notes into his jacket pockets. ESPN's cameras cut to the Montreal bench – the players and fans in the first rows behind them were stunned and dejected. Coach Yvan Cournoyer walked near the Montreal bench, hands in his pockets. Still, the crowd stood, and applauded both teams for their remarkable effort.

Fox waded into the group of players, caught Blum's attention, and pulled him off to the side for a post-game interview.

"I've got the man who took the last shot," Fox said. "Ken, it's just a matter of put the puck at the net. Hard-fought game, great way to end it for San Jose, obviously."

"Oh, this is a great game, you know anything could have happened," Blum said. "We just sat in the dressing room before we came out here – everything was going at the net. Just fire everything, anything can happen."

"Earlier in the game, it was you who turned the puck over," Fox said "It's got to be sweeter now that you're the guy that scores the winner."

"Oh yeah, I went from the goat to the hero," Blum said with a wide grin. "I can't explain it right now. It's just great."

"The goal that Blummer scored from the red line was very weird," said Mark Woolf later. "It kind of dipped at the last second. I don't know if he had a magic stick that night or something."

Woolf treasured the moment when RHI Commissioner Ralph Backstrom handed him the Murphy Cup as captain of the newly crowned champions.

"You think of all the nostalgia that comes with the Montreal Canadiens and the old Forum," Woolf said. "We grew up as kids watching Hockey Night in Canada, always watching the Canadiens against the Bruins and the Maple Leafs. To have Ralph come out, with all his Stanley Cup rings, and to be the last captain to raise a trophy in the Montreal Forum – that was pretty special."

"They curtained off the very top and ended up turning about 2,000 to 3,000 people away," said Rhino's owner Rich Shillington. "Doug Wilson [of the NHL's San Jose Sharks] was sitting beside me in the stands at that game, and it was one of the best sporting events ever. One lady, a season-ticket holder for about 25 years in the Montreal Forum, came up to Doug and said, second to the Russian hockey game [Summit Series] that they had in 1972, this was the best event she'd ever seen at the Montreal Forum. It was just an amazing game, it went into overtime, and after the game was done, everybody that was in that arena, the Forum, stood up and applauded. They enjoyed it that much. And you know what, that was kind of the pinnacle."

In a fine article for Roller Hockey magazine's November 1995 issue entitled, "In a League of Their Own," Warren Ettinger interviewed Roy Sommer.

"[Winning at the Forum] made things that much more enjoyable," Sommer told Ettinger. "I mean, you look up at all the Stanley Cup [banners] they've got and you know that's the last championship to be won there. That's going to go down in history, and I was just glad to be part of it. When they tied it up, I thought, 'Oh man, maybe what they talked about for all those years about winning the cup in here and the ghosts *are* true.' "

As Craig Minervini had said during an especially exciting moment of the championship game, "Roller Hockey International... in its third year... with games like this, it's going to be around for 100 more. It's been terrific, and then some."

The Anaheim Bullfrogs celebrate their RHI championship in 1993. Photo by Richard Neil Graham

One of the highlights of RHI was watching the fans' reactions and creativity at games. Photo by Richard Neil Graham

Chris McSorley, Tiger Williams, Grant Sonier and Chris Palmer before the 1994 All-Star Game in Vancouver. Photo by Richard Graham

The sun goes down on Cal Expo...and would soon go down on RHI as well.
Photo by JohnLymanPhotos.com

The logo from the 1994
All-Star Game in Vancouver.

July 9, 1994 All-Star
game tag.

A 1995 ESPN2 television pass.

Two views of a 1993 Bullfrogs
Championship ring.
Photo courtesy Mike Muckenthaler

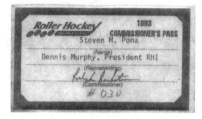

Steve Pona's 1993 Commissioner's Pass.

Promotional materials for RHI's
European Tour event in France.
Courtesy of Rui Russo

The Denver Daredevils had one
of the coolest logos in pro sports.

The Pro Beach Hockey logo.

John Vecchiarelli wins 1994 playoff MVP trophy. Photo by Richard Neil Graham

*The Eastern Conference won the 1994 RHI All-Star Game... and a free lunch.
Photo by Richard Neil Graham*

The Coconuts were a group of crazy Anaheim Bullfrogs' fans. Photo by Richard Neil Graham

Jeanie Buss was the hands-on owner of the Los Angeles Blades. She'd go to games and let her coaches know when she wasn't happy with the team's play. Photo by Richard Neil Graham

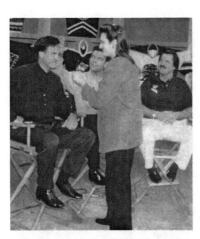

Brad McCaughey is prepared by the makeup artist for The Bullfrogs Report, while assistant coach Grant Sonier and GM Bob Elder look on. The local cable television show profiled the Anaheim Bullfrogs and their upcoming opponents. Photo by Richard Neil Graham

A champagne-soaked Chris McSorley celebrates after the Buffalo Stampede won the RHI Championship in 1994. Photo by Richard Neil Graham

Many former NHL players and others associated with the league were involved in Roller Hockey International. (From left to right) Dave Shultz, Paul Messier, Brent Callighen, Perry Turnbull, Bob Sirois, Bernie Federko, Yvan Cournoyer, Dave "Tiger" Williams, Bob Kelly, Warren Young, RHI Commissioner Ralph Backstrom, Garry Unger and Bob Crawford. Photo by Richard Neil Graham

Mark Cavallin makes save as Mike Callahan (#57) waits on the doorstep, 1994. Photo by Wen Roberts Photography Ink

Breck Wilson drew these cartoons for InLine Hockey News.
I'd come up with the ideas and Breck would do his magic.

Rob Laurie faces a shot by an Oklahoma Coyote player at a home game at the Arrowhead Pond in Anaheim. Photo by JohnLymanPhotos.com

Anaheim Bullfrogs star BJ MacPherson faces off against Steve MacSwain of the L.A. Blades. Photo by JohnLymanPhotos.com

Bob McKillop receives 1993 RHI Playoff MVP Award from Roller Hockey Magazine's Mark Brown and Robert Dean. Photo by Richard Neil Graham

Mark Major, the captain of the Empire State Cobras, in 1996, also helped the Buffalo Stampede win an RHI championship in 1994. Photo courtesy of Dan Delaney

Claude Scott, a comedian with a trumpet, or a musician with a great sense of humor. Take your pick. He pumped up the crowd at the 1994 RHI Championship Finals in Buffalo, New York. Photo by Richard Neil Graham

Manon Rheaume was one of the four female goaltenders in RHI, and she played in the RHI All-Star Game in Vancouver in 1994. Photo by JohnLymanPhotos.com

Draft Pick Round Girl, 1994. Photo by Richard Neil Graham

Steve Bogoyevac brings the puck up the rink, pursued by Victor Gervais of the Anaheim Bullfrogs. Photo by JohnLymanPhotos.com

Christian Skoryna poses with the RHI Championship trophy and Commissioner Ralph Backstrom. Photo by Richard Neil Graham

Inside the Arrowhead Pond, RHI's best facility. Photo by JohnLymanPhotos.com

Calgary Rad'z captain on Bauer ZT7 skates, 1994. Photo by Wen Roberts Photography Ink

Daniel Shank fights for position against Steve Wilson of the Los Angeles Blades in a game at the Great Western Forum. Photo by JohnLymanPhotos.com

Don Thompson, Max Mikhailovsky and Dennis Murphy as Max wins regular season MVP Award in 1995. Photo by Richard Neil Graham

Chris Nelson brings the puck out from behind the net in an L.A. Blades home game against the Vancouver VooDoo. Nelson used his skills and his status as an African-American athlete to pursue an acting career. Photo by JohnLymanPhotos.com

Portland Rage Player Director of Player Personnel Dan Delaney and a young Chris Valicevic in 1994. Photo courtesy of Dan Delaney

Mike Doers (33) looks for a loose puck in the crease against the Oakland Skates in a game at the Great Western Forum. Photo by JohnLymanPhotos.com

Young Vancouver VooDoo fans celebrate. Photo byRichard Neil Graham

Poor Parenting. Photo by Richard Neil Graham

Excellent Parenting. Photo by Richard Neil Graham

Mark Woolf of the San Jose Rhinos in 1994. Photo by Wen Roberts Photography Ink

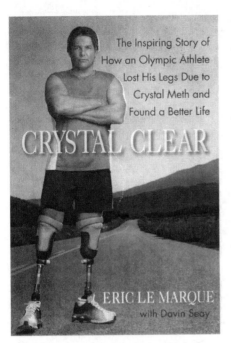

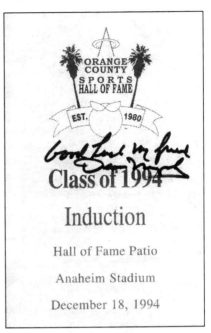

Crystal Clear, the autobiography of former RHI player Eric Le Marque.

Dennis Murphy was inducted into the Orange County, California, Sports Hall of Fame in 1994. I was honored that he signed my program.

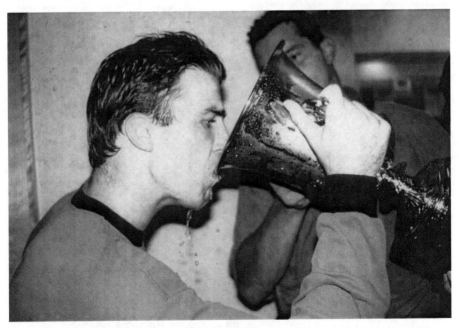

Joe Cook celebrates by drinking out of the RHI Murphy Cup in 1993 after the Anaheim Bullfrogs won their first championship. Photo by Richard Neil Graham

Brad Sholl makes a great
save on the cover of RHI 1995,
a video game of the league that
was never officially released.

Mark Messier poses with Stanley Cup wearing
his new RHI team's jersey. The Tampa Bay Tritons
lasted for one year.

RHI pogs portraying the
league's Central Division
lineup in 1994.

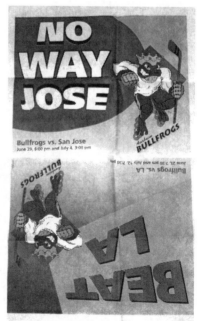

Promotional materials for Anaheim
Bullfrogs playoff games.

Perhaps the ugliest pro sports
event program ever designed.

An early RHI puck prototype – a roll of electrical tape with screws inserted that Anno Willison purchased at a hardware store.

RHI's Jofa SpeedPuck, the object of much controversy.

Ralph Backstrom and an advertisement for Super Street Skates. Backstrom is wearing his Los Angeles Kings jersey backwards because of trademark issues.

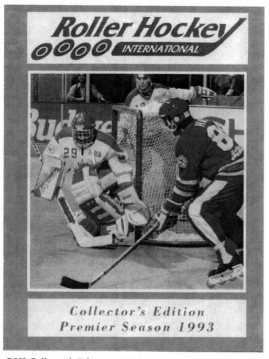

RHI Collector's Edition 1993 Program.

Max Mikhailovsky. Photo by Wen Roberts Photography Ink

The Christmas card that author Richard Neil Graham received from Orlando Jackals' owner Norton Herrick in 1996.

The cover of InLine Hockey News' October 1997 issue, after Team USA defeated Team Canada at the International Ice Hockey Federation Inline Hockey World Championship. Photo by Davis Barber Photography

The Anaheim Bullfrogs celebrate their 1993 championship. From left, Darren Perkins, Brad McCaughey and Bob McKillop. Photo by Richard Neil Graham

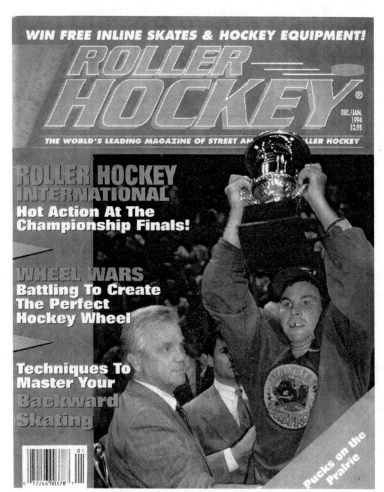

Kevin Kerr on the cover of Roller Hockey magazine's December/January 1994 issue. Photo by Richard Neil Graham

A player at the 2011 IHF playoffs at The 949 Roller Hockey Center in Irvine, California. A fantastic juxtaposition of modern inline equipment and old-school pro roller hockey. Photo by Tracy Robinson

Chapter 22

RHI's Front-Office Characters

The players weren't the only memorable "characters" in RHI – not by a long shot. The trio of Anaheim Bullfrogs' owners, Maury, Stuart and Nelson Silver, quickly come to mind as examples.

"The thing I remember the most about Maury is just his passion," said Bullfrogs' coach Grant Sonier. "He had the vision before anybody did; he was incredibly gracious and incredibly generous. Maury was very genuine and very passionate about the game of hockey in general. Anytime I ever question anything about money, Maury always said, 'Carte blanche. Anything you want. Carte blanche.' I'm not trying to say we were the be all and end all, but initially, if a player was going to come and give a summer up, they were going to come and play in Anaheim, because the word spread pretty fast that Maury was doling out the money."

"Maury was like a father to all of us," said Bullfrogs' defenseman Joe Cook. "He was just an incredibly kind, nice man. I think a lot of times, Stuart was made out to be the bad guy, but I think Stuart was the young buck that Maury would let deliver bad news, and Maury was kind of the grandfather. Everybody loved him. Maury was just a sweet, sweet man. Every time he saw me he had a smile on his face, he had something nice to say. He'd walk into the locker room, and he was just as excited when we won as we were. Just a really nice man. He knew your girlfriend's name; he knew your wife's name. He was good like that."

"I wore a headset, and it's very important, especially when you have TV and things like that – you start on time," said Chipper Righter, who served the team in a volunteer capacity. "We'd have people coming into the Pond, and Stuart would go, 'Chipper, hold up the game, we've still got people coming in.' I'd say, 'Stuart, if they're still coming in, they're going to be in. You can't hold the people that are already in to wait for those who are late.' But he wouldn't listen: 'Hold it up for eight minutes.' So the boys would be ready to play, and

McSorley or Grant downstairs would say, 'What's going on, Chipper?' Finally, they'd just say, 'We're going.' They didn't care what he said."

In 1995, Doug Jones worked for the Bullfrogs, using a walkie-talkie from the press box to report game stats and player information to Grant Sonier through Chipper Righter.

"Stuart and Nelson Silver had a walkie-talkie, too." Jones said, "So we would try to change channels because Stuart would be constantly on the walkie-talkie: 'Hey, we need to do YMCA. This crowd is dead. Oh, quick, there's a girl with big boobs in section 214, you gotta get the camera over there right now.' And Nelson would go, 'Stuart! Stuart! Relax!' and Stuart would go, 'Ah, you're just jealous because I'm better than you.' Nelson would fire Stuart, Stuart would fire Nelson, and then Nelson would say, 'Let's play 'Shout!' and get the crowd into it.' And then Stuart would go, 'No. Don't do 'Shout,' do the YMCA song. Everybody loves the YMCA song.' And Nelson would say, 'We're going to do 'Shout,' and Stuart would say, 'No, we're not.' And there was a girl upstairs, I think her name was Susan, she would do the music and she wouldn't know what to play. So she'd play 'Shout!' and then she'd do 'YMCA,' and everyone would get into 'YMCA' and no one would get into 'Shout!' and Stuart would go, 'I told you so, I told you so, Nelson. Look at everybody. They're up and having a good time while everybody sat still for 'Shout!' And it would be so funny, because Chipper would go, 'Jonesy, go to channel 4.' So we'd move to channel 4, and all of a sudden, Nelson and Stuart would be on channel 4, and the argument would continue."

Jones remembered that Stuart kept a gun in his briefcase. "Yeah, he called his gun 'Tony Montana.' He would pull his gun out and he'd say, 'Say hello to my little friend. This is Tony Montana. I never leave home without it.' "

In 2005, Stuart Silver was on a reality show called Boss Swap, in which Silver, according to a promo for the show, "a chauvinistic, tough-talking boss from an all-male car dealership who refuses to hire women for sales positions," swapped roles with "a supportive, laid back CEO of an all-women promotional firm."

"It was absolutely hysterical," Rob Laurie said. "During the show he has to work at an advertising company and he says, 'Hey, I've got a great idea that we could use to pump up the brand,' and they go, 'What?' And he says, 'I've got all these frogs.' He had these little green frogs. 'He goes, 'I've got thousands of them.' The girl who worked at the advertising company said, 'Why do you have thousands of these frogs?' Obviously, you know why he had them. He had them stashed in some warehouse somewhere and he was trying to find a way to pawn them off."

"In Stuart's office, he had photos of Muhammad Ali, Evander Holyfield and George Foreman," Doug Jones said. "And on Muhammad Ali's photo, it would say, in silver Sharpie, 'To Stu, beat the punch! *Michael* Ali.' And on the George Foreman photo, it would say something like, 'To Stu. You've got a hard left! George Foreman.' Paul Gibson, a huge memorabilia dealer in the day, used to go to all the rinks and sell autographs. Paul looked at those autographs and started laughing. He said, 'Stuart, you signed these yourself! First of all, you spelled the guys' names wrong, and it's Muhammad Ali, not Michael Ali.' We all got a laugh out of it, because we never really looked at them. All of a sudden, you go look at them close, and you go, 'Oh, my gosh, Stuart really did sign these!' "

"Nelson [Silver] always tried to stay away from the staff and stay away from the players," recalled former Bullfrogs assistant GM Chris Palmer. "He was actually a guy I could reach out to if I had a problem or a question, or like, 'Nelson, what the hell do I do?' He would actually take my call and give me advice. When I had Stuart telling me one thing and Maury telling me another, I could call Nelson, and he would sort it out and make it work."

The owner of the Bullfrogs' greatest rival, Jeanie Buss was also memorable to her players and fans of RHI.

"Obviously, Jeanie Buss was the hottest owner in the league," said L.A. Blades' center Simon Bibeau. "She was very involved for the team and she knew every player on the team. She did really care about the team and the guys."

"In the management side, Jeanie really knew how to treat the players and really make you feel like it was more than just playing for a team somewhere," Steve Bogoyevac said. "She made your feel like it was a family. She still calls us our kids. We try to get together once a year, she shows up and doesn't say too much, she's just smiling in the corner, digging it."

"I was very fortunate that I got to play for the L.A. Blades and Jeanie Buss, because she treated us as true professional athletes," said Blades' defenseman Chris Nelson. "We were treated just like the Lakers and the Kings. We had access to the training facilities, the locker room. From travel to accommodations, it was a first-class presentation, top to bottom. There are some horror stories about some other teams that were out there that were very different. I know that we had it very, very well. Jeanie Buss is a wonderful, wonderful person."

"Coming from the NHL and AHL straight to the RHI, I didn't take it too seriously at first," said Blades' forward Ralph Barahona. "So I was being a cocky jerk because I knew I had NHL experience. Jeanie doesn't know this, but I was nervous to meet her and she told me later that she was nervous to meet me as well. We actually hit it off, and I saw a true desire in her that was genuine. She had a true passion for this new sport that you don't see in most owners. So from that point on I felt there was a purpose and I knew I could help her by taking it more seriously."

Many of the league's coaches were also memorable personalities. Joe Cook never forgot his first experience with Chris McSorley, the Bullfrogs' head coach in 1993. Before coming to Anaheim that summer, Cook played ice hockey for McSorley in Toledo, Ohio. There was a fight in front of Toledo's bench, and the opposing player was getting the better of Cook's teammate.

"McSorley stands up on the bench and he kicks the guy that our guy is fighting," Cook said. "So the crowd goes nuts, and the ref throws him out. McSorley starts throwing sticks on the rink [and then] he rips his shirt off and throws it on the ice. That was my first pro hockey experience. I'm thinking, 'What the hell did I get myself into?' Chris was definitely a player's coach, and guys worked hard for him."

"Chris was a treat," said Savo Mitrovic. "He was a mind-game player. He will sit there and analyze and see how he can manipulate in order to create a certain situation. That's what he did best. Grant was just a sounding board. Chris basically ran that show. It was Chris' team. Grant brought in players. Grant brought me in, Bobby in. Grant did a great job, but it was certainly

Chris McSorley's team. He was a fiery guy. He would play mind games with ya. I remember one night, I think it was against L.A., and we were playing in Anaheim, and it was a playoff game, and he asked me what I think I needed to do in order for the team to win. He would do that systematically. He would grab a player every night, a player that he thinks he needs to talk to in order to create some kind of edge with that player. Whether that player being the weakest link, or at that time is not paying well, just trying create some kind of fire underneath that guy so he can go out there and make a difference. That's what he did, and he did that well. He makes sure that there's a balance in a room. He understands the heartbeat of the room, which a great coach always does. He knows how to steer that ship."

"When it comes down to hockey and knowing how to win games, he was a damn good coach," Rob Laurie said. "He gave me a lot of confidence, but he also made you feel like you were a part of something bigger than yourself. He didn't want any weak links. You're only as weak as your weakest link, and you didn't want to be that guy. Everybody was pulling on the rope. We had enough talent to win, so it was up to us not to lose. It was great to be on a team that allows you to do what you're supposed to do, win."

You were in good standing with Chris McSorley if you were a team player and played hard, as long as you picked the right rental car...

"I had Brad McCaughey driving a Corvette, I had Grant Sonier driving a Jag, and I gave Christian Lalonde the Mercedes 3ESL," said car dealer and team VIP Chipper Righter. "It's funny, because right after Lalonde got the SL, they canned him. So the joke was, don't drive the SL, because McSorley was also driving an SL."

"Grant was more of a strategist than Chris was," Joe Cook said. "Chris was a motivator, and Grant was more of a guy who taught us how to play the game of roller hockey. Chris was there for one year, I think I played for Grant for two or three. Grant had thoughts about how to play the game, strategies on how to cover guys. He really shaped the type of play that the Bullfrogs played with, more so than Chris did. I still talk to Grant to this day. Guys would kill for Grant. If Grant had an issue, he'd sit you down and talk with you. There were no real head games with Grant, ever. You never wondered where he stood. He was an honest coach, and a great guy. I loved playing for him."

Right after the 1994 All-Star Game in Vancouver, in which Sonier coached alongside Chris McSorley for the Eastern Conference, Sonier sang the national anthem before an Anaheim Bullfrogs' game at the Arrowhead Pond.

"Maury Silver was adamant that at every game, the national anthem had to be played," Sonier said. "As he usually did things with flair there, he had somebody lined up, and at the last minute they called in sick. They couldn't find the CD to play the national anthem, and Maury was losing it. I said, 'Maury, I'll go sing it.' He and his sons were looking at me, like, 'Are you kidding me? And I'm like, 'Trust me, I can sing. I'll honor America, don't worry.' We used to introduce the players individually, and we introduced the coaching staff as well, so I just slid along the wall and they didn't bother introducing me. And then the announcer came on and said, 'We have a special treat for you tonight.' The players didn't even know I was doing it. So I sang the national anthem, walked across the floor and coached the game."

After playing for Anaheim and Montreal, Mike Butters joined the Los Angeles Blades in 1995 to play for coach Bobby Hull, Jr.

"We played Oklahoma City, and I had two goals and two helpers and the eventual game-winner," Butters said. "Hully just said, 'That's it; you're here for the rest of the year.' I don't think I scored again that year." Butters, who grew up in Winnipeg, used to play ball hockey at the Hull's house.

"Bobby was a few years older than me, so he used to come home when Blake and Brett and I and a bunch of us were playing, and he used to rub my face in the snow," Butters said. "To this day, he says he doesn't remember that."

"We brought Bobby Hull, Jr. in as a coach, and it was absolutely just for the name," recalled Mike Altieri. "He was probably one of the most unorganized human beings I've ever been around, but quite possibly one of the nicest men you'll ever meet. He was completely all over the place. I found myself constantly picking up behind him as he went on his way. But I loved the guy. Just a gentle, great, fun, happy-go-lucky guy who was very appreciative of where he was in life at all times."

"When we were in Las Vegas with Bobby Hull, Jr. on the bench, we got a call against us," remembered Blades' defenseman Mike Doers. "I think it was a goal called back. I've seen coaches snap before, but Hullsy really snapped. He didn't just throw the puck bag out on the rink. He grabbed every water bottle, every single hockey stick and, I think, some of his clothing. It was all just lying out there. And he got the boot. It's always fun to see a coach snap anytime you're on the bench. That's funny stuff."

"Bobby Hull, Jr., was in a learning mode on the game, but he picked up the game very quickly," added Steve Bogoyevac. "He had a totally different way with players that got a lot out of the guys. He was your buddy and your friend, you could lean on him, but at the same time, he was 'The Man.' Everyone looked up to him. I remember him dressing for a game because we were short players, and he gets one shot on goal, from like center, and scores. So we were all doomed from there."

Mike Duffey said that the San Diego Barracudas had a memorable head coach as well.

"Steve Martinson made me cover people," Duffey said. "He would tell me, 'Use this line against so-and-so.' And I would write it on my hand as a joke, and then read the line off my hand to that opponent: 'You didn't make the NHL because you're an alcoholic.' And he'd say, 'You're trying everything tonight.' He ended up breaking my shoulder that night. Another time, Martinson told me to say another line to [another top player on the opposing team]: 'If so-and-so was here in the stands, your wife wouldn't know which way to turn her head.' " Though Duffey played for Martinson, he said that he was most impressed with another veteran RHI coach in the Western Conference.

"John Black, in my opinion, was probably the smartest coach in RHI," Duffey said.

According to Gerry St. Cyr, Black's strength as a coach for Portland in 1994 was his open mind.

"He was open to different things that the players thought they might want to try," St. Cyr said of Black. "That's why we were very successful. We respected him as a roller hockey guy and said, 'You know what? You're right. You know more about this game than we do. Teach us inline,' and in return, he's like, 'You know what? You know more about hockey in general than I do. Teach me that part.' He was very open to it. It was a very good relationship that he had with the players, and again, nobody had a chip on their shoulder. We all worked together, and that's why we were so successful that season."

However, St. Cyr said he first thought Black was crazy.

"The first couple of practices, all he's got us doing are these stop and start drills," St. Cyr said. "I'm thinking, 'What the hell is this guy doing?' We'd get into games early on in the season and play against other teams, and some of them didn't know how to stop. We were stopping on a dime. He basically coached us to play inline, while other teams we played against were taught how to play ice hockey in an inline game."

Dave Cairns, who coached with Tiger Williams in Vancouver, remembered a game where the VooDoo played the Sacramento River Rats in Kamloops, British Columbia.

"Sacramento came in, and I don't know if Tiger did it on purpose, but you had to get through this mountain to get from Vancouver to Kamloops to play," Cairns said. "Their bus didn't have enough power to get through the pass. They missed the warm up and got there just in time for the game. John Black came in and absolutely went off on Tiger. Sacramento proceeded to get their asses handed to them. They got blown out so badly, it was ridiculous. John Black said, 'The next time you come to Sacramento, you're going to be on the smallest frigging school bus I can find.' The next time we went to Sacramento, it was literally one of those short buses... with no air conditioning. We'd have to jam in all the gear and the guys would have to double up on the seats. Imagine trying to get to the airport, to the hotel, in those little buses. I give John Black a lot of credit. He did what he said he was going to do.

"Tiger Williams used to charge people $100 to skate with the team," Cairns continued, "and Tiger would skate with them. That was the thing; come out and skate with Tiger Williams. There'd be six hours of skating, and Tiger would do the entire clinic. He'd break them into three or four groups. Tiger was out there every single time. One of these guys comes the very first time, he's by himself, and he challenges Tiger to a fight. 'I'm here to fight you.' Tiger says, 'Who are you here with?' And he points to one buddy up in the stands. Tiger says, 'You don't have enough guys yet.'

"So, at the next clinic, the guy challenges Tiger again. Tiger goes, 'You don't have enough guys here.' This goes on until the final Saturday afternoon, and now the guy probably has 40 or 50 of his friends in the stands. This guy's a big guy. He goes, 'Tiger, when are you going to fight me? I've been telling all these guys that you are going to fight me.' They're right in the corner of the rink where the guy's buddies are in the stands, and Tiger says, 'All right, let's go.' And the guy can't get his gloves off fast enough. In a hockey fight, you grab a guy's jersey and you pull him forward. Tiger took this guy, grabbed him by the back of the jersey, instead of the front. The guy was on wheels, so he was off balance, and then, as the guy is going over backward, Tiger just pulls him forward, so now the guy's just completely off balance. Then Tiger hit him with one punch and just let him drop. The guy's 50 buddies just went bananas."

Unlike Williams, who would go out and drink with the Vancouver VooDoo players after games, St. Louis Vipers' co-owner and coach Bernie Federko stood a bit apart from the team's extracurricular activities.

"Bernie didn't really go out with the guys," remembered Scott Rupp. "He just kind of stayed with himself. He was an owner who was a coach, and he wanted everybody to win. Our second practice, we've only been on skates twice, and we're shooting on a goalie. You've got to control your skates or you're going to fall on your ass. Every shot he took scored. Here's a guy, he can't even stand up on skates, and it's goal, goal, goal. We're in a semicircle, so he's not moving much, but still, goal, goal, goal."

Rupp also had a story about Vipers' player-coach Perry Turnbull. "We blew a lead and we lost 11-10, and we're going to the locker room and our goalie stands up – he gave up 11 goals – and starts yapping about blowing the lead with about three minutes left basically cost each one of us $2,500," Rupp recalled. "Perry Turnbull stands up and says, 'Are you frigging kidding me? You couldn't stop a frigging beach ball tonight. Sit down and shut the hell up.' That kid put his tail between his legs and didn't say a word the rest of the year.

"Perry was all professional," Rupp added. "When it came to playing, you played hard, you played as a team and you stuck up for each other. You play as hard as you can and that's all there is to it. We were going to a shootout one night, and Perry went to shoot, and he couldn't move. The skates we wore were ice hockey skates converted over, with new rivets, so the sweat was just dripping through, all over your wheels. And Perry could not move. On a scale of 1-10, with a 10 as fast as you can go, Perry was going a 3. His speed was a 3, but his legs were a 15. He was trying so hard to get down the floor. He finally took a shot. I don't think he scored. He comes back to the bench and he goes, 'My goddamn skates are frigging leaking. I'm leaking!' "

Mario Sousa, a backup goalie for the San Jose Rhinos during the Rhinos' 1995 championship season, remembered the last regulation game of the season – and San Jose coach Roy Sommer.

"We just got thrashed," Sousa said. "We must have gotten beat 10-2. All I remember, I was so scared. I was 20 years old, and we walked into the locker room, and Roy Sommer went nuts. He came into the locker room, he started breaking sticks, throwing sticks and kicking fans. He was so upset. I remember him coming into the locker room and saying, 'Boys, if you guys have the guts to go out in the city of San Diego tonight you should be embarrassed for yourselves.' That was a huge turning point, because we went into the playoffs right after that. We beat the Bullfrogs and marched our way to Montreal. I really believe that game in San Diego was a turning point. Even though we got crushed, we still went out that night. As a matter of fact, we were partying with the Barracudas."

CHAPTER 23

Work That Slurpee
Machine at 7-11

I proved that I had no future as a sports bookie or fortune teller by writing the following prediction in my Editor's Letter in the December/January 1996 issue of InLine Hockey News:

"The 1970s were great years for the National Football League. In the '80s, the National Basketball Association flew high with the likes of Michael Jordan and Magic Johnson. In the '90s, it's hockey's turn. There has been growth in every aspect of hockey imaginable – from ice to street hockey to youth hockey to pro roller hockey and more. In 1995, manufacturers used inline and ice hockey imagery to sell products ranging from Old Spice deodorant to Alka Seltzer to Gatorade. If hockey wasn't hot, you can bet those advertisements would be few and far between. I believe that 1996 will be an even better year for inline hockey.... The future's so bright we gotta wear shades."

Who could have blamed me? The numbers were on my side. It seemed obvious to anyone who was watching that inline hockey was smoking hot. Speaking of hot, at the time Roller Hockey International was looking for something to spark its fourth season, rags, paint thinner and spontaneous combustion certainly fired up my life. On Sunday, April 28 of that year, I came home from a friend's birthday party to find the apartment I shared with my girlfriend consumed by flames. As I learned later, the landlord's son, the "manager" of our five-unit apartment complex, had been storing paints, thinners and other combustible materials inside his apartment, as he varnished a desk. Spontaneous combustion sparked the fire that suffocated our cat and burned up our belongings. It was incredibly painful at the time, but I still have to laugh at the letter sent by an IHN reader that was published in a later issue. Jeff Radoicic of Warren, Michigan, wrote: "When Richard Graham's apartment burned down, I felt for him. I made my wife read the article, too. She felt sorry for the cat."

Had I been more aware of the inner workings of the RHI leadership, I might have been feeling sorry for *them*.

While the San Jose/Montreal series had been a wondrous way for the 1995 season to end, Roller Hockey International was unable to corral that momentum. The turmoil and dissension that had plagued the league from the start of the season was never far away. Unfortunately, because RHI's management had offices in several different cities and its executives had competing personal agendas, many team owners filled the leadership vacuum by putting their own interests above that of the league.

The story of how RHI lost its national sponsorships might well be included in a book on the top sports blunders of all time. RHI's lucrative deal with Pepsi, Taco Bell and All-Sport disappeared after a team owner advertised PowerAde [a Coca-Cola brand] on the floor at his team's arena.

"Local team owners were shooting themselves in the foot by making their own deals," David McLane said. "We had a Monday night game with Taco Bell, Pepsi and All-Sport – all three brands under one umbrella – for a million-dollar-plus sponsorship of the league. For a young league to get this type of engagement was unheard of. We went to shoot a Monday night game and an owner had PowerAde on his floor." McLane asked the team owner how he could have put up an advertisement for a direct competitor to the league's major sponsor. "He explained that he, on his own, calculated the math of the national deal, divided by the split that we gave all the teams, divided by the number of teams, and then determined on his own that the value of his local Coca-Cola distributor deal for PowerAde was going to put $10,000 more into his pocket," McLane said. "So, after he'd invested over a million dollars in his team, for 10,000 extra dollars, he was going to jeopardize the entire league's million-dollar sponsorship from Pepsi-Co. Now, that's a genius."

RHI also lost a national hat sponsor because another team owner figured out he could make and sell team hats more cheaply and make a bigger profit, the health of the entire league be damned.

"David's efforts were constantly undermined by numerous team owners that simply wouldn't adhere to the national guidelines governing the equipment manufacturers' supplier pool, sponsors, and licensing companies and exclusive provisions," Dennis Murphy wrote in his autobiography. "One example, among many, was two teams selling their jersey logo rights to direct competitors of Taco Bell. Obviously moves like this by the RHI owners didn't sit well with David McLane, ESPN, or the sponsors and licensees. It was this constant interference and disregard for league marketing policy from a few of the league moguls that discouraged David McLane and eventually led to ESPN and David leaving RHI."

According to RHI Supplier Pool and Licensing Director Steve Pona, ownership defiance started two years earlier with the development of the RHI Supplier Pool. "Team owners were always looking to take care of themselves, even if that meant breaking a league contract," Pona said.

The supplier pool was designed to be a win-win-win for the league, team owners and equipment manufacturers. RHI charged a fee to manufacturers for "Official Supplier" designation and the right to sell equipment to the teams in various categories, including helmets, gloves, sticks, skates and wheels. RHI teams were only supposed to purchase these items from official suppliers. However, if teams still chose to purchase equipment from non-official manufacturers, they simply had to black out the brand name and logo of the company. If the equipment made it into a game and the logo was not blacked out, the piece of equipment was removed, the player was imposed a two-minute penalty and the team was fined by the league. Referees were instructed to police the league's supplier pool agreement by inspecting equipment before the game and between quarters.

But even though suppliers like CCM, Koho, Bauer, Labeda, Hyper and others were the most important partners to the league, many team owners disregarded them.

"Experienced team owners like Jeanie Buss understood the long-term value of critical supplier partnerships," Pona said. "But many of the entrepreneurial owners would rather save $200 on a stick order from a non-official supplier and hope they weren't fined. What they didn't know is that in addition to the referees, each manufacturer was also protecting their rights and would report violations to me after each game. The league had no choice but to make an example out of several owners by fining them and placing certain teams on a 'watch list' where referees were instructed to be especially vigilant. Sometimes it worked. Sometimes it didn't."

Pona added that some of the blame for the sponsorship miscues needed to be shared by the league.

"Many times, team owners just acted out of spite or to protest specific individuals in the league office that controlled those revenue streams," Pona said, referring to David McLane (sponsorship) and Alex Bellehumeur (licensing). "But the league office was pulled in so many directions at the same time, it was virtually impossible to give proper consideration and resolution to any one issue. Many times, we were bouncing from fire to fire without ever fully extinguishing any of them."

The league was not a united, one-for-all-and-all-for-one group. "Owners split into factions favoring Dennis or Larry, or in defiance against David or Alex," Pona said "Everybody supported Ralph – the hockey was untouchable. But depending on whatever issue was on the table at any given moment, you could guarantee that there was a fight for control of the business of RHI."

Pona said that the problem was magnified by the league's expansion from 12 to 24 teams in 1994 and the quick merger with the WRHL. "Nobody had time to unify under a ratified business plan," Pona said, adding that the team owners that brought in unauthorized sponsors may have done it to spite the league leadership, and not just in spite of it.

"With as much money that was at stake for the team owners and the league office, you would have thought that motivated and intelligent people could get on the same page," Pona said. "But petty personality conflicts and wayward politics diverted everybody's focus from a single unified vision of our game and our future. Everybody was running a different race. This experience is still the most disappointing and maddening of my professional career. If RHI would have taken a breath and developed a strong administrative base with solid owners, our league would still be operating."

European Vacation

After a year of planning, RHI held a European Tour from April 26 to May 11, 1996, that featured Team USA against Team Europe in a series of exhibition games. Grant Sonier, coach of RHI's Anaheim Bullfrogs, managed Team America, while San Diego Barracudas' coach Steve Martinson led Team Europe, a composite made up of European-born RHI players. Initially, tour organizers Dennis Murphy and Ron Byrne, RHI's deputy commissioner, hoped for about half a dozen events in eight cities in preparation for a full-fledged European League to start in May of 1997.

"It is our goal to feature our product on the tour and then to organize a full European League for the 1997 season," said RHI Chairman Dennis Murphy. "We feel confident that the European sports fans will love our game."

The tour that did come off had five games in four cities – and at least one major glitch. The tour's scheduled tilt in Ljubljana, Slovenia, was canceled when RHI didn't have a leg to stand on – Sport Court sold the floor that the tour intended to use before the game.

Just 400 curious fans turned up for the first game at the Patinoire Municipale de Tours in Tours, France, in which Team America defeated Team Europe, 9-8.

After the game, Stephane Desjardins put his language skills to good use.

"We went to a bar and I was translating what the girls would say in French back to the guys, trying to hook them up," Desjardins recalled.

More than 3,000 spectators saw Team Europe win game two, 7-6, at the new, 14,000-capacity Nynex Arena in Manchester, England. Leading up to the game, Manchester residents had seen satellite TV screenings of RHI's 1995 season highlights in the weeks before the tilt, helping them understand and relate to the RHI-style game.

Unfortunately, game three, held at the 11,000-seat Stadion an der Brehmstrasse Arena in Dusseldorf, Germany, slowed the momentum of the RHI Europe train. High ticket prices turned off fans and only about 1,100 people attended. Team Europe won the game, 8-4, but RHI might have lost the war, as the pace of the game was glacial and there wasn't a lot of hitting.

After the game, Desjardins, Steve Bogoyevac and Ralph Barahona rented a car and drove to Amsterdam. The car was broken into, but the three players had fortunately taken their hockey gear out of it. The next day, they drove back to the team hotel, but the team bus was gone.

"The guys got kicked out of the hotel because the league's credit card bounced," Desjardins said. "We had to go meet them in Munich."

Game four, held at Munich's historic Olympic Stadium Arena, drew 1,000 fans. Portugal, home to a very passionate following of Olympic ball-and-cane style roller hockey, was the location of the fifth and final game on the tour. That match drew 6,300 fans to the Pavihao Rosa Mota Arena in Oporto, and was notable for the fans who poured out onto the court after the game to have their pictures taken with the players. The score of the games four and five were apparently lost to history.

Anno Willison, an RHI producer of the tour, didn't recall the scores.

"I don't remember any of the games, because I was so busy," Willison said. "The rink we shipped to Oporto, I had to make it so it wouldn't fall down. It was terrible. And when we went to Tours, there wasn't anyone to help lay the Sport Court, and I had to do it with some of the little French helpers. The players were supposed to help, but they wouldn't do it. All they wanted to do was drink beer, get drunk and chase girls. We put on a bad game of hockey." Willison sold the players' jerseys afterwards to recoup costs.

"When the European Tour was all over, we couldn't pay the bills, and I sold the jerseys for $40 and $50, and they're going for $300 and $400 now," Willison said. "I sold them to anyone who'd buy them to pay some bills. The Team Europe jerseys were beautiful."

Overall, the European tour ended up as a bit of a disappointment. RHI's hopes for a European league in 1997 eventually fizzled, just like its plans for RHI-Japan had in 1995.

The Final All-Star Game

On July 7, 1996, RHI held what would prove to be the league's final All-Star Game at Anaheim's Arrowhead Pond. The game was shown on both ESPN and espn2, and although no one knew it at the time, it would be the last time that the league's very best players would gather together in one spot. Bullfrogs' owners Maury and Stuart Silver looked seriously stressed, and the announced crowd of 9,406 looked closer to 7,500, fewer fans than attended the 1994 All-Star game in Vancouver (16,150) and '95 All-Star game in St. Louis (about 9,000). Some felt that the game's timing was wrong, held so close to the July 4 holiday that potential fans were tapped out both physically and financially.

The Eastern Conference team was comprised of Rob MacInnis, Doug Lawrence, Kevin Plager, Chris Palmer, Samuel Groleau, Cory Laylin, Daniel Larin, Tony Szabo, Hugo Belanger, Alain Savage, Andre Brassard, Andy Rymsha and goaltenders Alain Morissette and Nick Vitucci. The Western Conference squad boasted Alan Schuler, Chris Valicevic, Doug McCarthy, Kim Maier, Mark Woolf, John Spoltore, Darren Colbourne, Joe Cook, Victor Gervais, Radek Hamr, Joe Burton, Kevin St. Jacques, Bobby McKillop and goalies Rob Laurie and Joe Bonvie.

A wild-west shootout ensued, as the two teams peppered 112 shots at the goalies, who could have sued their respective defenses for lack of support. As in 1995, Tony Szabo was named MVP, but this time for the losing squad. Szabo scored six goals for the Eastern Conference, but Anaheim's Joe Cook and Oakland's Kim Maier each scored three goals and had three assists to lead the West to a 14-12 victory.

Under the Table and Under the Radar

Under-the-table payments to players became another source of friction as the league moved forward. In his "It's Like This" column in the August 1996 issue of InLine Hockey News, Mark Madden wrote: "Here is a question from the SAT for RHI. Use a No. 2 pencil, please. And, as you'll find out as this column progresses, cheating will be tolerated. Believing that no RHI players get paid more than the league standard of $180 per game plus accommodations is akin to believing:

    a) O.J. didn't do it.

    b) That for every drop of rain that falls, a flower grows.

    c) That Elvis is still alive.

    d) All of the above."

Madden mentioned a rumor that Daniel Shank of the Orlando Jackals was supposedly earning $10,000 a month during the 1996 season. Where Madden heard that rumor, no one knows, but such rumors had dogged the league since the Anaheim Bullfrogs rocketed off to such a powerhouse first season. Madden wrote that paying players under the table was more stupid than immoral, since there were so many hockey players available to play in the league.

"So, if the old favorites want extra moolah, send them packing," Madden wrote. "Tell them there's still time to learn how to work that Slurpee machine at 7-11. No player in RHI has significant name value to sell even one extra ticket."

Madden revisited the topic in the October 1997 issue of InLine Hockey News, noting that L.A. Blades' coach Mark Hardy made on-the-record accusations of under-the-table payments by the Anaheim Bullfrogs to players after Anaheim added Hugo P. Belanger, Glen Metropolit, Bob Woods and Brent Thurston to its roster in mid season.

Blades' owner Jeanie Buss believed that where there was smoke, there was fire. Referencing 1994, when the league doubled in size, Buss said that it wasn't as if the league needed to create teams to create jobs.

"It was still hard to recruit quality players to play in our league," Buss said. "We couldn't afford to pay them a lot – at least the teams that weren't paying under the table. We set up a system that was based on prize money. Larry King's background was in tennis, and his argument always was that the most satisfied athletes are golfers and tennis players; every week you get paid exactly what you're worth. We were operating on the basis that everybody got paid the same amount, and the more you won, the more money you made," Buss said. "Besides expanding too quickly, problem number two in minor-league sports is cheating the system, paying under the table."

Buss could never confirm that other teams paid players against the rules. "I couldn't verify anything," Buss said. "Leave it to the players to even play us off each other – maybe they *pretend* that they're getting offers, and there's no way that I can prove that. Anytime anybody wanted that, I didn't want them on our team, because to me, that meant they were a cheater, and I didn't want cheaters on our team. It's as simple as that."

Several Blades' players said they had suspicions that Bullfrogs' players were making more than the league's mandated structure allowed.

"When I first got [to L.A.] and started hearing what the Bullfrogs were getting, and what we weren't, and I remember giving Jeanie a hard time," Blades' forward Ralph Barahona said. "We hadn't even met yet and I was on her case. Now I feel bad because she really didn't know what to do or offer the players, but all we knew was what the Bullfrogs were getting. Players talk, you know."

"The Blades never paid me extra; if they paid other guys, they kept their mouths shut pretty well," said Blades' forward Eric Rice. "I wouldn't doubt it. I think everybody pays under the table at every level. With salary cap in the NHL, I'm sure all the teams are doing it."

Blades' All-Star defenseman Steve Wilson said that he didn't know for certain if the Bullfrogs were being paid more, but he'd heard the scuttlebutt.

"There were obviously rumors out there that they were getting paid more than what the other teams were, but whether that was true…" Wilson said. "Maybe it was, but I still think that Anaheim had a great team. I think that our team was just as good; they just played well when they had to. When it came to crunch time, they were a better team than we were."

Dave Cairns, the assistant coach for the Vancouver VooDoo, said that Tiger Williams assembled that team honestly.

"He proved that you could put an entertaining, competitive team on the floor without having to cheat," Cairns said. "He did not pay under the table, and he was able to keep players loyal to him. He did that by giving players an opportunity. You know, you're going to come here; you're going to get noticed. He did that with Joe Charbonneau, he did it with Michael Kennedy. He gave players an opportunity, and then he picked up the phone and used his contacts and his reputation to move players into a better situation. I don't think anyone impacted the league quite to the extent that he did. He gave the league what it needed, and that was a flagship franchise in Canada."

Jason Klein, the co-owner of the Buffalo Wings, admitted paying players under the table during the 1997 season.

"We paid people under the table and we knew that we were violating the salary cap," Klein said. "But we knew that Buffalo needed a winner. We got pretty strategic about giving tickets away; by our 12th home game, we had 5,000 people in building, it was rocking, and we were more competitive."

During RHI's existence, the Anaheim's ownership always denied paying players extra money under the table. Years later, Bullfrogs, coach Grant Sonier admitted that the team definitely fudged the rules in 1993, the league's first year.

"I will say emphatically – we never ever paid the players anything more than what was part of the payroll system," Sonier said. "I said to Maury, 'These guys are not going to come out here for $400 a week, but they will come out for $800 a week, or $1,000 a week. Will you front the prize money? I'll guarantee that we'll win, so when the prize money checks come at the end of the year, they'll sign the checks back over to you.' And we did do that. But we did not pay them over and above what the prize money was allotted for… It was a big risk on my part, and on our part, that if we would have not succeeded, Maury would have been out all that money."

Bullfrogs' enforcer Mike Butters put a humorous twist on the serious and divisive issue when he described his arrival in Anaheim in 1993.

"I go to the hotel and meet the guys on the team – Brad McCaughey, Devin Edgerton, Victor Gervais, those guys," Butters said. "There's probably five or six of us sitting around. You put five guys on any hockey team in a room and you're going to know what everybody makes within 20 minutes. That's just the way it is. I'm sitting around talking to these guys and McCaughey brings it up first. 'Well, I don't know how to say this, guys, without pissing anyone off, but Mac told me I was going to be the highest-paid guy.' We all started cracking up. I go, "Really? Because I was told I was going to be the highest-paid guy.' So, every guy was the highest-paid guy."

Butters recalled earning $800 a week, twice the league-mandated amount.

"I know for a fact I wasn't going to come out for $400 a week," Butters said. "Come on."

CHAPTER 24

No Good Deed Goes Unpunished

Roller Hockey International's annual game of musical chairs took place again in 1996, with the league shrinking from 19 to 18 teams after losing the Detroit Motor City Mustangs, Chicago Cheetahs, Buffalo Stampede and Phoenix Cobras (who moved to Albany, New York and became the Empire State Cobras under new ownership), and adding the Long Island Jaws and Denver Daredevils. Teams staying put in their home cities but changing names included the Orlando Rollergators, who became the Orlando Jackals, and the Minnesota Blue Ox, who reverted to the franchise's 1994 name, the Minnesota Arctic Blast. Only Anaheim, Los Angeles, Oakland, San Diego, St. Louis and Vancouver remained from RHI's inaugural season.

One of RHI's major rule changes for 1996 was the end of the minigame as a way to determine playoff champions. Multiple complaints about the format led RHI to make playoff rounds three-game series.

"We felt that three-game series were a more realistic way of determining a real champion," RHI President Jerry Diamond said. [RHI would go back to the minigame format in 1997.]

The league also expanded its schedule from 24 to 28 games, increased the penalties for slashing, fighting and equipment violations, and cut the number of teams making the playoffs to eight from 16. And in news that was good for the best teams, but not so hot for the also-rans – only the top two teams of each division would participate in the playoffs. With each of RHI's 18 teams putting $112,000 toward the players' prize money, the prize purse would be $2,016,000 in 1996, making it the highest total in league history.

After being knocked out of the playoffs by the Anaheim Bullfrogs for the third year in a row, the Los Angeles Blades fired Bobby Hull, Jr. and hired former Los Angeles King Mark Hardy as head coach. Then the Blades traded forward Craig Charron to the Long Island Jawz for former Anaheim Bullfrogs' forward Bob McKillop. Additionally, Yvan Cournoyer resigned from Montreal Roadrunners in late 1995 to become an assistant coach for the Montreal Canadiens. Cournoyer's 28-15-3 record over two seasons, along with his 10 Stanley Cups with the Canadiens, must have looked quite impressive on his resume.

John Murphy, Dennis Murphy's brother and then the general manager of Roller Hockey International's San Diego Barracudas, had been admitted to the Long Beach Veterans Hospital on September 14, 1995, with a serious illness. On March 22, 1996, the large and gregarious man passed away, leaving a void in his brother's life. A memorial service drew a large gathering of Murphy's family, friends and colleagues, including RHI's Larry King, Ralph Backstrom, David McLane, Alex Bellehumeur, Dennis Murphy's right-hand man John Kanel, Anno Willison, Joe Noris and Red Rush.

"John Murphy loved hockey and he loved his players," said King at the service. "He loved to compete and he loved sports. He shared John Candy's humor as well as his stature. But above all else, he was a good sport."

"John Murphy was a really wonderful guy," said Jimmy Vivona, who played for the Connecticut Coasters in 1993 when Murphy was the team's general manager. "He was always there for the families of the players who wanted to come to the games. He was a visionary, one of the first people to believe that roller hockey could be a professional sport, even before RHI started."

In his autobiography, Dennis Murphy wrote, "My brother John stood 6′-2″ and weighed 400 pounds. He had a giant heart and the charm that could easily charm a snake. For 62 years, John brought happiness to most of the people he was associated with. He was Notre Dame and I was USC. We truly carried out that rivalry to the fullest."

After selling his ownership stake in Roller Hockey International in late 1994 to Larry King, Murphy had sunk his money into the Barracudas. That investment proved as disappointing as the Barracudas' 9-18-1 season record, and Murphy lost hundreds of thousands of dollars following the loss of his beloved brother.

Joe Noris, who was the Barracudas' president in 1995 and 1996, recalled the difficulties of making inline hockey succeed in America's Finest City.

Fred Comrie, who owned the team in 1993 and 1994, told Noris that he'd lost $600,000 on the Barracudas.

"It really came down to the number of home games we had, and we had a pretty slim budget, I think it was $600,000 for the whole year," Noris said. "We needed to gross – from everything – $40,000 a game" to cover the arena rent, players' apartments, rental cars, travel and office staff.

"It all adds up pretty fast," Noris said.

"So, at $8 a ticket, that's 5,000 people. When you're optimistically looking at it, you think you can get it. But when you get 3,000, in a 15,000-seat arena, it looks like nobody, and nobody wants to come. It's the same as you go to a club and no one's there; you don't want to be there."

The San Diego Sports Arena cost the Barracudas $6,000 per night, and the team received very little in the way of parking or concessions revenue.

"We would give away a lot of tickets to help promote to get people in to see it," Noris said, adding that the team's investors had conflicting ideas on how best to market the team.

"I personally ran into a lot of stone walls in terms of marketing ideas, some from Dennis [Murphy], some from the money guys," Noris said. "There were a dozen rinks in San Diego. We needed to go to them and cater to them and promote through them and work through people who play and work through the sport."

Noris thought that one idea, putting a four-page color ad flyer that offered two free tickets into every newspaper in San Diego, was a waste of money and time.

"I don't think we got 20 people," Noris said, regarding the promotion. "They ended up giving tickets away to the people at the rinks and then trying to promote to the rest of the city. I thought it was backwards and still think so today. I had a vision of how the marketing should be done. Unfortunately, Dennis would have to get investors, and they would come in with different ideas that had already been tried and had already failed."

Noris felt that the Barracudas should have been marketed and promoted throughout all of the recreational roller rinks in town.

"There were a dozen or so at the time," Noris said. "The sport, on a recreation level for youth and adult, was going great. I said we really need to cater to those people; we really need to get the players to go out to those spots. From my end, you could give me a 1 in 10 chance of winning a brand-new car if I went to the ballet, and I wouldn't go. So there was a contradiction there, because we spent a lot of money marketing to the entire San Diego County, having people pass out fliers on the boardwalk and that had been tried before. It's a small sport, but the hockey world is the hockey world, and that's what I felt we needed to go after first."

Small attendance numbers plagued most of RHI's franchises throughout the league's existence, especially in 1996. According to an article in the December 1996 issue of InLine Retailer & Industry News by Derek Moscato, "Empty seats at arenas across the country remained a source of embarrassment for the RHI, as many teams failed to reach attendance goals. Empire State closed out its season with a dismal average of 815 fans per game. Other disappointments included the Oklahoma Coyotes (2,820 average) and the Minnesota Arctic Blast (2,301). The Anaheim Bullfrogs, the league's marquee franchise, continued to lead in the category, with an average of 9,870 fans per game, followed by the Ottawa Loggers, who averaged a surprising 7,103 fans over the season."

Moscato's article also noted that ESPN's ratings for RHI telecasts were low, with the average rating for the league's weekly Monday night game on espn2 at 0.2, just 76,000 households per broadcast. As a result, ESPN was reevaluating its relationship with the league.

Teams pulled out all the stops to try and get people into their buildings. At Philadelphia Bulldogs' games, for example, a few lucky fans could sit in a hot tub at rinkside while being served free food and beverages.

The Players – the Wives – the Soap Operas

The 1996 regular season saw the Anaheim Bullfrogs and Minnesota Arctic Blast rocket to the top of the standings. The Bullfrogs were the class of the Western Conference's Pacific Division with a league-best record of 22 wins, four losses in regulation, and two overtime losses. The Arctic Blast went 22-6-0 in the Eastern Conference's Central Division and set league records by winning 16 consecutive games, including 13 straight at home. Other top regular-season teams included the Vancouver VooDoo (18-7-3), Empire State Cobras (16-7-5) and Orlando Jackals (17-9-2). Bottom dwellers included the Ottawa Loggers, who won just three games (3-22-3), the New Jersey Rockin Rollers (7-17-4), San Diego Barracudas (9-18-1) and the first-year Denver Daredevils (8-17-3).

The Orlando Jackals surprised a lot of people by quickly putting together a group of RHI's best players, including 1996 RHI scoring leader Doug Lawrence, 1996 top goaltender Corrado Micalef from Montreal, Daniel Shank from Anaheim, and Kevin Kerr, who'd last played with Anaheim in 1994.

According to defenseman Lance Brady, who'd played in Orlando the year before with the Rollergators, the Jackals did have quite an eclectic mix of players.

"The players – the wives – the soap operas," Brady said. "I think the team had every personality you can imagine on a hockey team. We ran the gamut from the pompous separatist to the greedy nationalist. We had Russians, Americans, Canadians, French Canadians and Latvians, but it was by far the most talented group of team players I played roller hockey with in RHI, possibly the best team ever put on the floor in the history of RHI. I know my boy Joe Cook and the Anaheim Bullfrogs would have something to say about that, but a case could be made."

Kevin Kerr, in particular, stood out, Brady said.

"Kerrsy was always in the brass' face about something, be it meal money, practice ice time, travel arrangements," Brady said. "Kerrsy definitely put the team number 1, well, 1A and himself 1B. That is not a knock. Any type of hockey can be a cutthroat league and you need to protect yourself; 24-hour contracts are not a fun way to make a living."

Brady said that the Jackals' players lived in an apartment complex with a large swimming pool, and when they weren't playing RHI games or golfing, they were out by the pool.

"To say this group of player wives was beautiful, that was an understatement," Brady said. "The 'wraparound' sunglasses were an absolute must by the pool. Combine fruity drinks and the strong-willed wives, and there was always a controversy brewing. It actually came to a pinnacle during, of all places, a home game at the O-Arena."

Two players' wives, who shall remain anonymous for reasons of propriety and lawsuits, did not get along. One was younger and bragged that her husband was going to the NHL, that her babies were beautiful, and on and on. The older wife became sick of the younger wife's pretentious attitude. It was a volatile situation, and it finally blew up.

"The fight – and I mean a fistfight – erupted in the stands right in the middle of one of our home games," Brady said. "The players from both teams were just staring in awe at first. Then it turned into a complete joke as the security guards came down to escort them out. Needless to say, that was one of the craziest things I had ever seen happen during a game."

While the Jackals were living it up and their wives were fighting it out in the stands, the Minnesota Arctic Blast were playing a fast and graceful style of roller hockey.

Probably because he led the Los Angeles Blades from a 2-7-1 start to a nine-game winning streak and a spot in the Pacific Division finals, Mark Hardy was named the Western Conference Coach of the Year. Scott Bjugstad won the same honor in the Eastern Conference for his record-setting season with the Arctic Blast. Hugo Belanger, in his first season on wheels for the Long Island Jawz, became the first player in RHI history to score more than 100 points. With his league-best 48 goals and 53 assists, Belanger scored 101 points in 25 games. Those statistics earned Belanger the 1996 Player of the Year award. Other award winners included Orlando Jackals' Daniel Larin, who was named Defenseman of the Year, and Los Angeles Blades' netminder Jeff Ferguson, who was honored with the Best Goaltender award. Larin led the league's defensemen with 32 goals and a plus/ minus rating of +35, while Ferguson went 16-11-1 and was stellar in net, helping the Blades win 11 of their last 12 regular-season games and make the playoffs.

One of the oddest incidents of the 1996 season was the "home" game that the San Diego Barracudas played against the Los Angeles Blades at the Great Western Forum – in Inglewood. On Monday, August 12, 1996, the game was played at 12 p.m. in a nearly empty arena… on purpose.

Because of a dispute with the management of the San Diego Sports Arena over the condition of the Barracudas' playing surface after a Gloria Estefan concert, Dennis Murphy decided that the team would play no more games in the Sports Arena that season. Since the Los Angeles Blades were in the midst of a run to make the playoffs, the Blades' management didn't want an unfair home-rink advantage, so the team purposely kept fans away. They didn't promote the game at all, and only San Diego fans were invited. Unfortunately, the media *did* hear about it, and Bill Plaschke of the Los Angeles Times showed up to his first RHI game in the league's four-year history to rip the Barracudas, the Blades and the league on the front page of the Times' sports section.

Plaschke noted that tickets weren't taken, the players outnumbered the fans, there were no concessions sold, and of the estimated 75 spectators in the building, one fell asleep.

Plaschke argued that the Blades effort to maintain the integrity of RHI actually undermined it, to which Blades' GM Tim Harris could only reply, "It's like, no good deed goes unpunished."

CHAPTER 25

Rinky-Dink Hockey International

David McLane brought ESPN to the league when he came to RHI in 1994. At the time, the sports broadcast company was testing the waters with its spinoff network espn2 and needed programming to fill air time. The emerging sport of inline hockey fit the bill perfectly. The network believed it could solidify espn2's broadcasting slate by signing fast-growing leagues like RHI. The league also fit in well with the National Hockey League, which at the time was the cornerstone of espn2's programming.

"The agreement we struck with RHI was a percentage of ownership for myself and ESPN," McLane said. "In return, ESPN would agree to broadcast a minimum number of games per year on Monday nights – 'Monday Night Roller Hockey on espn2.' And, we'd have a certain number of reruns on ESPN1, which is what they called it at the time. That was an off-shoot of our World Roller Hockey League agreement, where we showed all of our games on ESPN1 and rebroadcast them on espn2. But at the time, they were trying to grow espn2 and bring to it new sports, i.e., arena football, lacrosse... and roller hockey fit into that mix."

In 1996, ESPN and espn2 broadcast the league's All-Star, playoff and championship games in addition to the Monday night games. The company's aggressive and ground-breaking coverage created many firsts in televised pro sports.

"We had great timing to launch a new sport in conjunction with a new network, and ESPN agreed to provide all the funds to pick up production for all TV broadcasts for the first two years," McLane said. "That was unbelievable for a new, startup league. In today's market, that's unheard of. It was a great deal, a great foundation to grow the league by, and unfortunately, many of the team owners didn't appreciate the advantages that ESPN was providing to the league to grow itself."

At the 1995 RHI All-Star Game in St. Louis, McLane and ESPN wanted to do locker-room interviews.

"Someone was trying to prevent us," McLane said. "I know who that person was, but I'll avoid saying who – and they said, 'No cameras in the dressing room. That's not done in hockey.' Not having yet been to a National Hockey League game myself, I said, 'Well, who cares what they do in ice hockey? This Roller Hockey International and this is all new with new rules. We're putting mics on coaches and on the players.' They looked at me like I was nuts."

After being rebuffed by officials of the St. Louis Vipers, an angry and frustrated McLane went and sat in the stands to watch the game with colleagues from ESPN. That's when he decided that he'd move forward with his embryonic idea for another league.

"I'll never forget when I decided that Pro Beach Hockey was going to start," McLane said. "RHI team owners had been bitching at the league meeting that morning about not getting paid millions of dollars by ESPN. It was determined then that we should start an outdoor league and own all the sponsorships, own all the teams, and control everything for those advertisers that were looking to advertise and leverage the unique marketplace of inline skating and roller hockey. That afternoon was the start of Pro Beach Hockey."

ESPN's executives were just as frustrated, and after the 1996 season, the company decided not to exercise its option to renew the league's TV contract, citing the ratings for RHI broadcasts.

Jim Fox, espn2's color commentator for RHI games, greatly admired the job that ESPN did in covering the league, singling out the network's on-the-spot player interviews right on the bench.

"As far as I'm aware, RHI was the first sport to do that, the first that made it to any type of a major network," Fox said. "It was new, and there were some obstacles to overcome because of that."

Fox was as dumfounded as McLane at the lack of vision on the part of some of RHI's teams.

"I remember going to Montreal for the 1995 [San Jose vs. Montreal] finals," Fox said. "We get to the game and everything's all right as far as we know, espn2 had made all the proper contacts. I get to the game and try to get on the Montreal bench – Yvan Cournoyer was their coach – and it was just, 'No, you can't, you can't, you can't.' I said, 'Fine,' and I spent the rest of the game cheering for San Jose."

Fox said the bigger problem was that RHI's teams weren't all on the same page.

"That was maybe the best chance for that league's championship series to gain some type of promotion and some type of attention – and you come up with a roadblock like that," Fox said, shaking his head. "It was no exception to the rule; it happened all the time. You always ran into those types of obstacles where the individual team did not see the big picture of the league and where it was trying to go. The assistance and the help and the support that ESPN and espn2 were giving it just went over everyone's head."

Fox gave an example of one of ESPN's broadcasting innovations.

"One of the best things that ever happened had to do with being on the bench," Fox said. "We did a game in Buffalo, a player scored a goal, and we just happened to have a monitor on the end of the bench. So, he comes right off the floor, I have the mic right there, the replay's going and I say, 'Hey, tell us,' and he was able to analyze his own goal while watching the monitor right on the bench – as the puck was being dropped for the start of the game again. Even today we wouldn't get that type of access. That was something unique, it was great TV, it was great exposure, and I thought it was a great moment there – the ability to actually get the goal-scoring player 10 seconds after scoring, and go over it while the replay was going on. I thought that was groundbreaking."

Fox, who had been a color analyst on Los Angeles Kings' games since 1990, was also impressed with the equipment that ESPN brought to RHI games, including boom cameras, net cams and hanging cameras at different spots and angles in the arena.

"They spent a lot of money on it," Fox said. "They spent a lot of production on it. They tried and tried and tried to get the league to listen, to understand, to market."

Chris Palmer, who became RHI's television marketing coordinator, traveled to every televised game with McLane and Jim Fox.

"We couldn't believe it," Palmer said. "We'd go to these arenas and the players and the owners didn't get the value of television. So we'd go out for beers afterwards with the crew, and Jim Fox would say, 'I don't understand!' So it was a running joke the whole year."

"I just marvel," Fox said years later. "I'm disappointed that the league didn't go any further, and again, I'm disappointed more from the TV standpoint. ESPN was taking this very seriously. They put an effort into it. How much ESPN wanted it to work... I don't know if people realized that. I know that the RHI office did. But again, how you get that word out to the individual franchises?"

"Yvan Cournoyer is about as old-school as it gets," said Fox's broadcast partner, play-by-play man Craig Minervini. "We were in Montreal, which is a historic hockey city, and they weren't into the new-wave coverage that we were doing. It worked in California – Grant Sonier [coach of the Anaheim Bullfrogs] – we made him a household name. Roy Sommer was great with San Jose. They appreciated the exposure that they were getting, because for the most part, these guys were minor-league coaches and scouts and players, and even though it was roller hockey and it was a summer sport, it was a shot at the big time."

Minervini was greatly impressed by Fox's passion for the sport. "He was awesome," Minervini said. "First of all, what impressed me right off the bat, he would kind of like be in a crouched stance – he was so into it, it was infectious. He spoke with so much emotion. It was almost like his whole career was in RHI and not the NHL. I loved that about him, because it got me more intense."

There was a humorous side to the television equation as well. "They had us wired up on the bench," Sonier said. "ESPN used to bring the cameras right into the locker room pre-game and at intermission. They had to bleep out a lot of stuff."

Flip-Flop Follies

After once again vanquishing the Los Angeles Blades in the first round of the 1996 Western Conference playoffs, the Anaheim Bullfrogs ran up against the Vancouver VooDoo in round two. The VooDoo had spotted the Oakland Skates a 9-1 game-one win in Oakland before turning the tables in Vancouver, winning game two 5-2 and the rubber match 12-3. Playing at home in game one of the conference finals, the VooDoo defeated the Bullfrogs 9-5 and had a great opportunity to close out the series in game two in Anaheim. Unfortunately for the VooDoo, they lost a squeaker in game two, 7-6, setting up a win-or-go-golfing game three. Anaheim won that game 6-1 and moved into the RHI championship game.

In the first round of the Eastern Conference playoffs, the St. Louis Vipers pounded the Minnesota Arctic Blast at home in game one 12-6 before losing game two in Minneapolis/St. Paul 6-4. In game three, the Vipers continued to score goals and knocked out the Blast 9-5. It was only Minnesota's second home loss of the season, but it certainly came at the wrong time for the speedy Blast team. The other conference match up was between the Orlando Jackals and Empire State Cobras. The Jackals won game one 9-7 and lost game two 7-4 before crushing the Cobras in game three 11-5. Orlando's win set up a controversial RHI championship final between the Jackals and Anaheim Bullfrogs. Why controversial?

When Roller Hockey International's player draft and league meetings were held in San Francisco in October, 1995, the league decided that the Western Conference would be awarded the All-Star Game and the Eastern Conference would receive home-court advantage in the Murphy Cup Finals. On February 8 and 9, 1996, at the league's winter meetings in Boca Raton, Florida, however, that decision was reversed – home-court advantage would remain as it had always been: bestowed on the team with the best overall regular-season record. That changed *again* after Norton Herrick, the majority owner of the Orlando Jackals and Denver Daredevils argued that the San Francisco decision should be honored. The issue was the put to a vote that was evenly split – unsurprisingly – along geographical lines between the two conferences.

That's when RHI's executive committee upheld Herrick's protest and returned home-court advantage to the Eastern Conference.

The league's flip flop naturally angered Western Conference teams and effectively rendered the Anaheim Bullfrogs' regular-season record moot. Despite going a league-best 22-4-2 in the regular season, the Bullfrogs were forced to play two of their three championship finals games on the road in Orlando, where the Jackals had gone 10-4-0 in the regular season. The decision prompted Mark Madden to slam the league again in the October 1996 issue of InLine Hockey News:

"The '96 season was the most disheartening summer of the league's four-year existence, as RHI's management flunked Credibility 101," Madden wrote. "Reebok was late in delivering uniforms to the league's 18 teams, and many of the teams' jerseys looked cheesy. The espn2 channel refused to carry scores of RHI games on its sports ticker. Four teams had games on the day of the All-Star Game skills competition. Orlando received home-rink advantage in the Murphy Cup Finals even though Anaheim had the league's best regular-season record... Perhaps that's why a Bullfrogs' fan at game one of the Murphy Cup Finals held a sign that read: 'Rinky-dink Hockey International: We Make the Rules as We Go.' "

Though the Bullfrogs won game one at home, 9-8, Madden argued that home-court advantage gave Orlando an obvious edge because it gave Jackals' coach Jeff Brubaker the last change, allowing him to keep Orlando's offensive stars away from Anaheim's checkers for two of the final series' games. In game two, Orlando used that tactic effectively and won 9-6, tying the series at a game apiece. Despite playing away from the friendly confines of the Arrowhead Pond in Anaheim, the Bullfrogs still had a good chance to win game three – until it became apparent that their star forward Victor Gervais was injured with a pinched nerve in his back and couldn't play.

"He didn't even play the last game against Orlando because his back was so sore," said Bullfrogs' goalie Rob Laurie. "We didn't rest him during the season because were trying to get the number-one record in the league so we could have home-court advantage. We could have parked his ass on the bench or in the stands and saved him those last few games of the season and let him recuperate, but we thought it was more important to get home-court advantage."

Though Gervais badly wanted to play, Bullfrogs' coach Grant Sonier held him out of game three so as not to affect Gervais' ice hockey career in the International Hockey League.

"He told Vic, 'I don't want you to play, because I don't want you screwing it up worse and screwing up your ice hockey career for one roller hockey game.' Well, we ultimately lost the game, and we were missing our best player. Everybody missed him, Laurie said."

Though the game was tied at halftime, Orlando turned it on in the second half and won 8-4. In the seven games Gervais had played in, he'd scored 20 points.

"I didn't play the final game because I couldn't bend over to tighten my skates up," Gervais said. "I was in pain, but after warm up I went up to our coach, Grant, and I said, 'I'm going to play. I don't care. I want to play. I need to play.' I was pretty upset that I didn't play that game. I felt like I let my team down."

Orlando's Daniel Shank was probably the happiest person in the Orlando Arena after game three. Hurt and angry about being traded by Bullfrogs' coach Grant Sonier to the Jackals two weeks before the start of the season, Shank got his revenge. The fiery forward led all scorers in the playoffs with 12 goals and 27 points and was named Playoff MVP. During one game of the series, Sonier and Shank had a sizzling exchange of insults, with Shank telling Sonier he hoped he'd be out of a job. Shank, Daniel Larin (6 goals and 17 assists for 23 points) and Doug Lawrence (4-10-14) led Orlando in playoff scoring, while another former Bullfrog, goalie Bill Horn, led the Jackals with rock-solid play in net.

Lance Brady said that the turning point in the Jackals' season came about the same time as the femme fatale fistfight game in Orlando.

"We had a team meeting," Brady said. "We all agreed that we had the most talented team in the league. Who cares if the players, the wives, whoever, didn't get along off the ice? We had a championship team and we did not want that to go to waste."

Though some in RHI saw him as a disruptive force, Brady had nothing but praise for Orlando's team owner.

"Norton Herrick was one of the best, if not the best, owner I ever played for," Brady said. "He was around the team and the rink, but not too much, like other owner wannabees. He was a great businessman, and he treated his employees well. We were out after a game in Philadelphia with seven games left in the season, and Norton made the road trip with us. We needed to win six out of the last seven to make the playoffs. We had a player named Daniel Shank who always wore his AHL Calder Cup ring with the Adirondack Red Wings… a very nice AHL ring with an ample number of diamonds. Norton announced at that dinner, if we won it all, we would receive championship rings of that size. The man lived up to his word, as I have a ring to prove it."

There was fallout for the league after the Bullfrogs' controversial loss. The Los Angeles Times Orange County Edition decided it would no longer cover RHI, with reporter Paul McLeod blasting the league's lack of credibility.

The Jackals' championship win was also tainted in the minds of the Anaheim Bullfrogs and their fans.

As I wrote in my editor's letter in the October 1996 issue of InLine Hockey News, "I went to the opening game of the Anaheim Bullfrogs/Orlando Jackals series in the final round of the Murphy Cup Championship with my nephew Marc Quick and my little brother, Jared Adderly. The two 16-year-olds agreed that it was one of the best games of pro roller hockey they'd ever seen. The crowd was rocking, the game was fast-paced and exciting, and it was heartening to hear the crowd booing the announcements that said the final two games of the series would be played in Orlando. The league needs to listen to those boos. The fans – without whom RHI cannot survive – spoke loud and clear about the league's eyebrow-raising decision to give the Eastern Conference home-court advantage simply because Anaheim hosted the All-Star Game. There is no logical connection between the two events. RHI has created a great game that needs only minor tweaking to be superb, but it shoots itself in the foot with its unfathomable decisions from on high. Here's hoping the league gets its act together for 1997."

CHAPTER 26

Honey, I Shrunk the League!

The Toronto Wave franchise was expected to be an exciting new team in RHI's 1997 season, playing in Maple Leaf Gardens with Wayne Gretzky's brother Keith as coach, rock-solid Manny Legace in net and Cory Laylin to score heaps of goals. Unfortunately, it didn't turn out that way. The Wave never reached the shore, washing out for financial reasons along with three charter RHI franchises – the San Diego Barracudas, Vancouver VooDoo and Oakland Skates. The Philadelphia Bulldogs, Empire State Cobras, Long Island Jawz, Oklahoma Coyotes, Ottawa Loggers, Denver DareDevils and Minnesota Arctic Blast also left their fans in the lurch. The Blast's owners had intended to play at Blast Park, an outdoor facility adjacent to the Mall of America in Bloomington, but were unable to get proper permits from the city in time. The Ottawa Wheels replaced the San Diego Barracudas, and the Buffalo Wings came in as the league's newest team. The Wings played in the Marine Midland Arena, home of the NHL's Sabres and were owned by Buffalo stockbroker Jason Klein and California doctor Frances Edmonston. The league had shrunk to 10 teams from 18 and had fewer franchises than it did in its first season.

Adding to RHI's woes, RHI president Julian "Jerry" Diamond had passed away on December 16, 1996. The 68-year-old executive guided the league from January 1995 until his resignation in August 1996. Diamond was credited with stabilizing RHI after it had rapidly expanded to 24 teams in 1994.

RHI administrators and fans looked for a silver lining. Even Mark Madden, who loved to hold the league's feet to the fire, argued that fewer teams would mean tighter competition. In the May 1997 issue of InLine Hockey News, Madden wrote: "Look for a scintillating race for RHI playoff spots. Look for a tight postseason. But most important, look for great hockey every night in

RHI. And isn't that really the measure of a pro hockey league? Not a great championship series, not a glitzy All-Star game, not NHL has-beens as coaches, but great hockey every night. For the first time ever, that's possible in RHI."

At the 1997 player draft on February 13 in Boca Raton, Florida, change was the order of the day. First, RHI Commissioner Ralph Backstrom announced a comprehensive playoff system to avoid another controversy like the 1996 home-court advantage given to Orlando – in 1997, higher-seeded teams would have home court advantage in all playoff series. Second, the rosters of the now-defunct Ottawa Loggers and Vancouver VooDoo were raided by the teams that remained. Third, the San Diego Barracudas chose the VooDoo's Doug Ast as their number-one pick, but when the Barracudas eventually morphed into the Ottawa Wheels, Ast, who had been RHI's top goal scorer in 1996 with 50 goals (and 41 assists), ended up with the Los Angeles Blades. With the second pick, the Sacramento River Rats chose Andy Rymsha, reuniting him with Gerry St. Cyr and Chris Valicevic, his former teammates with the Portland Rage in 1993.

In the June 1997 issue of InLine Hockey News, RHI's biggest booster, CEO Larry King answered some of my questions on the state of the sport in general and RHI in particular.

"In another four years RHI will have a real average attendance of 10,600 per night at our current 23 percent growth rate," King said. "If our marketing alliance pays off and we secure a major marketing partner with major consumer products, our growth rate could double over what we have done to this point."

King glowingly proposed a future for RHI that included an indoor winter league that would start in 1998 and triple RHI's total attendance to 9 million per year by 2000.

"We should be making progress on taking RHI to Europe, Asia and South America by the year 2000, too," King added.

Just two months after that interview, Mark Madden (who else?) gave a blistering counter argument to Larry King's glossy assessment in "Roller Hockey International, R.I.P., Rest in Pieces," an article that he wrote in the August 1997 issue of InLine Hockey News. Madden likened RHI to a pyramid scheme:

"RHI isn't dead, not yet. But every time you blink, another piece falls off the body. Any league that loses over half its franchises over two years is a joke, pure and simple. It's the fallout of under financed, irresponsible ownership. It's the result of a maniacal money-grab by RHI's founding fathers. It's the by-product of letting anyone into the league who has the franchise fee with little or no regard to their long-term financial viability."

If RHI's official numbers seemed inflated, the lengthy list of inline hockey companies listed in the March 1997 issue of InLine Hockey News may have been an indication that the market was dangerously overextended. The proliferation of product surveyed in that issue's "Buyer's Guide" was a bit mind-boggling, with 14 wheel manufacturers alone. Apparel companies bloomed like algae in a warm backyard pool. There were other small companies that often offered just one-product and seemed to come and go like… well, RHI franchises, including Aggro Sport, 4 on 4, Face Off, Fastraxx, Go Sport, Grizzly Gear, Lazzy Legs, Ninja Skate Products, Power-Flite, Powerplay, Profect, Quadrax, Road Warrior, Rollerball, Rollergear, Speedfreak, Sportwerks, Stealth Products and Virtual Ice. This dizzying array of manufacturers was all searching for a market niche amongst the increasing mob of inline hockey players, and many, if not most, were destined to fail.

In September 1996, Dr. Frances Ann Edmonston and Jason Klein had purchased Roller Hockey International's Empire State Cobras to create the Buffalo Wings Roller Hockey Organization. Klein was a venture capitalist at Merrill Lynch in Syracuse, New York, and had always dreamed of becoming an NHL team owner.

"It was extremely vicarious," Klein said. "I'm an old goalie and I had played junior hockey in Toronto."

Klein started the Syracuse Hockey League and produced an RHI exhibition game in Syracuse between the Long Island Jawz and the Empire State Cobras, thinking it would help him decide whether to bring a team to Syracuse or to Buffalo.

"We had one thousand people paid in Syracuse with just grassroots marketing," Klein said. "It was very exciting, it paid the bills and we made a little money. I thought, 'This could be great.' We did our due diligence, ended up hiring people, and were very well financed, thanks to Frances Edmonston."

Klein and Edmonston enjoyed the ego boost that owning an RHI team gave them... for a while.

"It was very romantic in the business sense of it: 'We own a pro team; we'll be on TV!' " Klein said. "I thought I was going to retire from the brokerage business and make all this money."

When Edmonston and Klein signed their RHI contract two months before the season started, they realized it would cost $18,500 a night to play at Buffalo's Marine Midland Arena.

"It was originally $21,500 a night," Klein said. "Adelphia was to give us free TV ads, we could put up posters in arena, there were advertising concessions in building, but the contract was such that it was virtually impossible to get a penny from food concessions. We signed for $18.5k a night, and then we heard a couple of nights later that ESPN had decided not to renew. We had 100 season tickets at this point. We thought, 'What's going to happen?' We were sweating. I was constantly being called to be interviewed for radio, television and for magazine articles."

Klein and Edmonston spent several hundred thousand dollars on marketing between January and June 1997. They bought TV, radio, print and billboard advertising, but when the league's television contract fell through six weeks before the season started, they could not close deals with sponsors. According to Klein, he was never told that ESPN was going into its option year. While the Wings were able to get some breaks from an airline sponsor and a local restaurant named Mighty Taco, as well as some trade outs with Adelphia, they didn't have any cash sponsors.

"We had very little cash coming in when we were starting," Klein said. "This was scary – we couldn't sell season tickets. I thought we didn't have the right marketing staff. On opening night, Frances and I were sitting in the arena, 10 rows up behind our bench, with our heads in our hands. We had 997 paid. Two days previous, we had tried placing tickets in people's hands. The turnstile showed just over 2,500 people – and less than half of that number was paid. This is opening night – after spending several hundred thousand dollars on ads and staff and startup costs. My eyes welled up; this was not good. Then we proceeded to lose our first seven games. We had 500 people in a building with a capacity of 19,000. It was horrible. We had no expectancy that that this could happen."

Klein said he had heard stories about how successful RHI was in different cities.

"The league lied about attendance." Klein said. "If I only knew then what I know now. I remember Larry King or someone saying you'll get a lot of walkup – 'Buffalo is a big walkup city.' That's a line from Spinal Tap."

1997 Regular Season

During the 1997 regular season, the Eastern Conference's Orlando Jackals were the class of the league, posting record of 20-4-0. Orlando scored the most goals and surrendered the fewest, with goalie Sergei Naumov posting a league-best .854 save percentage. The defending-champions were the kings at their home rink, suffering only a single loss at the Orlando Centroplex. The New Jersey Rockin Rollers, boasting offensive stars such as Tony Szabo, John Vecchiarelli and Doug Lawrence, had the league's second-best regular season mark, 16-8-0, as well as the second-best home record at 9-3-0. The Rockin Rollers finished solidly in second place ahead of the Montreal Roadrunners (9-10-5 overall), mostly because they won all three of their overtime contests, while the Roadrunners lost all five of theirs. The Ottawa Wheels (10-12-2) and Buffalo Wings (6-18-0) rounded out the bottom of the Eastern Conference.

In the Western Conference, the San Jose Rhinos (15-7-2) were paced by the scoring of Jason Elders and the strong goaltending of Joe Bonvie. San Jose narrowly held off the Anaheim Bullfrogs (15- 9-0) to win its first division championship. The Los Angeles Blades (11-8-5), St. Louis Vipers (12-10-2) and Sacramento River Rats (6-16-2) followed. The Bullfrogs were hopping at home (10-2-0), but lost their spring on the road (5-7-0). The Bullfrogs had a late-season surge after acquiring Hugo Belanger and Glen Metropolit. Sacramento, which played its home games outdoors at the Cal Expo Arena, got an early season win by forfeit when Anaheim refused to play at the Cal

Expo rink.

Orlando's Bill Lund was the league's top point-getter, with 32 goals and 46 assists for 78 points. Radek Hamr of the Rhinos (19-56-75) and Frank Cirone of the St. Louis Vipers (34-39-73) rounded out the top-three scoring leaders. Other top scorers included Orlando's Kyle Reeves and Christian Skoryna, who both had 70 points. Reeves got his with 41 goals and 29 assists, while the smooth-skating Skoryna tallied 27 goals and 43 assists.

On June 6, in a home game against the St. Louis Vipers, Anaheim's Rick Judson, Darren Perkins and Marty Yewchuk scored three goals in a span of 17 seconds early in final quarter to lead Bullfrogs to 9-6 win. That broke the Vipers' record of three goals in 24 seconds against the Sacramento River Rats. (The National Hockey League record for three fastest goals was registered by Chicago Blackhawks' Bill Mosienko, who scored a hat trick in 21 seconds against New York Rangers on March 23, 1952, a truly amazing record.)

In mid-July, 11 RHI players participated in the International Ice Hockey Federation In-Line Hockey World Championships at the Disney Ice facility in Anaheim. This caused some soul searching on the part of some RHI team owners whose teams were battling for playoff position. The Los Angeles Blades went into a slump after three of its best players participated, but Blades' owner Jeanie Buss showed up to watch the event's championship game, which was held at the Pond. Her compensation was having Scott Drevitch, a Blades' star, on the gold-medal-winning Team USA. About the same time, Orlando's Daniel Shank became the first RHI player to score 300 points. Later that month, L.A. Blades' forward Doug Ast extended his goal-scoring streak to 15 games, tying the league record set by Tony Szabo of New Jersey Rockin Rollers one week before. Szabo's streak was stopped during a 10-6 loss to the Orlando Jackals.

Anaheim still led the league in attendance. On one night, RHI's largest crowd of the season (11,425) packed the Arrowhead Pond to watch the Bullfrogs score a sudden-death shoot-out 7-6 win over the Los Angeles Blades. But San Jose was the class of the league when it came to acquiring sponsorships and marketing dollars. With Burger King as a major sponsor, the Rhinos were able to offer fans free Whopper hamburgers whenever the team scored at least eight goals in a game. Whenever the Rhinos scored on their first power play of the game, the gas station chain Rotten Robbie offered five dollars worth of gas to every fan in one row.

While San Jose was a quality organization from the top down, the Sacramento River Rats raised eyebrows with their outdoor arena at Cal Expo. Roller Hockey International CEO Larry King had led the charge to have league games played in outdoor arenas, arguing that playing outdoors had been successful at the 1992 ball-and-cane roller hockey world championships in Portugal and as an exhibition sport in the Barcelona Olympics that same year. Unfortunately, the Cal Expo facility was not up to snuff.

"I'm not going to say playing outdoors sucks because no one's tried it," said San Jose general manager Jon Gustafson before the season began. "Who knows, it could be the saving grace of the league. You get parking money and advertising money, and the rent isn't as steep. But don't forget, one of the marquee things about this league is that a lot of the teams play in NHL venues."

Gustafson predicted that playing outdoors would "work big or fail big. No in-between."

Gustafson's words seemed prescient when the Sacramento River Rats posted their first win on June 19, a 1-0 forfeit victory over Anaheim when the Bullfrogs refused to play on a court they deemed soft and unsafe.

"That was our home opener," recalled River Rats' star Gerry St. Cyr. "They were literally screwing in boards and putting the rink together an hour before warm ups. The officials and the team coaches and managers were walking the arena and screws were sticking out inside the rink. It wasn't that safe. The Anaheim team just said, 'You know what? We're not playing. It's just not worth it.' "

St. Cyr thought it was ludicrous to expect players who'd experienced playing roller hockey in NHL arenas to "go backwards" and play outdoors.

"If it would have gone the other way, if guys never knew about the NHL arenas, it probably would have worked," St. Cyr said.

"Every night we opened at the Arco Arena we lost $10,000," said RHI CEO and Sacramento River Rats owner Larry King. "That's why we went out to form a rink at the Cal Expo, because it cost us $1,500 to be at Cal Expo and we didn't have the labor unions and everything else. We could actually make it at Cal Expo. At Arco, if we didn't have 5,000 paid, we couldn't pay for the ushers and the rent of the building."

Rex Fontenot, the PR director for the Los Angeles Blades that season, recalled one game he attended at Cal Expo.

"The place was packed and the crowd was rowdy," Fontenot said. "You pack 1,500 people into 1,500 seats, and it's a much better effect than putting 2,500 in a 16,000-seat arena. The fans really got into it. It really felt like this was an intense battle because of the way the fans were right on you and the place was packed and loud."

L.A. Blades' forward Eric Rice remembered an L.A. Blades' game at Cal Expo later that season.

"Once a summer, the crickets get wings, and they're attracted to lights that were illuminating the outdoor rink," Rice said. "They can't fly for very long, and so they fell on the court. Everyone was falling down because we were squishing crickets all the time. On the bench, they'd fall down the back of your jersey – everyone was squirming. At stoppages, kids would go down with the mops, which the crickets would jump over. It was the weirdest thing. Who'd ever think they'd play hockey on a cricket-covered rink? We still played, but the scoring decreased; no one could get going fast enough to get down to the other side of the rink."

It was a beautiful summer night, except for the bugs, recalled Blades' owner Jeanie Buss.

"It was the most disgusting thing I've ever witnessed," Buss said. "Bugs in the crowd and then the players slipping because they'd run over the bugs and then they'd squish and the court got wet. Oh, my God, that was a sight to behold."

Blades' defenseman Steve Wilson remembered the Cal Expo Arena for a much different reason.

"We were playing at that lovely outdoor makeshift arena they had there in Sacramento and Jeff Sebastian wound up with a full-fledged slap shot that went directly into my mouth," Wilson said.

Wilson's first thought was that all of his teeth were gone. Fortunately, the puck hit him below his teeth and then slipped up and hit him on the upper lip. Wilson ended up getting about 70 stitches.

"The thing that cracks me up about the whole thing is that the ref saw it happen and never blew the whistle,"

Wilson said. "I actually got up and had to continue to play because the guy didn't blow the whistle." The referee finally did blow his whistle, because all the players on the rink stopped out of concern for Wilson.

"The plastic surgeon did a phenomenal job," Wilson said. "To this day, I have a lot of other scars, from these hack jobs that these guys did quickly to get you back on the ice. But this guy, I thank him a ton, because he did a great job patching me up."

CHAPTER 27

I was Extremely Proud
to Be a Part of that Team

Eight of RHI's 10 teams participated in the post season in 1997. In several of the match ups, blowouts in game one were followed up by close second games. In each of the four series that were tied after two games, the minigames that decided who would move on to the next round were shutouts. As those minigames lasted only 12 minutes, it's not surprising that some goaltenders were able to shut down the opposition during that playoff season. Still, Doug Dadswell would continue to hold the remarkable record of the only complete-game shutout in RHI history, which he set in 1993 for the Calgary Rad'z against the Portland Rage.

Minigames were a thorny issue for RHI in every year of its existence except 1996, when a best-of-three format was used in the playoffs. Imagine working hard all season to gain entry into the playoffs, fighting other teams tooth and nail in two regular-length playoff games and coming out deadlocked, one win apiece – and then playing a 12-minute "game three" in which one borderline penalty might cost your team a championship. The system cut down on travel costs, but every time a minigame was played, controversy and bitterness ensued.

In the Eastern Conference quarterfinals, the 1996 RHI Champion Orlando Jackals had a relatively easy time of it, slamming the Ottawa Wheels 13-3 in the first game and 11-3 in game two. In contrast, the New Jersey Rockin Rollers narrowly got past the Montreal Roadrunners, winning game one 7-5 and game two 5-4.

In the Western Conference quarterfinals, the San Jose Rhinos spotted the St. Louis Vipers a 9-4 win before winning game two 8-6 and the minigame 2-0. The Anaheim Bullfrogs crushed L.A. Blades' hopes for the fifth straight year, winning the first game handily 7-2, dropping a 5-2 decision in game two, and beating L.A. in a contentious minigame 1-0. The Blades' record of futility against the Bullfrogs was extremely painful for the proud franchise just an hour to the north. The Bullfrogs had knocked the Blades out of the playoffs in the second round in 1993 and 1994... and in the first round in 1995, 1996 and 1997.

As there was no nationwide ESPN coverage for RHI in 1997, Jim Fox stepped out of the broadcast booth and joined the Blades as an assistant coach to Mark Hardy. Hardy, a former standout defenseman for the NHL's Los Angeles Kings, was in his second year as the Blades' coach. Fox, who had played 10 years with the Kings, was a straight talker who utilized what he'd learned about opposing teams' players and strategies when he studied them for his job as an ESPN color commentator.

"I had to prepare more for RHI than the NHL because I knew the NHL, more or less," Fox said. "In a league like RHI, constantly changing players in and out, you had to a little bit of work to stay on top of it."

Fox remembered a conversation that Blades' owner Jeanie Buss had with Mark Hardy at halftime of the first game of the 1997 playoffs, which the Blades lost by a large margin to the Bullfrogs.

"Jeanie had some words for Mark," Fox said. "She was not happy."

Whatever Buss said to Hardy, it must have worked, because the Blades came back to win game two, tie the series and put themselves in position to win it. Unfortunately, the Blades were given a penalty late in the 12-minute minigame, and the Bullfrogs scored on the ensuing power play to win the game. Though admittedly disappointed in the outcome, Fox was blown away by the Blades' character and heart.

"The quality of hockey was exceptional," Fox said. "To be able to line someone up and actually hit them, on inline skates, is incredible. That game was extremely physical, and it was heartbreaking. It was one of the few times in my life where I knew we gave everything we had. Even though we lost, and we were all upset... a half an hour after the game, I was able to completely accept the fact, because nothing more could have been done. Nothing. I was extremely proud to be a part of that team. It's been a proud sports moment for me because I don't know that there's any more that that team could have given.

I love thinking about that. It was a great series."

Prompted by a five-game losing streak in the middle of the regular season, the Bullfrogs had responded by signing players like 1996 RHI scoring leader Hugo Belanger, Glen Metropolit and goalie David Goverde just before the trading deadline. That raised the ire of the Blades and other teams in the league, and the Bullfrogs' bolstered lineup propelled the team to a five-game winning streak at the end of the regular season.

Alluding to the league-wide suspicion that the high-talent Bullfrogs' roster was composed of more than a few players receiving under-the-table payments in addition to the flat per-game fee that was their base pay, Fox said, "I guess when you look at it on paper, most people felt that Anaheim had by far the highest talent in the league. I'm sure you've heard some stories about how they got that talent."

New Jersey had changed its roster even more radically than the Bullfrogs. Except for bringing back Andy Rymsha, the Rockin Rollers started from scratch with an entirely new team. When Rymsha left the team after 13 games, the Rockin Rollers brought in playmaker and agitator Doug Lawrence from Orlando. They also added pure scorers Tony Szabo and John Vecchiarelli, and a goaltending crew comprised of Mark Richards, Marc Delorme and, late in the season, Nick Vitucci. Vitucci had won the 1994 Murphy Cup championship with the Buffalo Stampede, and he got the bulk of the action in the playoffs.

The architect that designed the team was Chris McSorley, who had led the Bullfrogs to the pinnacle of RHI in 1993 and won a second championship with the Buffalo Stampede in 1994.

"Chris was one of the best recruiters in roller hockey," said Vecchiarelli. "He knew his stuff, and he knew what he had to do to put all the pieces together."

Vecchiarelli credited Rockin Rollers' coach Doug Shedden for getting the best out of the highly talented group of players.

"Dougie was a really good coach, and he knew his hockey very well," Vecchiarelli said. "He was a player's coach who knew how to get us together and motivate us for every game."

Vecchiarelli singled out several players for the team's successful season, including former Buffalo Stampede teammates Mark Major and Nick Vitucci and new cohorts John Spoltore, Tony Szabo, Don Parsons and Doug Lawrence.

"Dougie was a big asset to the team," Vecchiarelli said. "He was a great roller hockey player. And putting all of us together on the same team – me, Szabes, Don, Johnny, Nick – it was a thrill to play together." (John Spoltore passed away from brain cancer at the age of 38 on April 30, 2010.)

"Johnny was a chilled-out, relaxed player who worked hard at both ends of the rink," Vecchiarelli said. "When he had his opportunities, man, he finished every single time… Johnny was a phenomenal hockey player. I'll never forget him."

Vecchiarelli remembered Don Parsons as an impact player – literally.

"Donnie Parsons was one of those guys who loved to hit and take the body," Vecchiarelli said. "If you had your head buried, look out, the train's coming to get you. He'd crush you like an ant. Donnie loved to throw the body around, and he was a good goal scorer, too."

And Tony Szabo?

"Tony liked the puck, we got him the puck and he buried the puck," Vecchiarelli recalled. "He put it on net every chance he had. That's what made him a great player."

In the Eastern Conference semifinals, the Rockin Rollers sent the defending champion Jackals to an 8-2 game-one loss before Orlando came back in game two to win a tight one, 7-6. That set up yet another series-deciding minigame, which New Jersey won 1-0, sending them into the championship finals. It was a bit of redemption for New Jersey, as the organization had experienced a horrendous 1996 season, finishing with a 7-17-4 regular-season record and out of the playoffs.

Following a similar big-win, close-loss pattern in the Western Conference semifinals, the Bullfrogs smashed San Jose in game one 9-1, lost game two 6-5, and scored two goals in the minigame to shut out the Rhinos 2-0. By winning both the first- and second-round series with minigames, the Bullfrogs certainly weren't choosing to do things the easy way. Still, their two minigame wins put them into their third RHI championship final series in five seasons. (The Bullfrogs defeated the Oakland Skates for the championship in 1993 and lost to the Orlando Jackals in 1996.)

Game one of the Murphy Cup Finals was held at the Arrowhead Pond in Anaheim. The Bullfrogs took advantage of New Jersey's aggressive play, which put the Bullfrogs on the power play time and time again. Scoring four goals with the man advantage, Anaheim tripled up on the Rockin Rollers 12-4, sending the two teams to New Jersey to play game two in front of season-high crowd of 9,160 at the Continental Airlines Arena. While the score was nominally closer at 9-5, Anaheim again wound up on top, giving the Bullfrogs their second Murphy Cup title and making them the first RHI team to win two championships. David Goverde, who stoned the Rockin Rollers every time they tried to make it closer in game two, was named MVP of the finals.

According to Vecchiarelli, Anaheim neutralized the Rockin Rollers' attempt to physically intimidate the Bullfrogs.

"Anaheim had a great team," Vecchiarelli said. "We wanted to play physical against them and wear them down. I think we were probably the tougher team than Anaheim, and when you play a team that's bigger and more physical, I think you can get intimidated, but their coach [Brad McCaughey] probably said, 'You know what, boys? Suck it up. Do what we have to do. Take the cheap shots and the hits and all that and we can beat them if they get in the penalty box.' "

In the championship round, New Jersey spent 56 minutes in the penalty box compared to Anaheim's nine. Vecchiarelli admitted that penalties put the Rockin Rollers into a hole they couldn't crawl out of.

"In roller hockey the puck went faster, and you can't stop like you do on ice hockey, so it was one of those games where a penalty can hurt you," Vecchiarelli said. "And in roller hockey, a penalty did hurt you – it almost guaranteed that you got scored on, every time."

Though game two was tied 3-3 at the half, Bullfrogs' goalie David Goverde's stellar play between the pipes kept the Rockin Rollers from mounting a comeback.

"David Goverde was a good goalie, but he stood on his head," Vecchiarelli said. "He kept them alive. He knew he had to step up and he stepped it up; he kept them in that series."

Immediately after the game-two win, Chris Newans attempted to give Anaheim coach Brad McCaughey a Gatorade shower – and then "totally just dropped the cooler on his head," recalled Bullfrogs' defenseman Tom Menicci. Menicci also remembered that Bullfrogs' owner Stuart Silver wanted to "make love to the Murphy Cup, but had to be beaten into submission to get him to put a few rounds of celebratory cocktails on his credit card."

Losing the L.A. Blades

There was fallout from the Los Angeles Blades' fifth consecutive early exit from the playoffs at the hands of the Bullfrogs. After the season, the Blades announced that they would withdraw from RHI. Dr. Jerry Buss, Jeanie's father, had always wanted his teams to win championships, and the Blades' playoff futility was more than he could accept. Disappointment with the team's inability to win the Murphy Cup wasn't the only reason for L.A.'s withdrawal, however. According to Blades' GM Tim Harris, trying to promote the team without national marketing and sponsorship support from the league wasn't economically feasible. Harris also complained about under-the-table payments paid to players on other teams and the lack of coverage given the Blades by the Los Angeles Times.

Blades' veteran forward Steve Bogoyevac lamented the team's exodus from the league in the January 1998 issue of InLine Hockey News – which was that magazine's final issue. Bogoyevac noted that the Blades were one of the league's best-run franchises and that RHI would have difficulty recruiting new teams once the Blades were gone. He also mentioned an inconvenient fact – the league's players had still not received a portion of their regular-season payments or any of their playoff bonus money.

"Where is that money?" Bogoyevac asked. "Everyone believes that inline hockey is here to stay, but at the professional level, someone needs to step up and run a league the way it should be run."

CHAPTER 28

In the Movies

One of the fringe benefits of being in the limelight of a new and vibrant professional sport for RHI's players was the opportunity to be in television shows, commercials and even movies. Advertisers like Gatorade and Ocean Spray tapped players to help them sell their products, and several movie producers utilized the players' skating and hockey skills in feature films. Ocean Spray's commercial gathered players from both the Anaheim Bullfrogs and Los Angeles Blades – Savo Mitrovic, Bob McKillop, Brett Kurtz, Mike Butters and Stephane Desjardins – all of whom took penalties on purpose just so they could sit in the penalty box and drink Ocean Spray Lemonade.

"They called a bunch of us to go to this ice hockey commercial, and we ended up booking this commercial for Ocean Spray, which was directed by Tony Scott, a pretty famous director ('Top Gun' and 'Crimson Tide')," said Butters. "We all went out there for a laugh, and we made some really good money on it. That's how I decided I was going to stay, instead of going home, and try and make a career of this. RHI was indirectly involved in that for me."

Butters has been a villain in horror movies and also performs improvisational comedy with his buddy Dave Coulier, but the comedy shows are not as frequent now that he works as a scout for the NHL's Tampa Bay Lightning and owns the America West Hockey League's Helena Bighorns.

"A lot of the guys in RHI came to see me do comedy – I remember Manon Rheaume and Gerry St. Cyr came to see me a few times," Butters said. "Luckily I didn't embarrass them too bad; they came back a few times. Hockey guys are like cavemen in a sense; when you're doing something like that, it's kind of an anomaly. So when your peers can see you doing something out of the box, it's kind of cool."

Rob Laurie, the successful longtime goaltender for the Anaheim Bullfrogs, played an ice hockey goalie in the John Claude Van Damme's 1995 action flick, "Sudden Death." Steve Wilson, a Los Angeles Blades' defenseman with a wicked slap shot, nabbed an after-school special purely by accident when Blades' teammate Steve Bogoyevac invited him to join him at an audition.

"Bogie was getting into the acting thing and he said, 'Come on this audition and give it a shot,' Wilson said.

Wilson had no intention of auditioning for "Smoking Sam," a film about a professional roller hockey player who had a contract with a tobacco company and set a bad example for the school children who saw him smoking.

"I'm like, 'I'm not going to do anything, but I'll come and watch the things that you do,' Wilson said. 'Well, they gave me these lines and the next day, I got a call back: 'We want you to come back and read again in front of the cameras.' "

Wilson got the lead part, and Bogie and Blades' goalie Brad Sholl had bit parts.

"It was something I never would have done if I didn't live in L.A.," Wilson said. "We filmed some stuff for ESPN, with Bogie and I in a convertible, showing off the sights of Los Angeles, and we got pulled over by the police. The policeman gave us a spiel about what we should do, and we're filming the whole thing. We included that whole bit in the ESPN skit, too."

Wilson said that when Jeanie Buss was profiled on "Lifestyles of the Rich and Famous," he and some of his teammates got to hang out with George Hamilton and Robin Leach from the show at a club in Hollywood. Wilson also met film stars such as Wesley Snipes and Tom Cruise. "It was just endless," Wilson said. "If you were playing in St. Louis or somewhere else, it just never would have happened."

Movie and acting work wasn't only for RHI's players. In 1994, Dennis Murphy sent Steve Pona from RHI's office in Anaheim to South Central L.A. to drop off a box of 150 pucks to a movie producer who was working on the movie "D2: The Mighty Ducks."

"Well, the next thing I know, the director was pushing me aside and saying I looked like one of the kids in the movie," Pona said. "He said, 'Do you skate?' 'Yeah.' 'Do you play hockey?' 'Yeah.' 'You're a double; you're in the movie now.' The next thing I know, I'm in wardrobe, they're fitting me with skates, with uniforms and they're getting me a stick. I'm getting rushed through the whole thing. I do a little screen test, and literally, I did all of the roller hockey scenes in the Mighty Ducks 2 movie in South Central. I got paid for it, and I still have the skates. I still use the hockey bag that was on set. I think I made $250 a day. I'm the one shooting the puck in the drum [that was used] for the goals; I'm getting crunched up against the fence on one of the body checks, and I'm the guy who shoots the knuckle puck."

Perhaps no RHI player was more successful in getting gigs in movies and television than Los Angeles Blades' African-American defenseman Chris "Nelly" Nelson. Jack White, a former hockey coach of Nelson's, told him about an opportunity on a television show, so Nelson drove to Malibu at 6 a.m., met an assistant director, was given a script and some clothes to wear, and was set up in a trailer.

"I took a nap, and when I woke up and opened the door, there were 16 of the most beautiful women I've ever seen in my life," Nelson said. "It was Baywatch. That was the first thing I ever did."

Later, Nelson signed with a talent agency and booked a commercial almost immediately. Nelson said he had no idea what he was doing at first, but he quickly picked up on the opportunity and ran with it.

"There was definitely value in being a person of color in the commercial industry, because I represented a demographic," Nelson said. "And so when the agency got a commercial assigned, I was always the black guy in their commercials. Not only that, I was also the best hockey player in all those commercials, too. So, not only was I the most qualified, but I'd won national championships, I played hockey on the U.S. National Team for roller hockey, I was also the best hockey player out there to begin with in the commercial industry, and I was a person of color. It was the Trifecta."

In addition to Baywatch and television commercials, Nelson was in movies like "Senseless," "Species II" and 1997's "Batman & Robin."

"Someone called me to this audition for this movie on the Warner Brothers lot in Burbank," Nelson said. "I skated around at full speed, and they pulled me aside and said, 'What is your background? Are you an actor?' I said, 'No, I'm a professional roller hockey player.' They said, 'Do you know anybody else that can skate like you?' I said, 'Yeah, I know about 14 guys.' They said, 'Go find those guys and bring them back and we will make a movie.' "

It was near the end of the Blades' season, and Nelson arrived late for practice. Blades' coach Mark Hardy asked him, "Do you want to be a hockey player, or do you want to do this movie crap?"

The Blades ended up losing to the Anaheim Bullfrogs in the playoffs, and the next day, Nelson took his teammates to the Warner Brothers' lot.

"They all got signed, and we all ended up working on Batman and Robin for about three-and-a-half months," Nelson said. "It was a blast. It was Stephane Desjardins, myself, Eric Rice, Steve Bogoyevac, Brett Kurtz, Mike Doers, Peter Kasowski… and we all did this movie, hanging out in this huge movie studio with Arnold Schwarzenegger, George Clooney and Alicia Silverstone. When we were done with that, we'd skate across the lot, hang out in the sunset for a little bit, and then skate back in. We got paid a lot of money to do that."

At one point, Nelson was approached by the movie's director, Joel Schumacher, who told Nelson that he had a clip from the movie that was going to be turned into a commercial. The problem was that all of Schwarzenegger's Mr. Freeze's henchmen – Nelson's teammates and other RHI players – were wearing heavy makeup and costumes that disguised their identities, and the studio needed to know who was who so they could pay the actors residuals for the commercial.

"I said, 'That one there, that's obviously me. That's Brett Kurtz, that's Mike Doers and that's Eric Rice.' And they're, 'OK, are you sure about that?' I said, 'I'm 100 percent sure.' They each made like $15,000 extra off the commercial. You couldn't tell who was who… Those were my boys, so I wanted to make sure those guys got paid. I don't know if I ever told them that."

In April 1996, Nelson made the cover of Roller Hockey magazine.

"It was the first time that I realized I was making a mark in the sport," Nelson said. "People were taking notice of me because of my skill *and* because of the color of my skin."

CHAPTER 29

A Great Rivalry

Just an hour's drive apart, the Los Angeles Blades and the Anaheim Bullfrogs had one of the best competitive rivalries in the league from 1993 to 1997, when the Blades dropped out of the league.

The competition between the two teams wasn't limited to the players – the owners got into the action quite frequently, too.

"Just like Batman needs a Joker and Superman needs a Lex Luthor, the Silvers were everything I needed in the league, because they were exactly the opposite of what I was," said Blades' owner Jeanie Buss about Maury, Nelson and Stuart Silver, the owners of the Bullfrogs.

"We were like the World Wrestling Federation – had we gotten along, I don't think it would have been such a rivalry," Buss said. "The rivalry went from top to bottom, and I admired the success the Bullfrogs had. Hands down, that was the model franchise in terms of their fan support. They were beloved in that town, and they were the first team to win a championship in that building. It was way before the [Anaheim] Ducks [of the National Hockey League.] And so, I couldn't have done it without them. Now, would I have done business the same way that they did? Probably not. Do I wish that we were still involved and in business together? Absolutely.

"It was exactly what the league needed in terms of a rivalry and two different philosophies and two different owners," Buss added. "Our focus was on developing American players; their focus was scouring whatever countries they could get players to come in from. They always put together a competitive team. They played a tough, physical style. We were more about scoring, with guys like Bogie and Kurtzy. We were like Yin and Yang. It was perfect."

"Steve Bogoyevac was absolutely my favorite," said Mike Altieri, the PR director for the Los Angeles Blades. "When he came onboard, I just could not pronounce his name. I became obsessed with making sure that everyone pronounced and spelled his name correctly. Talk about a guy with a presence and a magnetism. [He was a] good-looking young guy, but he was just so respectful to people. Talk about an example for athletes in general, how to carry yourself; this guy *got* it. I was constantly impressed with him. He could have been the biggest jerk in the world if he wanted to, but he was the sweetest, most thoughtful guy you could have as your leader and the top guy on your team.

"The Anaheim team, we just hated them and we could never beat 'em," Altieri added. "They beat us every single time. It was so frustrating. In our second year, we had Max Mikhailovsky as our goalie, and he had an unbelievable year. He was unbeatable. He was phenomenal. And I'll never forget the bus ride to Anaheim for the semifinals, and he could speak hardly any English, and he sat right behind me on the bus, and the whole way down there, I'm going, 'As long as we've got this guy, we've got it; we're going to beat these guys.' And he got absolutely shelled. I think they beat us like 6-1. He was awful from the minute the puck dropped. It was the most deflating feeling. Here we were, going into the building, we have the better goalie, and that was going to win it for us. I don't know if it was the pressure or what, but he literally had his worst game of the year in that game, and it killed us."

Blades defenseman Mike Doers, one of the team's best players, and one of the kindest and most considerate players in the league, said that it wasn't surprising that the Bullfrogs and Blades battled in every game.

"The Anaheim Bullfrogs were the Blade's greatest rival, absolutely, a cross-town rival," Doers said. "They were one of the better teams, and I think we were one of the better teams, so, naturally, you're going to compete hard against each other. The only frustration I can think of is not winning the league [championship.] We came close. I think you gotta give a lot of credit to the guys on the Bullfrogs, like Savo [Mitrovic] and Victor Gervais and Joe Cook. They had a bunch of guys that were all just tough to play against. And you were going to have bumps and bruises after every game playing those guys. It's just the way it was."

The Bullfrogs always had the best attendance in RHI. Their impressive arena had a lot to do with it, but so did the team owners' marketing ability.

"We played at the Pond before the Ducks did," said Joe Cook. "Part of the draw, initially, was the allure of people coming to see the building. But after the first season, after the Ducks started and we came back in 1994, we were still getting 11,000 people. I think, honestly, we were a lot more accessible than NHL players. We were in rinks, people were at our practices, and we'd sit and talk with them. I worked in a rink, so I dealt with a thousand people every 10 weeks at Stuart's Rollerworld, doing clinics and things like that. I think the Bullfrogs' success had a lot to do with the way the Silvers marketed the team; we used to *have* to go to these YMCAs and parking lots and clinics and to the beach doing stuff with people. So, they utilized the players very well. They got it. They were good marketers."

After winning a championship with the Bullfrogs in 1993, Bob McKillop played a second season with Anaheim before being traded to the Phoenix Cobras for Daniel Shank in 1995. McKillop ended up in Los Angeles with the Blades in 1996.

"It was weird to be in that division and play against the Bullfrogs and go to the Pond," McKillop said. "What a great experience. Anaheim was an unbelievable organization, first-class, and L.A. was the same. To get to play for both… what an honor that was. They were far and away the two best organizations in the league. I was a huge Lakers fan growing up, and I got to meet Magic Johnson, Michael Cooper and James Worthy. The fan base was a little bigger in Anaheim, but the L.A. lifestyle was a lot different. They paralleled each other. They both gave you what you needed to be professional. Anaheim had that cocky swagger, but they earned it. They were the organization to chase. Steve Beadle came over there with me. I was able to enlighten these guys on what goes on over there in Anaheim. It was Mark Hardy's first year coaching there, and we leaned on each other; it was a learning curve for everybody. I loved playing for both teams."

Both Blades and Bullfrogs singled out Anaheim's number-one goaltender for praise.

"Rob Laurie was a really good goalie," said Savo Mitrovic of the Bullfrogs. "He was my roommate our third year. Rob was quiet. He's a goalie. What else are you going to say about that? Goalies are always oddballs. There's nothing more you can say about a goalie than a goalie being a goalie. They're the ones that get the puck fired at them all the time. There's your answer about a goalie. Rob was a genius. I mean, he was a super smart kid. He had a degree in engineering. You could see him thinking. He'd be looking over at you and his mind is going 100 miles an hour. He thought his way through a lot of the things that he did as a goaltender, and that certainly made him one of the best inline goalies out there."

"Rob Laurie was just a phenomenal goalie," said Los Angeles Blades' defenseman Steve Wilson. "He was tough to beat. He showed up every year and played well for Anaheim. That's not an easy thing for a goalie to do, to show up year after year."

The Bullfrogs always had a bevy of big players to stand tall in front of Rob Laurie and to protect their star players.

"I always had guys to look after me," said Victor Gervais about Bullfrog enforcers like Barry Potomski, Mike Butters and Darren Langdon. "Darren Langdon? He was a beauty, that guy. Darren was a great guy. He was awesome. He was fun. He played in the NHL that next year. He didn't get too many challengers."

"Barry Potomski was probably one of the toughest players and one of the craziest kinds of nutty individuals that I ever played with, but was an absolute gentle giant," Cook said. "You'd never know if you met Barry in a bar, in a restaurant, at the pool, that he was a fighter on the rink. You never would have known it, because he was just a mellow guy."

"I always respected the guys with the talent and the scoring ability, but I always liked the guys that played the game extremely hard," said L.A. Blades' defenseman Steve Wilson. "They played hard, they hit, but they could also score. Victor Gervais, for me, was a great guy that I loved to play against. We yapped at each other, we battled each other, but at the end of the day, we both respected each other because of we did out there. He was probably the first one that comes to mind, because he was the total package. He did it all."

"There's an offensive force," said ESPN color man Jim Fox, agreeing with Wilson's assessment of Anaheim's longtime star. "I think he was as much mental as physical in his understanding of the game. He was gifted."

Eric Rice's story is a heart-warming one if you like, patience, humility, skill and down-right doggedness. Rice was nicknamed "Bones" in his freshman year at the Air Force Academy by his assistant coach. "I had lost 15 pounds and I weighed 135 pounds," Rice said. "The assistant coach, said, 'Man! You're just a bag of skin and bones.' "

"Eric Rice was just absolutely relentless," said Blades' teammate Steve Bogoyevac. "He was one of those guys who could get hit 20 times and still have the puck on his stick somehow. He didn't make the team, but he asked if he could stay, just skate, just come out and practice and be an extra guy. Sure enough, a couple of games later, there was an injury, he's in there, he earns his spot, and there's no looking back."

One thing I remember best about Blades' forward Brett Kurtz was a radio spot he did on L.A.'s KROQ radio station before a Blades' game against the San Jose Rhinos: "Be vewwy, vewwy quiet," Kurtz intoned. "Weer hunting whineocewous!"

"Brett Kurtz was one of the funniest, most outgoing guys on the team," said Mike Altieri. "It's funny, because he was one of the guys who probably had the closest taste to maybe getting to the NHL. He played college hockey at Wisconsin. You could just tell that he was a guy that players rallied around, a real vocal guy. He always seemed to get hurt, but he had some real talent. Another guy with a fantastic personality; he had so much confidence in himself. When we did TV, we got him in on the broadcasting when he was hurt, and he was fantastic. For a guy that never made it in the professional leagues, he was one of the most confident people I'd ever been around. To this day he's still that way. A great guy."

"Kurtzy was king of the backhand saucer pass," said Steve Bogoyevac. "He was really creative, and a great leader, too. He was involved in the beginning with putting the team together, working with the management to do that."

Named player/assistant coach for the Blades before the '94 RHI season, Kurtz's play prompted Jim Fox, color commentator for espn2's Monday Night Roller Hockey, to call Kurtz "the heart and soul of the Los Angeles Blades."

"Kurtzy could crack me up with his impersonation of Max Mikhailovsky," said Blades' owner Jeanie Buss. "Kurtzy had to take care of him, because he really didn't speak English. We had NHL scouts coming to look at him; he was a great goalie."

What Bogoyevac remembered about Mikhailovsky was "Max standing on his head many times," making impossible saves for the Blades.

"Brett Kurtz brought us Mike Doers, and when the players are arriving, they all come in about the same time for training camp," Buss said. "So I had to recruit my friends, whoever could pitch in and help. Doo Dog was coming in to the airport, and I had to ask my friend Stacy Kennedy to go pick him up. She said, 'How am I going to know who he is?' I said, 'All I know is his nickname is Doo Dog.' So she's at LAX baggage claim, walking up to every 20-year-old looking guy, going, 'Doo Dog?' People were looking at her like, 'What?!' Eventually she found Doo Dog. Doo Dog ended up meeting the woman he married, a friend of one of my friends. Those are the kinds of things you never forget – where people's lives changed because of their involvement in the league."

A pure goal scorer, Blades' forward Mike Callahan certainly impressed Steve Bogoyevac.

"He could find the net anytime during a game. Pretty awesome," Bogoyevac said.

"Mike Callahan was just a fun guy to be around," Doers said. "He was a guy's guy in the locker room who didn't have anything bad to say. He loved the game and played hard every night."

Jeanie Buss said that Callahan was "great with the puck. I liked him because he was old-school hockey; he was missing a couple of teeth. He had a passion for the game, and he was good at it, so he was a favorite."

"Mike was a really gifted hockey player," remembered his good friend, Blades' backup goaltender Brad Sholl. "People would say that he wasn't in great shape and that he was slow, but he had the best hands of anybody I've ever played with, whether it's roller hockey or ice hockey. You could always count on him to pot a couple of goals. The most amazing thing about Mike is that he can go all night long with the best of them and still put in three or four goals the next day. That to me is mind-boggling – how he could perform like that. He was a lot of fun. If you're still friends with a guy after your hockey is long past, those are your true friends."

Mike Doers said he'd never forget his 1993 Blades teammates Mike and Steve Ross.

"The first thing that comes to mind is ice fishing," Doers said. "That's all they talked about – shades of 'Slap Shot.' "

The Blades played the Bullfrogs in Anaheim in a 1995 game that players on both teams are unlikely to forget.

"We were on the power play, and the Bullfrogs had these new Hyper [logoed] towels on the bench," said Steve Bogoyevac. "Right before the power play started, Steve Wilson grabbed a towel to wipe the sweat off of his face, and went out on the floor. He didn't know it, but the ink had come off the towel, and his face was completely black. That's funny enough as it is, but to top it off, his own teammates and the Bullfrogs' players started laughing and yelling at him, "Hey Nelly!" [The nickname for Blades' African-American defenseman Chris Nelson.] But he had no idea – he was out there with the puck. It was pretty classic."

Nelson agreed.

"Wilson wiped his face and went out for a shift, and everyone just looked and jaws dropped in awe," Nelson said. "It was obvious that he had no clue what he looked like. It was as if someone had spray-painted him black. It was like a 1920s-style film where you see someone with white lips and black face. And he went out there for a shift or two, and both teams were dying in hysterics. It was one of the funniest things I've seen in roller hockey."

"I was just trying to wipe the sweat off of my face," Wilson said. "The next thing I know, the whole bench is just laughing their heads off at me. I'm like, 'What, are my pants coming down? What's going on?' I looked in the glass, and my whole face was almost all black from this towel."

CHAPTER 30

Sometimes You Only Get One Kick at the Cat

From almost the inception of Roller Hockey International, there were dreams of someday working hand in hand with the National Hockey League, filling NHL buildings with pro roller hockey in the summertime and using the NHL's marketing might to promote the game. Early in RHI's existence, the league's founders and some of its team owners felt that partnering with the pro ice hockey league could be mutually beneficial and grow both ice and inline hockey.

In the fall of 1994, RHI co-founders Larry King, Dennis Murphy, Alex Bellehumeur and Ralph Backstrom, along with Pittsburgh Phantoms' owner Howard Baldwin, met with NHL Commissioner Gary Bettman in the NHL's New York City offices to gauge the league's level of interest in RHI.

Backstrom said RHI's co-founders pointed out that roller hockey could be played just about anywhere – in parking lots, tennis courts and in the street. "Anybody with a street address can play inline hockey," was how Backstrom put it.

"We told Bettman that roller hockey would increase the popularity of ice hockey in the long run," Backstrom said.

The group also advised Bettman that the kids playing roller hockey in warm-weather states would come to identify with NHL teams and players as fans, and in the future, as ticket buyers.

"We had a very nice meeting," Dennis Murphy said. I just don't think that we were on as solid a ground as they might have liked."

That is not surprising, considering that many RHI team owners were hemorrhaging money. For example, only three of the league's 19 teams would show a profit in 1995. Teams needed a minimum of 5,000 fans to break even, and only a few were able to draw that.

The Anaheim Bullfrogs and St. Louis Vipers paid between $16,000 and $20,000 per game to rent the Anaheim Pond and Kiel Center, respectively. Fortunately, the Bullfrogs and Vipers drew enough fans to keep their owners from losing so much money that they dropped out of the league, and they would end up as the only two teams to play in every year of RHI's existence.

Larry King said that no arrangement was made between the two leagues was because the NHL was never really that interested.

"We met with the NHL twice," King said. "Because of the WHA days, Murphy had a hookup with Pittsburgh Penguins' owner Howard Baldwin, and Howard thought that this would be a good way to build the base for interest in hockey, and he was right about that. But if the NHL thought they could do it themselves, why did they need us? We met with them in New York, but nothing really came out of it. It might have been good for the NHL and it definitely would have been good for us, because we were still struggling. Every team lost money, some less, some more. It would have been a real shot in the arm for Roller Hockey International to align with the NHL."

Ken Yaffe, who was the NHL's vice president of fan development at the time, said that there were several reasons why the meeting didn't result in a groundbreaking agreement between the two leagues.

"At that point in the league's history, Gary Bettman had been in the commissioner's chair for one year; he was still studying and focused on priorities of the NHL," Yaffe said. "He was also heading into collective bargaining in 1994. We were looking at the notion of fan development and expanding and diversifying the NHL fan base, and there was a surge in interest and participation in roller hockey. We were certainly prepared to take a meeting and to look at opportunities and ways that we could broaden our fan base and touch more people with the game."

Yaffe said that street hockey and roller hockey were absolutely central to the NHL's marketing strategy at the time – building a generation of fans through an introduction to the game at the grassroots level. The NHL was also interested in RHI as an opportunity to fill facilities in summertime that were owned by NHL team owners, such as Howard Baldwin's Civic Arena in Pittsburgh, he said.

"But it was never sort of an all-hands-on-deck, laser-focused mission to try and find our way into the sport," Yaffe said. "We did plenty of things during those years. We established the International Ice Hockey Federation Inline Hockey World championship, we had the NHL Breakout Tour, and we were involved in licensing of roller hockey skates and protective equipment. Those were the priorities, not so much to own a league. That said, if we had ever seen a business plan or model that was sustainable, we would have jumped in."

Yaffe's last statement is quite exciting in retrospect. Fans of inline hockey can imagine where the sport might be today had RHI been able to make some sort of long-term business arrangement with the NHL. But Yaffe added that the NHL was in no rush to make a deal with RHI, because the NHL could afford to sit back and observe as other entities and private businessmen invested money in the roller hockey league.

"If we felt it was getting traction and would have been successful, we could have jumped into it," Yaffe said. "One of the big issues at the time was that we felt that the game wasn't, frankly, as good as it should be or could be. It wasn't as distinguishable from ice hockey as it should have been."

Three years passed as RHI continued to add and subtract teams, trying to find a formula that would keep the league alive.

San Jose Rhinos' owner Rich Shillington said he was sitting in the stands at a home game in 1997 in the San Jose Arena with Buffalo Wings' owners Dr. Frances Edmonston and Jason Klein, along with Rhinos' GM Jon Gustafson when Roller Hockey International CEO Larry King approached the group. According to Shillington, King said that RHI's owners had decided to go into the business of creating roller-hockey-specific facilities, and said that if Shillington wanted to go in the direction of the NHL, RHI would release the Rhinos from their contract so they could do so.

"I said, 'Fabulous.' That's exactly what I wanted to do," Shillington said. "I said, 'Well, you'll give me a letter in support of this to provide the release.' He said, 'Oh yeah, no problem, I'll give you the letter.' So, I went down the next day and met with Greg Jamison, the president of the Sharks, and he was elated. He said, 'Fabulous.' So he phoned Bettman. Bettman phoned me that day, and we probably talked for a good half hour on the phone, and then he said, 'Listen, I really would like you to come to New York so that we can meet on this.' I said, 'Fine, but I have a fellow that thinks very much similar to what I do in St. Louis, Dale Turvey, and I'd like to bring him to the meeting as well.' He said, 'No problem.' "

Shillington and Turvey made arrangements to go to New York and awaited the release letter from Larry King.

Shillington's expectation was that the meeting with Bettman would give him and Turvey an opportunity to "discuss the possibility of putting a league together – an NHL-sponsored league," Shillington said. "It was just to have preliminary discussions to develop a framework for moving forward."

Shillington said he kept phoning King, asking for the letter, but it didn't arrive before Shillington and Turvey flew to New York, so King faxed it to Gary Bettman. When he and Turvey arrived at the meeting, Bettman showed them the faxed letter from King, which stated that King "authorized Shillington and Turvey to represent RHI toward a merger, an amalgamation, between RHI and the NHL," Shillington said.

"Well, they were not interested in that one little bit, and it isn't what we were told [by King]," Shillington said. "So, we got knifed in the back really badly. And if King wouldn't have knifed us in the back, Roller Hockey International would be going very well right now. Because we needed the support, we needed the depth of the NHL behind us. It was the only way it was ever going to succeed."

Shillington said that the letter King faxed to Bettman derailed the meeting.

"He [Bettman] said didn't feel comfortable talking about anything, because that was not the essence of the meeting," Shillington said. "He was concerned about any legal ramifications. We didn't discuss anything thereafter other than the possibility of Bernie Federko going to the Hockey Hall of Fame."

Wouldn't an NHL-sponsored professional roller hockey league then have had to compete with RHI?

"No, no, no," Shillington said. "RHI would have been dead. What Larry had said was that they were going to pursue facilities, and that they were going to release us. Because I was always after King – 'This thing belongs under the jurisdiction of the National Hockey League, not us, because we were just not able to make it work.' It's like the WNBA, that's under the jurisdiction of the NBA, and that's exactly what roller hockey should have been."

Shillington said he envisioned professional roller hockey being played in the NHL's arenas during the summer time to the present day.

"Bettman was talking to me about all the interesting things he could see the NHL doing with roller hockey," Shillington said. "And quite frankly, it wouldn't bother me if the NHL had just said, 'OK, we're going to form our own league.' Which they would have, and I would have been a small part of it with the Sharks."

Shillington said he would have been happy with a minority ownership position with the Rhinos under an NHL roller hockey league.

"It is better to have a small piece of the action under a successful league rather than a full ownership within a failed league," Shillington said. "It would have suited me just fine. And it would have suited Dale Turvey of St. Louis just fine, too. Anyway, it didn't happen that way. If the people who were running the show, namely the Larry Kings and Dennis Murphys, knew what to do, it would still be going. But they didn't know how to take that success and manage. I thought Larry King's the one who killed the league. The big problem with roller hockey… you're only as strong as the weakest link in the chain. There were just too many weak links in the whole chain. It fell apart."

Shillington said that while the NHL wasn't interested in RHI in 1994, when Larry King and company met with the NHL in New York City, the ice hockey league was definitely interested in 1997 when he met and Turvey with Bettman.

"And one of the main reasons that they got renewed interest is that the San Jose Sharks just loved roller hockey because it was all part of them working and developing the South Bay area as a strong hockey area," Shillington said. "And it utilized their building during the summertime. A lot of young kids played roller hockey, so they were future Sharks' fans."

Shillington said that he came to realize that the RHI wasn't going to succeed on its own, and that the Rhinos' relationship with the NHL's San Jose Sharks was the key to his team's success.

"The Sharks were big supporters of ours," Shillington said. "They were involved in helping with the administration and all that sort of stuff. One year, we had $500,000 just in sponsorship revenues. We had a lot of support from the Sharks. I had always wanted RHI to get involved with the NHL."

Dale Turvey said that since both the Vipers' President Bernie Federko and coach Perry Turnbull had played for the NHL's St. Louis Blues, the Vipers had a connection to the NHL that not every RHI team enjoyed, and that the Blues supported any arrangement that the Vipers could make with the NHL.

"We had a great relationship with the Blues, and they were all for it," Turvey said. "And so, Rich and I went up there thinking we were going to cut a deal where the NHL was going to take over running the league and owning it. We thought we were all in agreement. We had spoken to Larry King and some of the other owners [of RHI] and we thought it was a done deal."

Larry King scoffed at Shillington and Turvey's version, reiterating that RHI was *always* interested in having the National Hockey League buy the league, including himself and Dennis Murphy, who saw the NHL as "the Holy Grail." Shillington's plan simply wasn't feasible, King said.

"Why would they [the RHI team owners] step aside?" King asked. "I don't understand this. I was the president of the league, I was representing the league, and I told them that I'd give them a letter so that they could negotiate for us, but stepping aside... impossible. I represented all the owners, but I couldn't make a decision like that for all the owners without consulting them. I was one owner amongst nine other teams at that time. That's impossible, but I could give them a letter authorizing them to negotiate for all of us, which I did."

King said that RHI wasn't planning on building roller hockey facilities.

"I don't know where the facilities stuff comes from," King said. "When you're a member of a league, you're an owner of the league. You're a partner with the other 10 teams in the properties, and you're a member of the nonprofit association that runs the league, so you can't release yourself from being a member of the league, but you *can* go negotiate for the group."

Never, King said, did he intend to let Shillington leave RHI with the Rhinos, let the league die, and have the NHL create its own league with some of RHI's teams. King added that he might have given Shillington a letter giving him the right to talk to a third party about RHI, without which Shillington would have been bound by the league's confidentiality agreement.

"I'm just going to kill the league and give Richard a letter saying that the league's dead and he can go negotiate for himself?" King said. "Right," he added. "That didn't happen. You can't write him a letter saying that he's out of the league," King said. "You would have to have an agreement for him to be leaving the league. You can't go negotiate a new place for yourself and leave your nine partners behind. It doesn't sound to me like either Richard was forthright to us about what he was doing or forthright to Bettman about what he perceived he could be doing. As I recall, we had a further meeting after that first meeting by Shillington and Turvey, and there were about nine of us at the NHL offices in New York. But that was under the auspices of Howard Baldwin."

King said that RHI "tried like crazy" to get the NHL to take the league over, "but for whatever reason, either with Howard Baldwin or with Gary Bettman, it all turned out to be a pipe dream from our standpoint. They didn't really have an interest in it."

King added that if the NHL *had* bought RHI, the league would still be around today.

"If the NHL would have taken us over, it would have guaranteed our success," King said. "If Richard [Shillington] had an entre to getting it done, we were going to give him any letter that he needed to make it happen, but obviously, we weren't going to have Richard go on without the rest of us. Yeah, 100 million dollars invested… just let Richard go off on his own… I don't think so."

According to Ken Yaffe, when Bernie Mullin became RHI's president in 1998, there were additional discussions between the NHL and RHI.

"When Bernie got there, we actually did have some more serious discussions where we might have signed an NDA [non-disclosure agreement] and, as I recall, started to look at some financial performance and a few different scenarios that might have led to an alliance or an ownership interest," Yaffe said. "This went on over a period of weeks, maybe months, but never really got a serious look in this organization. We were always enamored by the potential in roller hockey and the growth of the sport, but our focus was really at the grassroots level."

Rich Shillington recalled yet another meeting that he, Turvey and Mullin had with Bettman the following year, in 1999, RHI's final season.

"It just didn't go anywhere," Shillington said. "Bettman got so turned off about what had happened that he just wasn't interested. Sometimes you only have one kick at the cat."

What about the hope that lightning would strike twice? Several World Hockey Association teams had merged into the NHL. What about Dennis Murphy's hope that the NHL would buy RHI and run it?

"If anybody could have pulled that off, it was Dennis Murphy," King said, adding that Murphy had also merged American Basketball Association teams into the NBA.

"So I think there was a group of owners that probably entertained it," King said, "but the NHL management? I don't think that they ever entertained it for a moment."

Dennis Murphy said that some RHI team owners felt that the NHL liked RHI's product and wanted to take the league over, profiting on the hard work and financial risk that the original team owners' had incurred to build the sport to that point.

"From day one, we had two or three guys, led by Rich Shillington, who wanted to go with the NHL," Murphy said. "Rich always had it in the back of his mind to go with the NHL, because with the NHL's support, he felt that we'd turn the corner very easily. We had a couple of meetings with the NHL. To be honest, I think they thought we were a threat. We had a couple of guys who wanted to tie in and get extra exposure. They were right, but Gary Bettman didn't accept this at the time. They were not in the positive frame about that idea. Some felt that NHL was using us."

Despite the meetings between RHI's leaders and the NHL, no deal was ever consummated. Why, at the very least, couldn't an arrangement of some sort have been reached to provide the NHL with a pool of potential players, or conditioning and rehabilitation camps in summer for injured NHL players?

Maury Silver of the Anaheim Bullfrogs was one of the team owners who favored some sort of professional arrangement between RHI and the NHL.

"I thought that would be a great thing for everybody, and because the NHL knows how to run a league, the NHL would advertise it," Silver said. "We could benefit by advertising, that alone was worth $10 million."

Silver believed that the NHL had some interest in RHI, but that the league greatly overvalued its worth and turned off the NHL.

Steve Pona felt that a big part of the problem was that there were so many different potential scenarios for the NHL to work something out with RHI. Team owners like Silver salivated at the prospect of tapping the NHL's marketing might, while others, like Shillington and Turvey, wanted the NHL to buy the league lock, stock and barrel.

"There were so many possibilities between RHI and NHL," Pona said. "Certain owners held certain positions about what options they preferred, and Dennis knew how the ownership preferences sorted out. So, he would update Maury about news that pertained to his preference, Rich Shillington about his preference, etc. Some call that manipulation. I call it masterful diplomacy, because Dennis was able to take the temperature of each owner about different issues while still updating them and maintaining friendships and professional support. Sheer genius."

The NHL was certainly well aware of Dennis Murphy's abilities. The league had not forgotten Murphy's history in creating the World Hockey Association and how some WHA team owners made a pretty penny when the WHA folded and their teams merged into the NHL. That alone would have raised warning flags in the minds of certain NHL team owners and league administrators.

Though Pona passionately wanted a deal to be struck and felt optimistic about the possibilities, he anticipated that the timing may not have been quite right. On one hand, there were many old-school NHL owners at the time that weren't ready to make that kind of an investment in a non-traditional game like inline hockey. On the other hand, there were several RHI team owners who hoped to recoup their losses with one check. When combined with the lack of a unified league growth strategy, the mix proved to be too volatile.

Pona felt that RHI floundered because the founders' original business plan wasn't a long-term strategy.

"RHI's management and ownership were, from day one, hoping to revisit the success of the WHA and be purchased by the NHL," Pona said. "Their early strategy was to be big enough to hold off competitors and to have enough money in the bank to hold out until the NHL was interested. Their strategy probably wasn't off base, mind you. The NHL was expanding to the Sunbelt where inline skating and roller hockey were already part of the lifestyle, and ice rinks were scarce to nonexistent. NHL owners owned their buildings in the south, and they needed tenants in the summer, desperately."

Many people, including St. Louis Vipers' coach Perry Turnbull, felt that RHI missed a great chance.

"It's very unfortunate that RHI's leadership wasn't able to make the marriage with the National Hockey League." Turnbull said. "The NHL could have used inline hockey as a training tool. Roller hockey has been a great skill-building tool. Look at Paul Stastny in Colorado. He's a top-20 NHL player, and he was from the Midwest Fighting Saints, our travel kids' team. There are lots of guys, there's Brad Boyes here [in St. Louis]; these kids all played at the high level of roller hockey also. I don't care if you're playing shinny hockey on your knees or playing out on the street with a pair of shoes and a ball, you're still thinking hockey, and that's what I wish we could do a little bit better with the roller side... connect with the St. Louis Blues."

Anaheim Bullfrog's goalie Rob Laurie expanded on the theme.

"San Jose was getting 6,000 fans a game in 1997; that's pretty damn good," Laurie said "They were tying it all in with the Sharks and cross-promoting. I think the NHL missed the boat; they should have gotten that going. Larry King was pushing outdoors venues, and it tanked. Give him credit for trying to start new things, but it didn't work. It was the wrong way to go, and the San Jose way was the right way to go. Most fans are just hockey fans. What else are you going to do in the summer time? Roller hockey was a perfect avenue to be different, but similar. Roller hockey was another way to get people to the rink. You can't deny that people liked watching those games."

Laurie noted the excitement created by RHI's 4-on-4 style of play, which the NHL incorporated in its overtime periods.

"You go to an NHL game now, and in five minutes of overtime you see as many scoring chances as you do in the whole rest of the game," Laurie said. "And people are on their feet at the end of the game because there could be a 2-on-1 and then going back the other way a 3-on-2 and then a breakaway back the other way. I mean, everybody's just going, 'Oh, my God, it's unbelievable!' Because it's 4-on-4. And that was the whole game of RHI."

"The founders had a lot of good ideas and understood the need to build the grassroots of the sport," said David Smallwood of Karhu, who added that RHI worked hard to bring players into the sport and build the league's fan base. "They tried to do a lot of good things, but like many businesses, there were a lot of issues that go into whether they're long-term successes or not. You look at soccer, you look at indoor football, minor pro hockey leagues – some are very successful, but others fail. The NHL is still working hard to succeed at what they do."

Mike King, the original owner of the Vancouver VooDoo, said that RHI should have had more of its ducks in a line before approaching the NHL.

"I think that we approached the NHL too early," King said. "If the league had been around for a longer period of time and had proven itself in terms of popularity, attendance, TV ratings and so on, then they might have been in a better position. The NHL didn't want to buy something that was going to fail. I don't think we'd been around long enough to establish any credibility yet."

"We were believers," said Larry King, of RHI's founders. "That's the problem. We went in as promoters and came out believers... and left two or three million dollars behind. We had a great time doing it, too. You gotta admit; we had a great time doing it."

CHAPTER 31

One Part Slapshot, Marx Brothers, and Spinal Tap

In an article in the November 1997 issue of Roller Hockey magazine titled "Starting a Riot: Major League Roller Hockey, a renegade professional league whose first season was one part Slapshot, one part Marx Brothers, and one part Spinal Tap," Bill Jensen wrote about his experiences in the first season of MLRH.

"From bodies flying through the boards and onto the sidewalk at Chelsea Piers in New York, to players bleeding on the bench waiting for a team doctor that would never come... the growing pains and pleasures of a fledgling pro roller hockey league affected its young players from day one," Jensen wrote. "Major League Roller Hockey's first game took place amidst the truck stops and motels of the minor-league city of Carlisle, Pennsylvania. As a member of the New York Riot, a team comprised of the best amateur players in New York, we had arrived the night before the game to terrorize the local Best Western and plan our next day's attack. But as they dimmed the lights, brought out the smoke machine and introduced the Pennsylvania Posse, we weren't thinking about hockey, we were thinking about hitting. We went out to play old-time hockey and line up the perfect open-court hit, forgetting about the puck in the process. I put on my best Ulf Samuelsson mask and got in the record books by mugging Posse leading scorer Jay Mazer and receiving the first penalty in MLRH history."

Jensen's article described a season that so frustrated league co-founder Bill Raue that he erased its history from the MLRH website (http://www.MLRH.com) which still exists today. MLRH has continued, off and on, in one form or another, ever since.

Four years after playing in Roller Hockey International for the Connecticut Coasters, Jimmy Vivona played with Jensen on the New York Riot in 1997.

He said that the team's rink in Long Island was a hostile environment for visiting teams.

"I remember having a big game against the Philadelphia Posse when one of their players, who was obviously pissed off, elbowed me in the face, opening a gash above my eye," Vivona recalled. "The captain of my team, Joe Tamburino, immediately started pounding the guy, but that wasn't good enough for some of the fans. I actually had to talk a few Brooklyn guys out of waiting to introduce themselves to the player who elbowed me. They felt that since I had to go to the hospital, he should have to join me. The scary thing was that they were 100 percent serious!"

Vivona added that the young fans of the league looked up to the players and were happy when they were given sticks and T-shirts – even if Vivona and the other MLRH players had to worry whether their checks from the league were going to clear.

"I often get angry that this season has disappeared from the books of roller hockey history," Vivona said. "I had 15 goals and 37 assists in eight regular season games, and yet it seems to have been wiped away. Well, they can't take away my fond memories of that season, nor the scar above my right eye that I will have as a lifelong keepsake of 'The Lost Season.' "

Bill Jensen described dodging fans while dressed only in a towel to get to showers at the other end of the rink, dealing with injuries ranging from shattered kneecaps to facial gashes and even broken legs, and having his team painted as the villainous rivals for the Washington Power, a team that benefited greatly in accommodations and equipment from its connection and close proximity to the league offices in Alexandria, Virginia.

"We're part rock and roll and part roller hockey," Raue had told Roller Hockey magazine in "Summer Thunder," an April 1997 article describing MLRH's plans. "We're taking our show on the road."

"We will play in smaller arenas, coordinate it with youth hockey leagues and clinics, and get intimately involved with the community," said Raue's partner, Dr. Arnold Willis, in an article I wrote in InLine Hockey News that same month. "We hope to develop grassroots support, leagues and clinics for kids, locally. There's a lot of interest from sponsors, because we're linking it to youth development programs. I have three sons who skate and play roller hockey. The key to our potential success is for every franchise to own an equitable amount of the league; teams have to be able to make money on their investments. We're asking teams for a 3-year-or-better commitment."

The league's "Rollin' Thunder Tour" was intended to be a six-team traveling roller hockey festival, with two games a day in the East Coast and Canada that would include games against European teams. The league would begin play on July 5, and franchise fees were to be $50,000 a pop. Those initial expansive plans morphed into a four-team North American league – the Washington Power, New York Riot, Carolina Copperheads and Pennsylvania Posse – along with a team from England that was flown in to participate in the league's playoffs.

"The league was run by the seat of the pants," Jensen recalled later. "I remember the jerseys we had. Raue had bought these jerseys in bulk, so the Riot jerseys were these weird colors – he just got a deal on them. He had a background in graphic design, so he did some really cool logos. I liked the logos a lot. He would do these logos and match them up with these jerseys he'd bought in bulk."

Jensen remembered buying the British team Cokes when they were flown out for the playoffs – "they were so happy" – but he didn't recall the league having any medical insurance for the players.

"I broke my wedding ring finger and had to get my ring cut off my hand. I think I just paid for that out of my pocket," Jensen said.

Longtime roller hockey entrepreneur Charley Yoder ran the Pennsylvania Posse.

"He had two sons who were really good," Jensen said, speaking of CJ and Jami Yoder, who would both later play in Roller Hockey International. "They were excellent. Jami nailed me during a tryout. I remember basically just flying through the air. I'd never been hit like that before, and never since."

What Jensen remembered most about the league, however, was having a great time after the games.

"The young players on the Riot were experts at two things in life: roller hockey and having a good time," Jensen wrote. "On the rink, they were some of the most talented players I've ever seen. Off the ice, they could party in a morgue. Watching them buying each other beers with their hockey money while hitting on every girl that walks by, I had to smile for them. Even though we felt like lab rats, given skates to see if we could get out of this wacky experiment of a hockey season, we felt like professional players for five weeks. We may not have gotten a lot of money, but we got our dream. Our dream and our chance."

CHAPTER 32

It'll be Baywatch on Wheels

In December 17, 1997, Daemon Filson, my boss and the publisher of InLine Hockey News, called and told me to clean out my office in Santa Monica by the end of the year because Sports & Fitness Publishing was going out of business. A little more than a month later, I interviewed Roller Hockey International CEO Larry King for InlineHockeyCentral.com, a web site I'd quickly put together with Jon Niola, a webmaster and friend. After having spent the better part of seven years writing for such publications as Hockey Player, Roller Hockey Magazine, InLine, InLine Retailer & Industry News, IHN and others, I wasn't quite ready to walk away from the sport. I figured that it was as good a time as any to start my first business.

I asked King what RHI needed to do to have a sixth season in 1998. "The only thing we need to survive is money," King said. "The only measure of success for a pro league is survival."

King said that he was waiting on a $1.5 million bridge loan that would help clean up RHI's balance sheet so the league could go public, raise $10 million dollars with an IPO, and not be so dependent on the number of teams in the league for its operating costs. Despite the league's precarious financial situation, King was confident that the league would play with eight teams in 1998, even if RHI wasn't able to put a schedule together until as late as April 1. (That confidence was probably not shared by the RHI players who had yet to receive their playoff bonus money for the 1997 season. The league had spent the $151,000 in prize money to keep the Ottawa franchise solvent during the season.)

With RHI's future up in the air in early 1998, it seemed that everybody and his brother were creating new leagues to replace it. Original RHI co-founder Dennis Murphy, along with Maury Silver, the owner of RHI's Anaheim Bullfrogs, had joined with a group of North American businessmen to create

Professional Inline Hockey. Murphy explained that the new league was necessary because RHI appeared ready to throw in the towel on a 1998 season.

"Schedules, sponsorships, TV contracts, lease dates, the supplier pool and team configurations are not in place, and the 1998 season is quickly approaching," Murphy said. "Many of us at the New York meetings have spent millions of dollars to bring RHI into its sixth year, and we feel the RHI leadership has not fulfilled its duties. We must protect our interests and go a different path."

Murphy added the Anaheim Bullfrogs would play in PIH, with team owner Maury Silver as league president.

Throwing another acronym into the mix on January 26, 1998, the eXtreme Hockey League (XHL) held a press conference in Buffalo's Marine Midland Arena to announce that the Buffalo Wings, who had played their inaugural 1997 season with RHI, was the first team to sign up with the XHL. Wings' owners Frances Edmonston and Jason Klein decided to jump from RHI because the league's salary cap of $5,000 per team per week made it difficult to add star players who demanded more money to play in Buffalo. The XHL would have a weekly salary cap of $6,000, but top players would be able to earn more money. League COO and Commissioner Phil Kershaw was also considering allowing XHL teams to carry a "marquis player," whose salary would not count against the salary cap.

The dueling announcements about PIH and XHL created conversation and confusion, but in the end, neither league got off the ground. Within days of Murphy's pronouncements about PIH, the Anaheim Bullfrogs signaled their intent to join Bill Raue's Major League Roller Hockey for that league's second season. Not long after, the Buffalo Wings dropped their plans to play in the eXtreme Hockey League and they too joined MLRH. Adding a touch of irony, RHI's hoped-for bridge loan from New York investment bank BlueStone Capital Partners *did* come through, but not in time, and the league went on hiatus for the 1998 season.

While RHI, PIH, XHL and MLRH fought it out in boardrooms and in the media, David McLane's new league burst onto the scene in the spring of 1998. Pro Beach Hockey was graced with such gimmicks as a two-point shot, the seven-foot-wide nets that McLane had used in his World Roller Hockey League in 1993, an outdoor court that sat on the sand next to the Huntington Beach Pier, no offsides, a dance troupe called the Slammin' Dancers… and ramps behind the goals. McLane created six teams with no geographical affiliation – Salsa, Dawg Pac, Heavy Metal, Web Warriors, Gargoyles and Xpress – and their games were taped for later broadcast on ESPN, which signed up for three years of coverage. Pro Beach Hockey also used a ball instead of a puck, perhaps to set itself apart from Roller Hockey International… or to avoid lawsuits from Alex Bellehumeur.

Irritated at the loss of the national sponsors he'd helped RHI attain and disappointed that some RHI team owners didn't understand or appreciate the value of the league's television deal with ESPN, McLane had been thinking of his new league for some time. As early as May 1996, Mark Madden was writing about McLane's planned league in InLine Hockey News. Apparently, RHI's most-successful coach, Chris McSorley was going to be involved, and he was enthusiastic about Pro Beach Hockey. "It'll be Baywatch on wheels," McSorley said. "It'll be a cool game under a hot sun."

Like RHI, Pro Beach Hockey played with four skaters and a goalie a side. Unlike RHI, it emphasized the players' personalities and looks as well as their hockey skills. Playing at the beach in late spring also enabled the league's camera crews to scan the bleachers for bikini-clad spectators to give the event's likely viewers (who weren't necessarily *hockey* fans) another reason to watch. McLane even hired McSorley as the league commissioner.

Perhaps the oddest aspect of the league in its first season was Pro Beach Hockey's decision to sign a sponsorship and licensing agreement with V-Formation, an inline skate company. The deal required all league players to wear the company's uniquely designed skates in which each wheel was alternately angled at 16 degrees, like a hillbilly's teeth. The skates' shortened wheel base was designed to give players a quicker turning radius in tight quarters. In races for the puck in open court, however, players using the skates seemed slow.

To many people, it seemed odd that Roller Hockey International would permit one of its principal executives to create another league. So as not to conflict with a potential RHI season, Pro Beach Hockey games were played in May, with the first telecast shown the first week of June and the best-of-three championship series aired on August 22. Even though Pro Beach Hockey didn't directly compete with RHI, InLine Hockey News' resident curmudgeon Mark Madden excoriated RHI in the January 1998 issue of InLine Hockey News for permitting PBH to even get off the ground, arguing that McLane had "successfully pulled off one of the most amazing examples of conflict of interest ever when he handled RHI's TV and marketing affairs while preparing the launch" of Pro Beach Hockey. Apparently, RHI's Larry King had blessed PBH.

"RHI never saw what I did as conflict of interest," McLane told Madden. "Larry King feels that the more exposure roller hockey gets, the better for all roller hockey." McLane also told Madden that "the teams aren't geographically positioned, they're psychographically positioned. For example, the Salsa might be the favorite team for people of Mexican or Spanish descent. Computer nerds might root for the Web Warriors."

People either loved PBH or hated it – there was really no in between. To this day, on web sites like InlineHockeyCentral.com, inline hockey aficionados debate whether the league was a positive force that kept the league in the public eye or a joke on wheels that gave the sport a black eye from which it never recovered. I was a skeptic myself, but I tried to be as fair as possible. While I personally felt PBH was a distraction from what RHI was trying to accomplish, I was glad that there would be some form of professional roller hockey to cover in 1998 – and I greatly appreciated the advertising support McLane gave Inline Hockey Central one year.

On May 4, in an article on IHC titled "Pro Beach Hockey Passes First Test," I wrote: "A live band (an alternative group called Velvet Chain) played between games, and the atmosphere was circus-like in the best sense of the word. Spectators included Manon Rheaume, Cammi Granato, Bobby Hull, Jr., and Jeanie Buss, former owner of the Los Angeles Blades of Roller Hockey International. Except for the flooring (plywood covered with Roll-On), the event received few complaints from the players, many of whom had played in RHI or were local Southern California beach hockey pick-up players. Though the heat was definitely a factor, especially for the goalies, the players didn't seem to let it bother them."

Proving that Roller Hockey International had no problem in providing players for McLane's league, participants included Los Angeles Blades' players such as Steve Bogoyevac, Eric Rice, Chris Nelson, Mike Butters, Brad Sholl and Stephane Desjardins, as well as other RHI veterans like Tony Szabo, Chad Seibel, Ralph Barahona, Christian Lalonde and Andy Rymsha. Top amateur players included Brian Watanabe, Rob Chornomud and Matt and Marty Mullen. In my article for IHC, I added that "the event is unlikely to appeal to fans of 'old school hockey,' but it did seem to capture and hold the attention of most of the spectators in attendance."

At the end of Pro Beach Hockey's first month-long "season," the Tony Szabo-led Web Warriors defeated the Chris Nelson-captained Dawg Pac in two straight games, 7-5 and 12-5, in the Pro Beach Hockey Championship series. Nelson earned the league's MVP award, and the Web Warrior's Roman Hubalek led all playoff scorers with nine points. Szabo, who was a player/ coach for the Web Warriors, scored eight points, while Stephane Desjardins and Jason Jennings each added seven. Web Warriors' netminder Rob Laurie was named the tournament's top goaltender. Laurie, an original Anaheim Bullfrog, had joined the Web Warriors mid-tournament, adding yet another inline hockey championship to his resume.

Major League Roller Hockey

Bill Raue, the wild man behind Major League Roller Hockey, with his out-of-control white hair, much resembled Dr. Emmett "Doc" Brown from Back to the Future movies. Perhaps no one in the sport gave more of his heart and soul than Raue, and the bruises he received in return, whether rightly or wrongly, showed that he wore his hockey heart on his sleeve when he attempted to scrub Major League Roller Hockey's first season (1997) from the historical record. Just the same, in 1998, in what was MLRH's true second season, Raue stepped into the breach to give roller hockey fans something to cling to after Pro Beach Hockey's short May "season" – at least until RHI came back in 1999.

It all began with a $1 pair of inline skates that Raue's wife Lindsay had purchased at a yard sale in the summer of 1996. Apparently, the previous owner had broken his wrist during his first outing on the skates. Convinced that they were cursed, he offered them to the first taker for the bargain-basement price of a dollar. Lindsay Raue's purchase indirectly led to the creation of Major League Roller Hockey. Bill Raue, a self described "old goalie from Wisconsin," jumped into the sport of inline hockey feet first, literally. From that day, Raue, the owner of a graphic-design firm in Alexandria, Virginia, was hooked.

"We'd go out and play on basketball courts until the authorities chased us off," Raue said. "I was the oldest juvenile delinquent in Alexandria, Virginia."

The lack of a suitable roller hockey rink prompted Raue's involvement in rink construction and then "one thing just led to another" – including dasherboard manufacturing, Sk8 Magazine and, eventually, Major League Roller Hockey.

Following the league's four-team 1997 season, Raue hired Shawn Jones, the former executive director of the National In-Line Hockey Association, as MLRH's commissioner. Upon the announcement of his hiring in April, Jones said that MLRH would play in the United States, Europe and Canada, and that RHI's Anaheim Bullfrogs would join the league as its flagship franchise. That was definitely a coup for MLRH, as the Bullfrogs still drew the greatest number of fans of any team in the sport.

What became quickly apparent about Major League Roller Hockey's 1998 season was its stunning lack of parity. The league's top five teams beat up on the rest of the league, and the top three teams – Anaheim, Columbus and Orlando – had only three regulation losses and two overtime losses against, *combined*, out of 60 regular-season games. Those same three teams had the league's stingiest defenses and best goaltending, each giving up fewer than 100 goals – 82, 84 and 93, respectively. Anaheim was a veritable all-star team, with such former RHI players as Bullfrogs' Darren Perkins, B.J. MacPherson and Glenn Stewart; San Jose Rhinos' Mark Woolf and Darren Colbourne; Minnesota Arctic Blast's John Hanson and Bill Lund. In net, the Bullfrogs had Rob Laurie to carry the load. Columbus boasted Joe Bonvie, who'd played 33 games for RHI's San Jose Rhinos the previous two seasons. Orlando had Steve Vezina, who would become infamous the following year and give the sport of roller hockey a ton of mainstream press it really didn't need. Anaheim's potentially perfect regular season was marred by one shootout loss to the Surge.

"In RHI, especially in California, all the teams had a lot of talent, and I think there was a lot of parity," said Bonvie. "But in MLRH, there wasn't. There were three or four good teams and that was it. If you didn't play those three or four teams, you were kicking their ass."

The Virginia Vultures, MLRH's fourth-best team, lost just four games all season and led the league with 290 goals – an average of 14.5 goals per game. On August 7, 1998, in a game that put the league's lack of parity on display for all to see, Vultures' forward Hugo Belanger tallied an incredible 26 points on 11 goals and 15 assists in a 38-6 pounding of the Philadelphia Sting. That night, Belanger set MLRH individual game records for points, goals, assists and plus/minus (+26).

Looking back without a box score to check facts, one has to wonder: Where was Sasha "The Pit Bull" Lakovic that night?

Lakovic, who'd quickly gained a reputation as an ice hockey enforcer in his first pro season in the Colonial Hockey League with 235 penalty minutes in 28 games for the Chatham Wheels, also scored 24 points in 11 games for RHI's Vancouver VooDoo in 1993. After playing just seven RHI games in 1994 for the Oakland Skates and Vancouver VooDoo, Lakovic played 17 games for the Oakland Skates in 1995 and the San Jose Rhinos in 1997 before joining Major League Roller Hockey's Philadelphia Sting for the 1998 season. He averaged a goal a game during his RHI career, so he could put points on the board as well as fight. That was shown in early July 1998, when Lakovic scored four of the Sting's five goals as they defeated the Carolina Crushers, 5-4.

CJ Yoder, who played for the Pennsylvania Posse that season, watched from the stands as a fan one night as Lakovic killed a penalty in a very unique manner during a game between the Sting and the Washington Power in Philadelphia.

"Lakovic goes out there for a penalty kill – he'd already put a guy over the boards with a hit – and he sits the puck behind him along the boards and stands like this [shoulders up, elbows out] for two minutes straight," Yoder said. "Nobody went near him. I'll never forget sitting in the stands. I wouldn't have gone after it either! He was another one of those guys I never wanted to run into in an alley."

It might have been safer in an alley with Lakovic than in the stands if you were MLRH President Bill Raue. Before one MLRH game in Canada between the Toronto Torpedoes and the Bullfrogs, Raue was in the stands having a meeting when a puck caromed off a goalpost during warm ups and struck Raue in the head. No one claimed responsibility. The Torpedoes also figured in a fun MLRH game story when they traveled to Washington, D.C., for a game against the Washington Power. Filling out biography sheets on game day that took advantage of the Power's unsuspecting announcer, Washington's fans were informed that the Torpedoes' players hailed from Afghanistan, Jamaica, Chernobyl and the Philippines.

Yoder also remembered the Rough Rider puck that MLRH used, and not fondly.

"We still have a box of them in my dad's roller skating rink in the basement in a box that will never be touched," Yoder said. "Nobody's ever touched them. They've got dust on them. That puck was *bad*."

The MLRH 1998 Finals

After what turned out to be a fairly pointless regular season, considering the strength of just a handful of MLRH's 20 teams, the entire single-elimination-style playoffs – quarterfinals, semifinals and finals – were held at the Arrowhead Pond of Anaheim in late August.

The Orlando Surge defeated the Virginia Vultures in the quarterfinals and then ended the Columbus Hawks' 15-game winning streak and season by squeaking by 5-4 in the semifinals. Jamie Cook, who had led all MLRH defensemen in scoring during the season, potted two goals in the third period to pace the Surge.

In their quarterfinal match up, the Anaheim Bullfrogs dispatched 1997's MLRH champion Washington Power, 20-4, firing 68 shots in the game against the Power's shell-shocked goalie. In the semifinals, the Bullfrogs met the Brighton Tigers of the league's six-team United Kingdom Division. The Tigers had received the dubious "honor" of playing the league's top team in the semifinals by virtue of their 6-1 record against other British teams. The Bullfrogs, led by Glenn Stewart's seven goals and six assists, crushed the Tigers, 37-2, setting up the championship game between the Surge and the Bullfrogs on August 26.

In the regular season, the Bullfrogs (19-0-1) and Orlando (18-1-1) were evenly matched, with each team winning a shootout in the other team's building, but Anaheim raced out to an early lead in the final. The majority of the announced crowd of 7,158 fans cheered for the home team, and the Bullfrogs didn't disappoint – building a 5-1 lead before hanging on to defeat the Surge 5-4.

The win gave the Bullfrogs the MLRH Jason Cup, which had been named for 15-year-old goalie Jason Daniel Kostelnik of Washington, D.C., who had died in 1997 after a heart transplant operation. It was the Bullfrogs' third professional roller hockey championship – they'd won RHI's Murphy Cup in 1993 and 1997. Bill Lund was named the tournament MVP, and his hat trick in the first half of the championship final jump-started the Bullfrogs.

Though Orlando's furious comeback fell short, the one-goal game wasn't decided until the final ticks of the clock, and a Surge shot hit the post in the last 45 seconds. It was, according to one reader of Inline Hockey Central, "roller hockey's most exciting game... period." A post-game incident spoiled what had been a great championship final, however. Anaheim's Chad Wagner cold-cocked Orlando's Alex Alepin in the post-game handshake line and broke his nose, bloodying the floor and tarnishing a longstanding tradition of sportsmanship. That punch overshadowed a brilliant season by Anaheim's netminder Rob Laurie, who was the league's best goalie in the regular season, posting a 3.93 goals-against average.

"MLRH was very Mickey Mouse, in retrospect," said Jason Klein. "The name did not beget the reality. I've often thought that Raue and Dennis Murphy were two of a kind. They both had really good ideas, but they didn't have the business sense or the deep pockets. Raue meant well, but if you call something Major League... there's a very negative impression, it lacks integrity when you use phrasing like that. It's unfair in the long run. Anything that lacks integrity, I believe, is destined to fail."

Major League Roller Hockey had stepped in and gave many of the players a place to play in the summer of 1998, but a crummy puck that bounced like a super ball hampered play, and the lack of parity was disappointing. It was fun, but it certainly wasn't Roller Hockey International.

CHAPTER 33

It was Like Somebody Just Ran Over His Dog

In early 1999, Roller Hockey International was preparing to return from hiatus, Major League Roller Hockey was making its plans for a third season and David McLane's Pro Beach Hockey was set for its second made-for-television event on the sand in Huntington Beach. As in 1998, PBH games featured a ball rather than a puck, an outdoor ink with ramps and plexiglass behind the nets to redirect the ball back into play, and a two-point shot. Dispensing with the patchwork painted-wood flooring from 1998, McLane went with a floor that Ice Court's Nicholas Johannes created especially for the event. The flooring's black-matte finish was popular with the ESPN cameramen – it didn't reflect the sun or buckle in the heat.

The same six teams from 1998 were put together for the event: Heavy Metal, Xpress, Gargoyles, Dawg Pac, Salsa and the defending PBH Champion Web Warriors, led by Tony Szabo. Other players of note included 1998's MVP, Chris Nelson of the Dawg Pac, Rob Laurie, Chad Seibel, Mike Butters and Rob (The Hammer) Harmer. (Upon his introduction to the crowd, Harmer came out on the rink waving a rubber mallet.) The games featured crunching action, cheering kids, music from a live band, and bikini-clad go-go dancers gyrating on top of the scaffolding high above the bandstand. The infamous ramps behind the net seemed less of a factor than in 1998, as many players simply waited for the Franklin ball to roll down the ramp before playing it. Boasting four former Los Angeles Blades – Steve Bogoyevac, Brett Kurtz, Eric Rice and Mike Callahan – the Xpress won the event, defeating Heavy Metal two games to one. The games were shown on ESPN later that summer.

Major League Roller Hockey still intended to compete with Roller Hockey International for an apparently shrinking audience of fickle inline hockey fans in 1999. After RHI had canceled its 1998 season, MLRH stepped into the breach. However, just the opposite happened in 1999 – on June 25, Major League Roller Hockey Commissioner Bill Raue announced on the league's website that the league had called off its planned third season. RHI would play in 1999, MLRH wouldn't.

"A last-minute financing package fell through, and we had no assurances that MLRH could complete the season," Raue wrote. "We deeply regret the inconvenience to fans, players, and sponsors, but there are no alternatives. To those who believed in me, I will always be grateful. I'm sorry there could have not been a happier ending."

Rumors had been flying about the league's imminent demise for weeks. At a MLRH league owners' meeting, at least one team was accused of non-payment of league dues and franchise fees, and several teams immediately dropped out in anger. Commissioner Shawn Jones quit after the raucous meetings, but Raue attempted to rebuild the league with the remaining teams.

"We had trouble putting a schedule together; it was no one thing," said Raue, who angrily defended his handling of the league. "The recent events have been a good lesson for me," he said. "I was there for the sport and kept the pro game alive at a personal cost of about $800,000. I allowed Anaheim to play when they had nowhere to go in 1998."

Before RHI's season could get under way, however, Raue fired one more quixotic shot across the older league's bow. A company called the Pacific Sports Hockey Group had acquired the rights to the Anaheim Bullfrogs and announced that the team would play in RHI, and not MLRH. In early June, Raue claimed that PSHG had previously negotiated with MLRH in bad faith and that the company used MLRH to gain access to the Anaheim Pond, and he threatened a lawsuit.

"We wasted an entire off-season with these guys," Raue told Inline Hockey Central. "It cost us the opportunity to develop a West Coast division and sponsorship dollars because we could not confirm a team in Anaheim."

Nevertheless, Anaheim did play in Roller Hockey International in 1999, and it was Major League Roller Hockey that ended up "on hiatus." As Roller Hockey International prepared to return from a year off, Bernie Mullin, the former vice chancellor for sports and wellness for the University of Denver, who had been hired as RHI's president in May, 1998, had been busy. Mullin designed a single-entity ownership plan in which RHI would own the eight teams participating in RHI in 1999 – the Anaheim Bullfrogs, Buffalo Wings, Chicago Bluesmen, Dallas Stallions, Las Vegas Coyotes, Minnesota Blue Ox, St. Louis Vipers and San Jose Rhinos – and provide an average of $350,000 toward each team's payroll, equipment and travel costs. The league expected corporate sponsorships and hoped for a national television contract with Fox Sports Net (that never came through) to provide the necessary revenue. The league would also keep expansion fees from any future teams.

"The game and the product and the fan support were there, but the finances weren't there [in 1998]," Mullin said in an interview for Inline Hockey Central on January 28, 1999. "The league ran out of money because it used its money to bail out a couple of bad franchises."

Under RHI's new plan, players would all receive $300 for each win and $200 for each loss, with bonuses for playoff success.

Jon Gustafson, general manager for the Rhinos, praised incentive pay as a great idea. "The guys have to perform to make money," he said. "The more games you win, the more money you make."

Gustafson argued that the new payment structure would create incentive and urgency, the players could make as much as $12,000 by winning the championship in RHI's three-month season.

When two proposed RHI teams, the Detroit Racers and Florida Jackals, dropped out of the league after the player draft on March 3, those teams' players were dispersed to the league's remaining eight teams in a supplemental draft at RHI's spring meetings May 2-3. In a random drawing, the Buffalo Wings won the first selection and picked Bill Lund, a former star for several RHI teams. Lund dished out an RHI record seven assists in one game, and had led the league in scoring in 1997 with 78 points for the Orlando Jackals. RHI's newest teams were the Dallas Stallions and the Chicago Bluesmen. The Bluesmen name was based on The Windy City's status as the "Blues Capital of the World." The team played at Fox Valley Ice Arena and had an appropriately named mascot: Sax-Squatch. The Dallas Stallions played at Reunion Arena in Dallas.

The Las Vegas Coyotes, taking the team name and logo from the Oklahoma Coyotes, who played in RHI in 1995 and 1996, became the league's second team to play in Sin City. The first was the Las Vegas Flash in RHI second season, 1994. Another retread team, the Minnesota Blue Ox, which had previously played in the league in 1995 at the Aldrich Arena, would now play at the Mariucci Arena on the University of Minnesota campus.

Rounding out the league in 1999 were the San Jose Rhinos and two original RHI franchises – the Anaheim Bullfrogs and St. Louis Vipers. [In January 1999, the San Jose Arena Management Company – which ran San Jose Arena, home to the Rhinos and the NHL's San Jose Sharks – had purchased a 50 percent ownership in the Rhinos.]

As Mullin explained it, a local promotional rights owner (PRO) in each city would pay arena costs, pay the league for the right to market the team, and make money through ticket sales and merchandising. The idea was to bring in stable ownership to the league and avoid fly-by-night owners and the shaky economics of the league's past. Mullin added that the plan would help promotional rights owners like the Bullfrogs' Pacific Sports Hockey Group turn a profit, help stabilize the league and attract the interest of NBA and NHL owners and arena operators.

Mullin rejected the suggestion made by some journalists that with the league hiring all of the teams' coaches and signing players, such micromanagement might potentially affect outcomes of RHI games.

"Local promoters won't allow it to become a 'show' rather than a sport," he said.

RHI 1999 Regular-Season Rumblings

While the first-year Bluesmen and Stallions sunk to the bottom of the standings with identical records (7-17-2), the Western Conference's Anaheim Bullfrogs once again raced to the top of the standings during the 1999 regular season, going 21-3-2. The Bullfrogs were followed by the Eastern Conference's St. Louis Vipers (17-8-1) and the West's Las Vegas Coyotes (16-7-3).

CJ Yoder liked the league's payment system to players that season, considering his team's successful record.

"We were very good, so it was great for us," Yoder said. "You got $300 if you won and $200 if you lost, so every game meant a little bit to the guys. I liked that idea. We played about two-and-a-half games a week, something like that, because it's jam-packed into a three-month time period, and guys have to go back to ice hockey. So, we were winning a good amount of our games, so I made good money that year."

Still, there were obstacles to overcome, Yoder said.

"There was one time we were sitting in the Kiel Center and someone came in and said, 'Hey guys – right now, the league doesn't have any insurance. You don't have insurance if you go out there. Do you still want to play?' I'm a roller hockey player. I was playing without insurance all the time," Yoder said. "We may have been playing the Chicago Bluesmen – and their roller hockey guys played. I think Danny Costanza stayed on the rink the whole game because only four or five of their guys would play."

The minor-league ice hockey players on the team sat on the bench so they'd get paid, but didn't go out and skate.

"A guy blows a knee out and ruins a career," Yoder said. "We might have had one or two guys that sat out, but not too many."

Fearing an injury is one thing. Fearing a coach was another. Longtime RHI forward Gerry St. Cyr said that there was one game in Las Vegas that season that he'd never forget – which included a half-time, locker-room tirade by Las Vegas Coyotes' coach Chris McSorley.

"He came in and was basically screaming at everybody – how the other team was kind of walking around us and no one was playing defense," St. Cyr said. "He always liked to have a tough team. So, he was screaming at us and yelling and saying, 'If these guys are coming down on ya, they'd better not be making it to the front of the net. You better be chopping off their arm and their leg, and if they're still hobbling around on one leg and one arm, you'd better chop the other one off.' It was probably a good 10-minute rant, from as soon as we got in the locker room to two seconds before we had to run back out on the floor. It was pretty funny. It caught everybody off guard, and the team definitely deserved to be yelled at, but it was like somebody just ran over his dog and we did it on purpose. It was one of those things you don't see too often. So it was kind of funny under your breath, but at the same time, you're thinking, 'Holy shit. Is this guy's head going to pop off or spin around?' You don't know what you're dealing with there."

Slinky Anaheim Bullfrogs' forward Hugo Belanger was probably one of the players who had cut through the Coyotes' defenses that season. Belanger led the league in scoring with 37 goals and 43 assists for 80 points, followed by Ken Blum (36-39-75) and John Vecchiarelli (28-43-71) of the Buffalo Wings.

One of the season's highlights came on June 27, when Minnesota forward John Hanson tied an RHI record with seven goals as the Minnesota Blue Ox defeated the St. Louis Vipers, 11-7. Hanson tied the record established by Brad McCaughey of the Anaheim Bullfrogs against San Jose on July 15, 1994; John Vecchiarelli on August 31, 1994, in the playoffs against the Portland Rage; and Gerry St. Cyr of the Sacramento River Rats against San Diego on August 15, 1996.

While players were taking care of business on the court, the same couldn't be said for RHI's front office. As early as mid July, there were rumblings that players weren't being paid.

On July 19, 1999, in an Internet newsgroup about RHI called Plaidworks, a representative of one of the eight RHI teams posted anonymously that players' checks, which were paid by the league, had bounced.

"RHI having serious problems. Not really sure there will be a next year for the RHI. Been told by a few players that their checks from the league have bounced. If they don't have the money to pay the players, then who's going to play next year?"

That problem continued at least into early August, when some fans of the Minnesota Arctic Blast noticed that several of the team's best players, including Bill Lund, Taj Melson and John Hanson, had missed a home game. Instead of playing for the Blast, the trio had played in the "pro" division at the North American Roller Hockey Championships, an elite amateur tournament best-known as NARCh, in Atlanta. This minor mutiny was certainly not a vote of confidence in RHI.

Pan Am Pharmaceuticals

It was always a challenge for Roller Hockey International to get much mainstream media attention outside of each team's individual market, unless there was a controversy like those involving Berkley Hoagland being told to play basketball or Christian Skoryna purposely scoring on his own goal. Both those incidents made it into USA Today and other major newspapers. However, on August 1, 1999, RHI got what might have been the most concentrated, unwanted and *worldwide* media exposure ever, even though the league was only indirectly involved.

That summer, inline hockey was included in the Pan American Games for the first time, hosted by the city of Winnipeg. In the championship final on July 27, Steve Vezina, a 23-year-old goaltender for RHI's Buffalo Wings, led Team Canada to a 7-6 victory over Team USA. Unfortunately, Team Canada's celebration was short lived when Vezina was randomly tested for drugs after the game and showed positive for three substances, including pseudo-ephedrine and extremely high levels of an anabolic steroid, Nandrolone. Vezina said he was taking the drugs to gain weight for the upcoming ice hockey season. On August 1, Canada was stripped of its gold medal, and for a time, RHI was stripped of its cloak of anonymity in the mainstream press.

When the news about Vezina hit, John Hopkins, the public relations director for the Buffalo Wings, was swamped with phone calls from the Canadian Broadcasting Company, the Winnipeg Sun, the Toronto Star, the Toronto Sun, the Globe and Mail, Hamilton Spectator, The Sports Network (Canada's version of ESPN), French-language papers in Montreal, the Buffalo News, the Canadian Press, The FAN 590 in Toronto, the Montreal Gazette, the Associated Press, local outlets and more. Buffalo coach Lou Franceschetti was interviewed on CBC television and in a radio interview with a Toronto sports station.

"We made the very front page of the Buffalo News, a franchise first," Hopkins said at the time. "If there was anyone in the Buffalo area that didn't know of the Buffalo Wings, I'm sure they do now."

The day before the news broke, Franceschetti told Hopkins that there was a rumor that Vezina had tested positive for a banned substance.

"He told me he would be surprised because Steve didn't have the physique that would indicate he was taking something to put on muscle or weight," Hopkins said. "He also pointed out there was no real competitive advantage a goalie would receive from taking an anabolic steroid or over-the-counter product. This was something Lou repeated many times in the following days, to newspapers, television and radio."

Hopkins blamed the Wings' tiny (1,862 capacity) non-air-conditioned Buffalo State Hockey Arena for Vezina's drug use, stating that Vezina, with his heavy, sweat-soaked goalie gear, was losing several pounds of weight per game in the heat.

"The arena was *hot*," Hopkins said. "We had industrial-size fans in all four corners of the arena to help circulate the air. I officiated in our amateur league, and knew how hot it was skating at a normal speed; I could only imagine what our pro athletes were dealing with."

At the time of the drama over Vezina, the Wings were suffering through an 8-13 season, and Franceschetti was about to resign from the team. Benny Gulakiw took over for Franceschetti as interim coach on August 6 for a game against Dallas – Vezina's first game back in goal since the Pan Am Games. Requests for media credentials began to pour in.

"Buffalo was still reeling from the Dallas Stars' Stanley Cup victory, especially since many believed that Brett Hull's Cup-winning goal should not have counted because he plainly – and illegally – had a foot in the crease," Hopkins said. "The Stallions' appearance would be the first by a Dallas team since Lord Stanley's Cup had been awarded, and we took advantage of this fact. We hyped it up in local ads. The return of Steve Vezina helped, too. A full house awaited as the teams took the floor."

At halftime, the Wings had a contest on the Sport Court.

"We selected a handful of father-son teams," Hopkins said. "Each team had their legs tethered for a three-legged race. Starting from one goal line, the son had to stickhandle a puck the length of the floor and shoot the puck in the empty net at the other end. The catch: The father had to put his free foot in the crease before his son could shoot. The crowd roared with laughter when the rules for this contest were explained."

Another wrinkle appeared when the Stallions refused to take the floor for the second half.

"RHI rules required the home teams to take care of visiting teams," Hopkins said. "There were two options for feeding the visitors: Provide a $25 per diem per player or arrange for them to be fed at the home team's cost."

The Wings had arranged for the Stallions to eat at a local establishment, but the Stallions were not happy with that arrangement. Many players in RHI would eat on the cheap in order to pocket the remaining cash, and the Dallas Stallions had no intention of taking to the floor without their $25.

"They knew we had a full house, and there was a lot of media in the building," Hopkins said. "We were essentially held hostage. We couldn't let them walk out. Intermission was usually 12-15 minutes long and we were up to 20 minutes already. Our CEO, Jason Klein, made an emergency trip to an ATM machine and took out the necessary money to pay the Dallas players. After about half an hour, just as the media began to ask questions about the hold-up, the teams returned to the floor."

Though it was a close game until halftime, the Wings turned it on in the second half and helped Vezina to a 7-3 win. The disgraced goalie made 35 saves and picked up an assist in front of 1,643 at the Buffalo State College Hockey Arena. Despite the turmoil surrounding his positive test and the unexpected leave of absence that Wings' coach Lou Franceschetti took soon afterward, Vezina helped the Wings take off. After all, he hadn't broken any RHI rules, because the league did not have a doping policy.

The next night, at the Kiel Center in St. Louis, Vezina won again, backstopping the Wings to an 8-7 overtime shootout win. After making 35 saves in regulation, Vezina made three more in the shootout, helping the Wings come all the way back from a 4-0 first-quarter deficit to victory.

Before the Pan Am Games, the Wings had lost seven of their previous eight games. After the hoopla surrounding Vezina's trials and tribulations, the Wings won their next two games under interim coach Benny Gulakiw and assured themselves a playoff spot.

CHAPTER 34

It Couldn't Have Been Better If We'd Scripted It

In 1993, when Chris McSorley stacked the Anaheim Bullfrogs with minor-league ice hockey players, most players who had grown up without extensive minor-league ice hockey experience were shut out of Roller Hockey International. But CJ and Jami Yoder were two of the few inline hockey players who got their chance and made the most of it. The sons of Charley Yoder, a roller hockey rink owner in Middletown, Pennsylvania, were rink rats since day one. The Yoder brothers' passion for the game was stronger than any obstacles placed in front of them.

"There's a picture of me on skates at two years old before I could even walk," Yoder said. "I could stand, but couldn't walk at that point, and they got me on skates. So, that's my big thing. I could skate before I could walk. My father has always owned a roller skating rink, and I absolutely loved it. I remember skating at my father's little rink at three o'clock in the afternoons, sweating like crazy and the puck's rolling toward the red line and I'm like, 'I'll make RHI this year if I can beat that puck to the red line' or something like that."

Yoder said he'd never forget when he finally did get picked up by the St. Louis Vipers in 1996 and played a game against the Philadelphia Bulldogs at the CoreStates Spectrum.

"I think they closed down Middletown, Pennsylvania, when I played that one game, and there were almost 50 people there to watch me play," Yoder said. "I'll never forget that opportunity. Walking into the locker room around all these guys – they seemed like big dudes to me, you know? And I'm like, 'I don't know whether I should be here.' Seeing number 82 up there [on the scoreboard], that's just something that brings a smile to my face every time."

Yoder enjoyed playing in RHI's major arenas.

"The Pond was awesome, the Shark Tank [San Jose Arena] was awesome," Yoder said. "I just remember taking it all in like that in every building that we went into. It was just something that I would never have gotten to do in ice hockey. Playing ice hockey, I'd be a minor-league ice hockey player all my life."

After Yoder played his first RHI game, the Vipers told him that they wanted to keep him, but their next game was at home in St. Louis. They'd put him back on the roster for the following game, in New Jersey.

"I saw that the game was on espn2 and I said, 'I'll pay for myself to get out there if I'm going to play!'" Yoder said. "I ended up flying out there myself just so that I could be on espn2."

The game was shown about a week later.

"I remember being in a bar in Harrisburg, Pennsylvania, one night," Yoder said. "It's a pretty big club, I'm some 21-year-old kid, and somebody stops me and says, 'Hey, you're on TV out there!' The place is packed, and I'm, 'Oh, my gosh, that's embarrassing.' But I get in my car that night, and I'm like, 'Oh, that's pretty cool.' Because of RHI, I was on TV."

"With the RHI, mostly, you'd recognize guys' names from ice hockey, from minor pro somewhere," said Christian Skoryna, a St. Louis Vipers' center and Yoder's teammate. "They'd have a history. Someone would know someone by 10 degrees of separation. Everyone knew each other somehow, just because of the affiliation with the minor pro leagues, but Jami and CJ were kind of unknown in that respect. I was pretty young myself, but I remember thinking, 'These guys are kids.'"

Ron Beilsten, a longtime quad skate roller hockey player and coach, was amazed at how open-minded Bernie Federko and Perry Turnbull (former NHL players) were about bringing roller hockey players to the St. Louis Vipers. Beilsten first heard about CJ Yoder at an amateur inline hockey tournament at the Odeum in Chicago. Beilsten's son JP told him about this hotshot player who was "the real deal." Ron Beilsten mentioned Yoder to Vipers' coach Turnbull and asked him to take a look at Yoder at practice. At the time, the Vipers were scheduled to play an away game in Philadelphia. The team arrived in town late and didn't have a chance to practice, so Turnbull put CJ Yoder into the lineup, sight unseen.

"To this day, Perry was like, 'Dude, this kid was dazzling guys,' and CJ was with us from that point on," Beilsten said. "But this was a roller kid. They were open. We brought many roller guys along. And the team never questioned it… They had an open mind that these are real players in their sport… One thing this sport was missing was its own stars, and I think we were so close."

"Ron brought them in and said, 'Listen, these guys are studs in their local rinks and they're great on their wheels and they understand the game of roller better than most,' and Perry was willing to take a chance on them," Skoryna said. "I watched them both mature over the few years I was there with them, and CJ probably weighed about 145 pounds when he first came to the team. I could tell right away, Ron was right on in the way that they understood the game of roller hockey very well.

"They grew into more of a defensive role," Skoryna added. "CJ never really played any power play or took an offensive position on our team. They were great penalty killers and they were huge being so successful that last year. As soon as we got a penalty, they were the first two on the rink. It's impressive to me that CJ blossomed into such an offensive weapon from the defensive role he was thrown into early. For a guy who wasn't used to the [physical intimidation] ice hockey side of it, that must have been terrifying. Hats off to him for showing the toughness to stick it out and stay with the game."

Yoder recalled being awed by playing for former NHL players like Bernie Federko and Perry Turnbull… and by Turnbull's intensity.

"I remember him screaming at Doug Lawrence because he gave somebody a whack, 'How tough do you think you are?' you know, from behind the bench," Yoder said. "I'm like, 'Oh, my gosh, he's yelling at the players like that?' Ronnie probably had to talk him into picking up this scrawny little roller hockey player. By the end, he'd talk to me all the time."

Turnbull got a kick out of it when Yoder changed his own wheels at halftime, Yoder said. "He'd be in the locker room, and when I change my wheels – I don't ask our trainer to do it – I've got a wheel here with spacers and bearings and the hardware there, and it's laid out for when I come back during the game. Perry just loved it. He'd laugh at me and give me shit, but I love that guy."

In 1997, CJ Yoder tied Vipers' leading scorer Mike Martens in plus/minus, with a plus 45, despite posting 23 fewer points than Martens. His brother Jami put up 30 points in 18 games.

One and Done

Since there were only eight teams in the league in 1999, the Chicago Bluesmen and Dallas Stallions did not qualify for the playoffs because they finished last in their respective divisions. And as St. Louis and Anaheim received first-round byes for finishing atop theirs, the first single-elimination playoff games were played between the second- and third-place teams. In the Eastern Conference quarterfinals, the second-place Buffalo Wings beat the third-place Minnesota Ox 8-3. The Wings' celebration was short, however. In the semifinals, the St. Louis Vipers ended Buffalo's controversy-marked season with an 11-7 win that was closer than the score indicated. Definitely not a goaltenders' duel, the teams traded goals before the Vipers pulled away at the end.

In the Western Conference quarterfinals, the San Jose Rhinos outlasted the Las Vegas Coyotes 6-5, but were knocked out of the playoffs in the semifinals when Anaheim easily handled them, 6-2, in Anaheim. That set up a finals matchup of the two teams with the best regular-season records.

The Bullfrogs were considered the clear favorite, based on their 21-win regular season (the Vipers won 17) and their suffocating defense. While St. Louis had scored 221 goals in the regular season compared to the Bullfrogs' 197, Anaheim had an obvious edge on the back line, holding opponents to just 127 goals in 26 games. The Vipers had given up 168 goals.

The tournament-style playoff games were all held at Anaheim's Arrowhead Pond, and the Bullfrogs' faithful fans could have probably been forgiven for taking the Vipers lightly based on a combination of their powerhouse team and home-court advantage. As it has been said many times before, however, the playoffs are a completely different season. Despite what the Bullfrogs and their fans thought, the Vipers were a confident team and never really accepted the second-best status that had been thrust on them.

"We were pretty big underdogs in the mind of everybody in the league,"

Skoryna said, recalling the conversations he overheard when the players hung out at Anaheim's National Sports Grill. "If I were to judge by talking to guys on other teams, everyone was thinking Anaheim would walk away with it. It was a large misconception, I think, that the west was a much stronger division than the east."

Many of the players considered the semifinal between Anaheim and San Jose to be the "real" final, and that the Vipers would be a formality for the Bullfrogs in the RHI championship game.

"We certainly didn't buy into or believe that," Skoryna said. "We all had a lot of faith in one another and had gone through a lot that year, as far as the ups and downs of our season. But if I were to judge by what everyone else was saying – we didn't really have much of a chance going into that game."

"That game" was held on August 22, 1999, in front of an announced crowd of 6,143. The Bullfrogs got off to a bad start when Bullfrog defenseman Chad Seibel was ejected for "intent to injure" after kneeing first-year St. Louis defenseman Ryan Aikia. In addition to having Seibel kicked out the game, the Vipers were awarded a penalty shot and a five-minute power play. Though Rob Laurie stopped Christian Skoryna on the penalty shot, the power play was another matter. The Vipers scored three goals to take an early 3-0 lead.

Many teams would have fallen apart or folded after such a disastrous sequence of events, but the Bullfrogs pulled together and responded with three straight goals. The Bullfrogs took their first lead of the game, 5-4, when Roman Hubalek scored his second goal of the game with 6:23 remaining in the third quarter. All seemed right with the Bullfrogs and their fans until Jami Yoder tied the game with just over a minute left in the third quarter. The home crowd's hearts sunk again when Ben Gorewich took advantage of a rare miscue by Bullfrog goalie Laurie and stole Laurie's weak pass before scoring on a wraparound. That made it 6-5 Vipers, but the Bullfrogs still had life and another comeback left in them. Sean Whyte popped in a rebound given up by Vipers' goalie James Jensen with 3:43 left in the game, and it was tied again, 6-6. Unfortunately for the Bullfrogs, Jami Yoder set up Mike Martens for a booming slap shot a minute later that got past Laurie, making it 7-6, and Martens put a final nail in the coffin with 1:12 remaining with an empty-net goal. The Vipers had defeated the Bullfrogs in their own barn 8-6 and thwarted Anaheim's hopes for a third RHI championship.

One of the biggest smiles was on the face of Vipers' goaltender James Jensen, who'd been Rob Laurie's backup in Anaheim the previous year in Major League Roller Hockey. Jensen held the Ralph Backstrom Cup high over his head as he was surrounded by his happy teammates.

Christian Skoryna said that the championship probably meant as much to Jensen as any Viper.

"It was kind of retribution for him, given the fact that he had been a backup to Robbie the entire time he was on the West Coast," Skoryna said. "I think that Robbie served as sort of a mentor for him, a guy he looked up to and learned a lot from when he played behind him. For him to be able to step out from behind his shadow and for us to come together and win that was a huge thing for him. As it was for all the guys. I mean, it couldn't have been a better finish if we could have scripted it."

"One thing that comes to my mind about that series was how big a deal it was to our goalie James Jensen," said Viper's assistant coach Ron Beilsten. "Jenner was part of that team at one time, from that area, and we picked him up in the off-season. I remember saying to someone, 'This is his Stanley Cup.' I mean, it really was. It's a championship at any level. And sure enough, he had a rooting section. There was a big crowd that night, and he was up for it."

After Michael Martens of St. Louis was named the playoff MVP, the Vipers got off the floor and rolled into their small locker room on the opposite side of the Pond from the Bullfrogs' glitzier digs. One might have expected the Vipers to be jumping with joy. That's not how Christian Skoryna remembered it.

"It wasn't a mood of going crazy with jubilation," said Skoryna. "Everyone was reflecting in their own mind the way the season went – the pride of it all coming together in the end, overcoming the doubters, and the underdog role that we had assumed, but that we didn't necessarily embrace. For the first few moments after we won, I think it was just a feeling of reflection and taking it all in and quietly saying, 'We did it, boys.' Guys weren't going nuts screaming. It was more of a quiet reflection and a quiet satisfaction of taking in the win."

Jamie Kompon, a St. Louis Viper who would go on to become an assistant coach for the NHL's Los Angeles Kings eight years later, didn't play in the final game against Anaheim, but he remembered being in the locker room before the game started.

"I remember a few players saying, 'Hey, there's no pressure on us. Let's just go and play our game,' " Kompon said. "I think that was the biggest thing. Just believe in your teammates, believe in each other. Look across the room. We're all going to be there, and when it's all said and done, we're all playing for one goal: to raise that cup when it's all over."

Kompon shared in the Vipers' celebration.

"There are certain things in life you just can't describe," Kompon said. "I've been through a few of those, and it's just total elation. It's that coming together and sharing that special moment."

The Call

Naturally, much of the post-game discussion centered on the controversial penalty call that referee Jean-Claude Caisse made on Chad Seibel.

"We scored three goals on it, and that was pretty much the tone of the game," Vipers' assistant coach Ron Beilsten said. "We exchanged goals back and forth the rest of the way. That was just a huge start."

Bullfrogs' goalie Rob Laurie defended his teammate.

"You can't say that Chad Seibel cost us a championship, because we still had chances to win that game, and everybody could have done something better," Laurie said. "I did a lot of things in my career that didn't help us win, or whatever, and it's just something that happens. I mean, Vic Gervais took a penalty another time when we were playing San Jose that didn't really help us, either. It's just one of those things that happen. All those things have to come together, you know?"

"After the first half, we were in the locker room, and the owner of the Bullfrogs [Pacific Sports Hockey Group's Rob Montag] came to give me a bunch of bullshit," Caisse said. "He was very upset, but the commissioner of the league, Ralph Backstrom, said, 'You had no choice but to call that kind of penalty.' He backed me up."

Caisse and his linesmen had agreed to referee the game, despite being owed a substantial amount of money by the league, and demanded that they be paid in cash before the game started. That didn't happen, so Caisse stunned his colleagues by washing the game off his back at halftime – literally.

"I was in the shower between the first and second half when there were all these people in the stands, and I was all packed up and ready to go home because they couldn't keep their word. The linesmen were looking at me like I was crazy."

Caisse and his linesmen were paid and the game continued. Had Caisse made his stand before the game, perhaps the league could have found replacement officials. Had he waited until after the game, he and his linesmen might never have been paid. Whether one agreed with Caisse's call on Seibel or not, he deserved credit for a brilliant negotiating ploy.

Full Circle

It also seemed appropriate, in hindsight, that the game was held at the Arrowhead Pond, the site of the Bullfrogs incredibly successful opening-night game in 1993, which helped RHI gain valuable exposure and credibility right out of the gate. It also seemed fitting that the Bullfrogs and Vipers had met in the championship game, as they were the only teams to play every year Roller Hockey International existed.

"That made the championship even more special," Ron Beilsten said. "Dale Turvey was our premier owner, and I asked myself, 'What is this guy doing in this crazy league, spending a lot of money?' What made me appreciate winning anything was probably him at one point. He was so committed to winning – at any level – a championship. He didn't need a championship to validate himself; he was a very successful businessman. But when it got down to that game, he was like, 'I would give anything to win this thing.' It was *so* important for him to win."

Turvey attended the game along with some of the team's other investors. "We were so excited," Turvey said. "We couldn't have been happier if it was actually a Stanley Cup. We put a lot of time and energy and money into it, and guys like Bernie and Perry and [Ron] Beilsten were all dedicated. It was really exciting and a lot of fun. It kind of made the whole trip worthwhile, because, frankly, in that year, in 1999, after we sat out in '98, our attendance had dropped down, you could kind see, 'Well, hey, maybe this isn't going to continue,' so it was a great way to finish up."

Along with Ron Beilsten and Bernie Federko, Vipers' coach Perry Turnbull had also been in the league with the Vipers from the very start. Turnbull said that the championship win was the highlight of his RHI career.

"I would have loved to have done it as a player, but I can get some satisfaction at least out of coaching them," Turnbull said. "That was a wonderful thing."

CJ Yoder was the roller-hockey rink rat that the Vipers had taken a chance on and given a lot of playing time to, relying on him and his brother to shut down the Vipers' opponents' biggest guns.

"Not being an ice hockey guy was a big deal," Yoder said, "and a big deal for the sport, too – that there's a roller hockey guy playing in RHI."

Yoder remembered skating around with the Ralph Backstrom Cup on the rink, and then backing off and just soaking in the surroundings that night.

"I was still young then, and I remember being overwhelmed," Yoder said. "I couldn't have gotten any luckier than being where I was, and just wanting to do the best that I could. That last game was one of the neatest experiences of my life. Winning the championship was huge. I remember celebrating a little bit and then taking time by myself and just looking around and like, 'Look where I am right now, and what I've gotten to do.' I never would have had that opportunity to go play in the Pond and all the rinks that I got to play in. RHI was just phenomenal. I remember looking around, just trying to take it in, not knowing if it would ever happen again."

CHAPTER 35

RHI Personalities

Although many people argued that one of the reasons Roller Hockey International didn't succeed was because it didn't have "stars" that the general public could latch on to and bring the league mass media attention, it definitely had its share of fascinating characters. Whether it was Bob McKillop outperforming the Anaheim Bullfrogs' cheerleaders, TV sitcom star Tony Danza singing the national anthem before a Philadelphia Bulldogs' game, or the St. Louis Vipers' goalie who was arrested and carted off to jail, RHI's players, owners, referees and even fans created some memorable and often hilarious stories that should not be lost to the sands of time. Here are a few of them.

Fast Friends

Mike King, who played for Team Canada on RHI's inaugural tour in 1992 and ended up buying the Vancouver VooDoo, remembered when he first met Dennis Murphy – and being a little surprised at Murphy's lack of height and excess of girth.

"I walked into the Pacific Coliseum here in Vancouver – and you know what Dennis looks like - Dennis didn't look like your average sports marketer," King said. "I looked at him and I said, 'Man, I'm not sure that this is the right place for me.' They couldn't find any pucks, so Dennis came over to me and asked me if I had a car. I said, 'Yes, I have a car,' and he says, 'Come on, you've got to drive me to a sports shop, we need to pick up some tape,' because there wasn't anything to use as a puck for the tryouts. Literally, out of his pocket, he was buying all the pucks and rolls of tape he could at a local sports store. It was almost like it was destiny, because from that point on, Dennis and I became close friends."

Right-Hand Man

John Kanel, a kindly person who wore glasses and spoke softly – most of the time – eventually became Dennis Murphy's right-hand man in many of his sports ventures. In the 1980s, Kanel was the mayor of Cypress when Murphy was the mayor of Buena Park. When Murphy tried to annex the Los Alamitos Race Course, a major source of tax income, for his city, Kanel's quiet manner changed.

"He found out about it and put a stop to it, Murphy said. "He called me everything but the kitchen sink. He said, 'I'm going to fix you guys,' which he did. It would have meant money to us and I tried to sneak it by him, but he didn't let me do it. He said, 'If you come through Cypress, I'll have the police pick you up."

Kanel ended up worked with Murphy in sports for many years.

"He'd take the blame for things that I should have taken the blame for," Murphy said. "We used to pay the players in RHI and they'd line up at the bank. He was the guy who was always putting money in the bank, so everybody was nice to him because he was their bread and butter."

Fit to Be Tied

ESPN play-by-play announcer Craig Minervini was a dedicated follower of RHI fashion, purchasing a tie made by fashion designer Nicole Miller.

"She was pretty well known in the fashion industry," Minervini said. "Well, unbelievably, she made a tie with all the RHI logos on it and I have it. Of all the weird things, Nicole Miller makes an RHI tie. She was kind of hip in the '90s there with the products she made. Occasionally I wore it to work when I did a broadcast."

He Could Relate

Jeanie Buss remembered a playoff game between the Los Angeles Blades and the Anaheim Bullfrogs at the Arrowhead Pond that she attended with her father, Dr. Jerry Buss.

"There was one person who had a sign that said, 'Jeanie Buss is a bimbo,'" Buss recalled. "I said, 'Dad, can you believe that? Look at that sign,' and he said, 'Well, you know, they have a point.' My dad could always make me laugh. Any time there was criticism in the media, I could go to my dad and he always knew the right things to say. He had to go through it, running the Lakers and the Kings, and all the criticism he got in the media from the fans, so to have his kids go through it, made us closer as a family, because we could relate to the same experience."

Wild Bill's Entrance

Anno Willison said that "Wild Bill" Hunter was one of the greatest hockey promoters ever, as well as one of Dennis Murphy's very best friends. Willison recalled a league meeting in 1994 when Hunter, then working for the league's Edmonton Sled Dogs, was a guest speaker.

"We had a hockey meeting at the Crown Plaza," Willison said. "When Bill went to make his entrance on the stage, he slipped, fell down, threw his briefcase and all of his papers all around and got up and very casually dusted himself off and went to the mic and said, 'Wasn't that a great entrance?' He did it on purpose."

Kid Reporter

HockeyTalk magazine came up with very creative idea, a column by "Kid Reporter" Grant Hatfield. For the magazine's October 1, 1996, issue, the youngster interviewed Anaheim Bullfrogs' coach Grant Sonier. It was a day when the Bullfrogs were to travel by bus to the Great Western Forum to play the Los Angeles Blades. The perceptive adolescent took note of Sonier's Corvette convertible and proved to be an astute interviewer, able to draw quotes out of the most hardened inline hockey warriors: "On the bus to the Forum to play the Blades," Hatfield wrote, "the players have a choice of sleeping or watching a movie. I asked the players what they like to watch. They answered, 'Bambi' and 'The Lion King.' (Yeah, right!) The game that night was fast, furious and intense. There were fights, arguments and colorful language that the players didn't learn from watching Bambi!"

Free Shower

In 1994 the Bullfrogs were scheduled to play an away game against the Calgary Rad'z. Bullfrogs' radio play-by-play man Lew Stowers went out for a walk that afternoon on a hot and dry summer day, and noticed a big wet spot on the sidewalk in front of the Bullfrogs' hotel.

"All of a sudden I hear some noises or laughing going on, and I look up, and there's Savo and McKillop and Cookie and some other guys – just in time for a trash can full of water to hit me in the face from 10 floors up," Stowers said. "They were just laughing and screaming and hooting and hollering and having a good time, and I'm head-to-toe drenched like I jumped into a swimming pool. I had to walk through the lobby, with all the people looking at me; squish, squish, squish."

Blind Man's Bluff

During a 1994 home game with the Los Angeles Blades, Steve Chelios, Chris's younger brother, tilted his helmet down over his eyes, turned his hockey stick upside down for use as a cane, and walked around the rink pretending to be blind. The organist started playing "Three Blind Mice." I'm not sure if the organist received a penalty, but Chelios certainly did.

Phantom Phone Call

Fred Hetzel, a fan of the Pittsburgh Phantoms in 1994, wrote a letter to someone in the Phantoms' organization during their season, telling them how much he was enjoying the team's games and accompanying hoopla. The next game, a cheerleader came up to him with a cell phone and said that he'd won a free long distance call to anyone he wanted. He called his sister in Atlanta.

St. Louis Sellout

Dale Turvey, an owner of the St. Louis Vipers, received the shock of his life in 1994 when the Vipers were preparing to play their final game of the season. The team was fighting for attendance, averaging about 3,000 fans a game, and

Turvey thought his leg was being pulled when a staffer came in to his office and said that the parking lot was full. It turned out that Camel X, a popular local radio station, had announced that it was the last game that would ever be played at the Checkerdome, as the team was moving to the Kiel Center in 1995. With Major League Baseball out on strike, people flocked to the arena.

"I go out in the parking lot and the parking lot is packed and people are lined up," Turvey said "Because we didn't have enough ticket takers, we just let all those people in – there's like 12,000 people – and we didn't make a penny off it. We didn't care; we were just thrilled it was full. I called up Bernie, who was the coach, and I said, 'Bernie, you can't start the game.'

He said, 'What can I do?' I said, 'The parking lot is full; we've got to get these people into the game. Pretend like you're having a heart attack or something.' Somehow he delayed the game; I don't know how he did it."

Killer Dance Moves

Chipper Righter, who became a jack-of-all-trades for the Anaheim Bullfrogs, remembered a time when Bob "Killer" McKillop was injured.

"Killer hurt his knee, we were traveling by Southwest Airlines, and we were pushing him in a wheelchair. We finally got him to where he could stand up, and the flight attendant said, 'Are you OK?' He said, 'I'm fine.' She said, 'Yes, you *are*.' "

McKillop was a huge Michael Jackson fan during RHI's heyday.

"Yeah, I was one of those guys," McKillop said. "You gotta understand; I could care less about what anybody thought about that. I was who I was and I had a lot of fun doing it [dancing and singing to Jackson's hits]."

"Bobby McKillop could sing," said teammate Christian Lalonde. "He'd do all the moves. He was really, really slick. He would do the whole routine. He had a great voice."

"I walked in one day and I saw the image of the TV on and I said, 'Bleep. I left the TV on last night,' recalled Anaheim coach Grant Sonier. "I'd been watching video the night before, and I walked in and I saw Killer watching a Michael Jackson concert that he had taped – two inches away from the TV. He loved Michael Jackson. Doesn't make him a bad guy; you'd just never think a hockey player would love Michael Jackson. The moral of that whole story is that I never ever thought any less of Bobby McKillop as a hockey player because of that. I think that's why we had a great rapport. He knew I knew what he was capable of – players like Bob McKillop who played major junior hockey – all had that dream of playing in the NHL. RHI *was* the NHL for some of these guys. It was the coolest thing, really. It was five years of unbelievable ups and downs and great relationships."

"Killer can dance like I've never seen," recalled Chipper Righter. "The Polliwogs had auditions, and we wanted to have the right girls and the right look, so we would have practice and auditions and the boys were working out in the gym and they'd come check out to see – and Killer came out there. And people are a little bit shy when they first try out, because you're not used to being in front of people, you're holding back a little bit, and Killer would say, 'Girls, come on! Give it some energy!' They said, 'If you can do any better, come on out.' They put on a song and he went out there and danced, and he blew them away. Leg pops and arm locks, and he had on a little hat like a taxi driver. Whatever he was watching on those videos, he wasn't just watching; he was educating himself."

On the Air

"Victor was hysterical," Righter said, discussing Anaheim forward Victor Gervais. "I think we're in San Jose, and he had been thrown out of the game prior, so he couldn't play, so he was drinking all day. Come game time, he was just sauced. So Lew Stowers, who did such a great job for us, asks him to come up and do color commentary. So he gets up there, and Lew's very professional: 'Well, Victor, that first period was pretty exciting. What did you think about the way so and so were playing.' 'Holy bleeping A, did we!' Lew turned off the mic, 'Victor, we're live. You can't cuss.' He was so sauced, he didn't know. They just had to get him completely out of there."

Practical Joker

"I had just started Burly Hockey and we were doing the jerseys for Orlando and Anaheim, and it was literally two nights before opening night, because we were doing the sublimation for the Jackals," said Jason Lauderdale. "Orlando's goalie Billy Horn and Robbie Laurie had played together on the Bullfrogs the year before. Robbie came into our work at midnight and helped us put the numbers on. We had a heat press and I had a couple of guys doing the stitching, and Robbie goes, 'Hey, let me do these,' and he starts going. Well, I get a call after Fed Ex landed in Orlando the next day. I think they were playing their home opener that night, and Robbie had put Bill Horn's name on backwards and screwed up his number. Horn said, 'What the heck were you guys thinking?' and I said, 'Robbie Laurie did your jersey.'"

Snack Time!

"Robbie Laurie was on the bench one day, not playing," said Chipper Righter. "I was always on the right gate, and I kept turning around and seeing him with his lips tight, laughing. I couldn't figure out what was so funny. So I decided I'd close the gate, but I'd watch to see what he did the next time – he was eating a hot dog on the bench. He was turning his head, taking a bite, and then turning back around."

"Chipper loved that one," Laurie said later. "I would give one of the kids that were helping a buck, because I wasn't playing, and say, 'Go get me a dog. Get me something because I'm hungry.' On game day, you eat about 12:30 p.m., 1 o'clock, and all of a sudden it's 7 o'clock, 8 o'clock, and you haven't had any dinner. Chipper is sitting next to me working the door while I'm sitting on the bench. He's to my right and I'm ducking my head down to my left, and he doesn't really see anything, and it goes on for a while, and finally, he's like, 'Hey Robbie, what are you doing?' And I'm like, 'What am I doing what?' and I can barely talk. And he says, 'Why do you keep ducking your head down? What have you got in there?' And he looks, and there's only a quarter of a hot dog left in my catch glove. He just started cracking up and I started laughing, too."

Hockey Highlight

"I was roommates with Randy Smith for the St. Louis training camp [in 1994]," said Lance Brady. "We drove to some backwoods town that just so happened to have the electricity go out that night. We saw two monster trucks with their top lights on, driven up right in front. All I could think of was 'Deliverance.' We walk in seeing mostly the locals, and then in the back, on one of the stools, was Brett Hull. Hanging with Brett Hull that night was definitely one of the highlights of my first pro year, and definitely the highlight of my St. Louis Vipers experience."

You Call *that* Intimidation?

Before playing in RHI in 1993, Jimmy Vivona played quad-skate roller hockey in a league in Fort Hamilton in Brooklyn, New York, that boasted future National Hockey League Hall of Famer Joe Mullen and his brother Brian.

"It was five-on-five, small rink, all excellent players, but a lot of these guys were criminals," Vivona said. "They were treacherous, treacherous people. They'd put a stick in my face and threaten to blind me during the course of the game, and I gotta tell you, I absolutely believed 'em. When it came to the toughest league, no question, it was in New York. That's why in RHI, when you're playing against these Canadian kids or these East Coast League guys, when they were trying to intimidate ya, I used to laugh because, my god, this is like a massage compared to what we used to get in Fort Hamilton. RHI was a pleasure to play in. You wanna fight and just drop the gloves? No problem. I don't have to worry about being shot after the game? It got so bad that Fort Hamilton was actually featured in Sports Illustrated years and years ago. They actually had to land a frickin' helicopter on the rink during one of the brawls in Brooklyn – a police helicopter landed on the rink. Just imagine that; that's how bad it used to get."

Up Close and Personal

"We had Charlie Simmer [a former star for the Los Angeles Kings] doing the radio commentary for the Bullfrogs," remembered Anaheim goalie Rob Laurie. "Charlie Simmer! Are you kidding me? He'd go on trips with us and he's talking about roller hockey. This is Charlie Simmer. We should be talking about *you*."

All Fright Airlines

Larry King was a pilot, and Jeanie Buss once had to fly to Denver with King for a meeting with RHI Commissioner Ralph Backstrom.

"He landed the plane in Hawthorne and picked me up," Buss said. "I've been on a private plane, but not that kind of private plane where I was literally the co-pilot. I had to do all the switches. It was only two hours to two-and-a-half hours, but in little planes, you've got to stop and refuel, so it means another landing, another takeoff. That trip put me over the edge. I can't even remember the meeting because the flight was the scariest thing I've ever been on."

Airport Follies

"Going to airports was always fun," said San Jose netminder Joe Bonvie. "One of the favorite things was to take a five-dollar bill, take some dental floss, and put it through the middle, and when you're at your gate, you put it in the middle of the aisle and you watch people come in and lean for it... then you gotta yank it away from 'em to see the reaction. At some point, the whole gate is in on it. Everybody's kind of snickering, waiting for the next person to do it, and then a whole lot more people than the team... the whole group of people waiting to get on the plane are starting to laugh. You know, some people get mad, some people laugh it off, so it's kind of funny."

Team Bonding

"For some reason, the difference between ice hockey teams and roller hockey teams at the time – the tight-knit part of that – you didn't get that in ice hockey like you got in roller hockey," said Steve Bogoyevac of the Los Angeles Blades. "I don't know if it was just the chemistry we had, or if it was the game itself, but it happened. We'd spend every day, the whole day, together. My best friendships were created during roller hockey. The guys I remember and the guys I hang out with now are guys I played roller hockey with, and not necessarily ice hockey. Personally, [there was] absolutely not one negative. Not one drawback. It was a great time in my life."

Who's the Boss?

TV sitcom star Tony Danza, a co-owner of RHI's Philadelphia Bulldogs, sang the national anthem as part of the pregame ceremonies at the team's CoreStates Spectrum home opener in June. According to Roller Hockey magazine's August/September 1996 issue, "He hit every note without fail after introducing the anthem with, 'Hey, if I mess this up, you can't do anything about it because I own the team.'

Tasty Trade

"Ron Beilsten was the assistant coach for the St. Louis Vipers when he noticed that Jeff Blum of the Detroit Motor City Mustangs wasn't getting much playing time during the 1995 season. He suggested to Vipers co-owner and coach Bernie Federko that the Vipers make a trade for Blum and got the green light. Beilsten called Detroit's GM and suggested a trade.

The GM said, "We don't need anybody, you got any money?"

Beilsten said, "No, we don't have money. You're not getting any money. You're not playing him. We need him. Let's make a deal."

The Detroit GM said, "Here's the deal. You stay at the host hotel and you buy two pre-game meals on your next road trip."

"Sure enough, the deal went through, they sent him down, he comes on a plane and I pick him up," Beilsten said. "There was a big joke for a long time: 'You were traded for two pre-game meals.' That's one of the best deals in hockey, because he played his heart out for us and was a huge player in some of our good years."

Leave Your Motor Running

"At the end of the season, lo and behold, one of the cars we rented to our players wasn't turned in," said Joe Noris, the general manager of the San Diego Barracudas in 1995 and 1996. "We tracked it down to which player had it last and found out it was one of the guys from Quebec. I'm not going to name names because he's still in Southern California… and we couldn't find the car. I finally got in touch with him in Quebec and said, 'Where's the car? He said, 'Well, I was really running late and it was really hard on me, so I just left it in front of the airport.' I said, 'In front of the airport? Not in the parking lot?' He said, 'No, I didn't have time for the parking lot. I left it in front of the airport.' "

Scoring Machine

"In the first game of the RHI 1994 championship series in Portland, Oregon, on August 31, 1994, John Vecchiarelli scored seven goals and added three assists, setting a league record for points in a playoff game, as the Stampede defeated the Rage, 11-8. Leaving the team hotel before the game with teammate Mark Major, Vecchiarelli felt tired, so he talked Major into going to a café.

"We drank about five or six espresso coffees, and we then went out and played that game and it was phenomenal," Vecchiarelli said. "They called me Espresso Vecchiarelli after that. I don't know if anyone ever beat the record of 10 points in a playoff game. Coming back to Buffalo for the championship game and winning and being the MVP was great. It was a highlight of my life."

A Foggy Notion

"The funniest thing that I wish I had on videotape, was – I guess it would have been year two [1994] – we were playing Vancouver and they probably had 10,000 or 12,000 people at the home opener," said Jon Gustafson, star goaltender for the San Jose Rhinos. "We were all on the bench waiting for the VooDoo to come out, and they decided that they were going to use this oil-based fog. They had this big banner of the VooDoo and the guys were going to skate through it and onto the floor. Well, the fog came out and settled onto the floor and it was like grease. The cheerleaders came out first and they all just, I mean – yard sale! There were six or seven girls on each other, short skirts, some of them crying because they were hurt. The players don't know that yet – this is a televised game; nobody tells them – so these guys come flying through this big paper VooDoo thing onto the floor and they run into all these girls. They've all got this stuff on their wheels and they couldn't stand up. It was 10,000 people absolutely dying laughing, and this is on TV, so they had a 30-minute break and they had to figure out how they were going to get this stuff off the floor. We're sitting on the bench. I felt bad for the players, but it was one of the funniest things that I've ever seen."

Bring on the Dancing Girls!

"Everybody still can't believe that we had the Laker Girls at all our home games," remembered L.A. Blades' backup goaltender Brad Sholl. "That was pretty amazing. We'd sit on the bench and see these girls out there and they're wearing your jersey. The guys would always look forward to halftime [when they did their dance routines] and no one really wanted to go into the locker room."

Popular Frogs

After the 1993 season, the National Hockey League's Mighty Ducks of Anaheim began playing in the Arrowhead Pond with the Bullfrogs. Bullfrogs' coach Grant Sonier remembered a Ducks' game when Bullfrogs' stars Bob

McKillop and Savo Mitrovic were in the building.

"Their faces came up on the Jumbotron," Sonier said, "and the audience started chanting Savo's name, 'Savo! Savo!' It was during an NHL game! That's how popular these guys became. We went to restaurants where people knew who I was. We had a cable show [The Bullfrogs Report] that won a cable award. People really grabbed onto this."

Rob Laurie remembered going to the Red Onion, a local bar that sponsored the Bullfrogs [and later became the National Sports Grill]. Laurie noticed some of the Mighty Ducks' players who'd recently come into town at the bar.

"We'd already been out here for the majority of the summer, and those guys rolled into town and didn't know anything about anything, you know?" Laurie said. "They were in town to get ready for training camp. The guy at the bar would like, 'Hey everybody, we've got a bunch of the Bullfrogs here!' And people would go, 'Yeah!' And then he'd go, 'Yeah, we've got some of the Mighty Ducks, too.' And everyone would go, 'The who? The what?' "

The Ramada Inn was Hopping

One of the first deals that Chris Palmer made as the assistant GM for the Bullfrogs was to arrange a trade out with a local hotel.

"The players stayed at the Ramada Inn," Palmer said. "I traded out rooms for the guys in exchange for dasher boards and tickets and all that kind of stuff. We just partied back in the rooms till 1, 2, 3 o'clock in the morning. The ownership of the Ramada was actually very tolerant of all of that. They never got so much business at that CC's [the hotel bar] until the Bullfrogs came to town. That place rocked afterwards. That place was like a frat house. Let's just say that those guys had no problem getting the ladies."

According to Christian Lalonde, he, Bob McKillop and Steve Beadle would get the key from under a teammate's doormat and rearrange the entire hotel room. 'We'd switch all the furniture in the living room with the furniture from the bedroom, and when they returned, they thought they had walked into the wrong hotel room. They'd come back and we'd be laughing our asses off," Lalonde said.

"At the Ramada, the TV remotes all operated with the same code," Lalonde remembered. "Barry Potomski would be in bed watching TV, and we'd sneak up on the outside balcony and change his channel through the window. He'd go, 'What's going on?' and he'd change it back and go back and sit down… and we'd change the channel again."

Mike Butters recalled how he and Victor Gervais "did some stupid, stupid things" that summer. "We gutted our hotel room, put all this furniture poolside, and we had a bet to see who could stay out there the longest and we were sleeping out there," Butters said.

"We had a little parrot that you put batteries in, and when you'd say something, it records it and repeats it, but in a parrot's voice," recalled Bullfrogs' VIP Chipper Righter. "Savo was a guy that loved to sleep in, I mean, till noon or 1 o'clock, all his drapes drawn, dark. So we would say 'Savo, get up,' and the parrot would yell, 'Savo, get up. Savo, get up.' It would repeat it twice. And Savo would say 'F---ing go away!' and the bird would go, 'F---king go away, f---ing go away!' "

In the Line of Fire

Rex Fontenot, the PR director for the Los Angeles Blades, had the opportunity to stand in for Jim Fox as the Blades' assistant coach at a game in San Jose that Fox was unable to attend in 1997.

"It was one of those beautiful things that can happen in minor-league sports," Fontenot said. "I remember the team skating out in San Jose Arena and the fans are screaming at me, 'Beat L.A.' They were throwing popcorn at me, and I'm like, 'Yeah, this is great. I'm loving it.' "

Hockey Trader

Dan Delaney was a director of player personnel three RHI teams, the Portland Rage (1994), the Ottawa Loggers (1995) and the Empire State Cobras (1996).

"One of the funniest things was when professional ice hockey players tried to make the transition to the wheels for the first time," Delaney recalled.

"Falling, going into the boards, slipping and sliding wasn't uncommon. I remember Portland Rage Russian forward Vadim Slivchenko saying to me, "Dan, I love hockey, but what the hell have you gotten me into?" Philadelphia Bulldogs' GM Al MacIssac once gave Delaney the highest compliment: "Dan Delaney is the type of guy that would trade his own grandmother and a bag of pucks if he knew he could get a good deal on a player."

Goalie in a Cage

In 1997, the St. Louis Vipers had a game in Orlando against the Jackals that conflicted with Vipers' goaltender Alain Roy's wedding to the daughter of Vipers' team owner Dale Turvey.

That's when it was determined that Viper's coach Perry Turnbull would attend the wedding and assistant coach Ron Beilsten was charged to take the team to Orlando. That weekend, one of the team's goaltenders had too much alcohol and got out of control – to the point of being arrested and hauled off to jail.

"So we let him sit overnight, and the next day, he's calling me like crazy," Beilsten said. "He told me, 'Go in my room, use my credit card, go get money, get me out of here.' So I got his credit card and got cash like crazy – and I had to take a taxicab, because nobody's got a car – to get a guy out of jail. I spent half my trip at the Orlando jail getting my goalie out."

Unfortunately, the Viper's other backstop, Mark Cavallin, had a pulled groin.

"We got just beaten down by these guys [Orlando], because Cavallin can only make leg saves on one side," Beilsten said. "All the players are like, 'Are you going to put him [the recently sprung-from-jail goalie] in?' And I said, 'No, I ain't putting him in.' The one and only time that I'm the head coach, right? Perry said, 'I let you take the team one time and look what happens.' "

CHAPTER 36

Aftermath

Roller Hockey International began its inaugural season on July 1, 1993, and by the end of its fourth year, 1996, more than 3.8 million fans had attended RHI games, an average attendance of 4,259 fans per game. From 1994-1996, the league's fans across the country watched RHI games on the sports cable channels ESPN and espn2, including a "Monday Night RHI Game of the Week" and broadcasts of the All-Star, playoff and championship games. But while the sport continued to grow, RHI's inability to keep a stable roster of teams harmed its credibility. There were 36 teams in the league's first four years alone.

"I made a lot of mistakes," said RHI co-founder Dennis Murphy. "I had some owners that should not have been owners. You don't know what to expect, so you grab whatever you can get a hold of. Most of the owners figured it would take five years before turning the financial corner, but the ones that hoped to make a quick buck were hugely disappointed as their losses mounted."

Murphy was 66 years old when RHI had its inaugural tour in 1992.

"One reason for the failure of RHI, in my case, was getting older," Murphy said. "You don't take care of the details like you should. There was also a lot of politics. Larry King is a good lawyer, but he's not a good organizer. People started going off in their own directions, and the league fell apart. You need someone to take charge. Some guys have to give up the ship. They can't run it, so give them a franchise. Just don't let them run the league."

It didn't help that key founders didn't get along and were unable to work together. Alex Bellehumeur and Larry King nearly came to fisticuffs, and everyone in the league offices seemed to have a different idea of how RHI should proceed.

"The reason RHI failed was that too many of the individuals comprising of the league had self-interest which prevented everyone from working as a cohesive unit and team," said David McLane. "Without everyone pulling in the same direction, the ship was bound to break apart.... and it did."

"The people involved in the inline game, basically brought the game down themselves," said all-star forward Gerry St. Cyr, who played in five of RHI's six seasons. "It was a great game. You can't tell me that when the RHI was in its prime that people wouldn't rather watch an RHI game on TV than darts or pro bowling. I turn the TV on and see darts on and pro bowling guys run out through the smoke and I just shake my head at how bowling can be on TV and not professional roller hockey. There's got to be a reason for it, and my opinion is that there were too many people at the top driving the ship in different directions."

Another reason for RHI's downfall was its biggest drawing card – the large and expensive stadiums that many of its teams played in. Having arenas like the Arrowhead Pond of Anaheim, Montreal's fabled Forum and the Kiel Center in St. Louis added glamour and credibility to the league, and attracted fans and the media. But the rents for teams that didn't own their buildings (the Los Angeles Blades in the Great Western Forum were one of the few that did) were exorbitant for a fledgling league. Even when teams successfully drew 5,000 to 7,000 fans for a game, the cavernous NHL barns made the crowd appear much smaller. When even fewer fans attended a game, as often occurred, it felt more like being in a vast lecture hall than a sporting event, no matter how exciting the action on the court.

"Those buildings they played in put them out of business," Paul Chapey said. "They were both the best thing they had going for them and the worst thing they had going for them."

Chapey argued that RHI needed smaller venues in which the team owners had control over concessions and parking. "If they had those kinds of buildings to play in, then they would still have a pro league," Chapey said.

Rapid expansion from 1993 to 1994 also contributed to Roller Hockey International's demise.

"The people who were in charge of running the league needed to drive revenues, and at that point in time, the easiest way to get revenue was to find franchises," said San Jose Rhinos' GM Jon Gustafson. "You are only as strong as your weakest link. Not to say that the people who were owners had the wrong intentions – they all had the right intentions – but you need to have some staying power, and you need to get over a couple of hurdles to make sure that the entity is strong. We had too many weaker sisters and too many people in the league office who didn't do their due diligence well enough."

For one bright shining moment, however, RHI had a potential connection with the National Hockey League – perhaps professional roller hockey teams could be playing in NHL arenas in the summertime today.

"The NHL was definitely kicking the tires," Gustafson said, "and I think that they totally missed out on that. For instance, the best part of the game right now in the National Hockey League is overtime. What is it? It's four on four. You're really seeing the fruits of RHI right now in California. All of a sudden, you have all of these young kids that are signing NHL contracts. They're being drafted. They're getting Division 1 scholarships. That is as much a part of Roller Hockey International as it is the NHL, because all those kids started playing roller hockey. And then it's just an easy progression to ice hockey. In Southern California, we've seen a very large percentage of very high-quality kids. One of the main reasons is that there is another avenue, and the other avenue is roller hockey."

Buffalo Wings' co-owner Jason Klein felt that RHI failed to properly market its stars, develop local talent through amateur leagues, or spend enough money on promoting the league in the media.

"There was a lack of professionalism in the league's administration," Klein said. "Marketing was suspect; there was no RHI business plan pre-1997. You have to spend marketing dollars on media. That's a cost of doing business. RHI did a really bad job of that."

Klein suggested that RHI may have been more successful had it emerged later, when YouTube, MySpace, Facebook and other social networking media came into existence, adding that RHI simply could not continue to exist once it lost its national television contract. "You cannot succeed at a pro level without television," Klein said.

Los Angeles Blades' owner Jeanie Buss said what the league needed most was more time, and that the kids who were eight, nine and 10 years old when RHI started would eventually become ticket buyers.

"I needed 10 years until they were going to become the consumers of a professional league," Buss said. "We just had to dodge the bullet for 10 years. If we could survive 10 years and not fall into the same problems that other potential leagues fell into – allowing underfunded owners to own teams – we could have people who were dedicated to growing the sport and not trying to stab each other in the back and pay players under the table and the craziness that goes on in every league. I've been through many leagues, and I've seen it all happen… if we could just bite the bullet and make it to that 10-year mark…"

Even though Roller Hockey International disappeared more than a decade ago, its reverberations are still being felt today.

"Dennis Murphy did some things that changed a ton of people's lives," said Joe Cook of the Anaheim Bullfrogs. "I think he deserves a certain level of respect for that, whether you agree with the way Dennis ran things or you don't. At the end of the day, he did a lot of great things for people. The people who built the sport gave a lot of people jobs and careers and made changes in people's lives. We may be without a pro league today because of the way things were run, but at the end of the day, the guys that were involved in that [league] made a difference in our lives."

"The thing I loved about it was the risk, the way everyone dove in and risked their reputations on a new thing," said Craig Forrest, who played for the Los Angeles Blades in 1993 and later became an executive at Hyper Wheels. "It was exciting to play in the Forum and to have our locker room in the Kings' locker room. People were in the stands."

"People still talk about RHI to me," said Jon Gustafson, who currently manages the San Jose Sharks' ice and inline hockey rinks programs. "I've never left San Jose, and it's really amazing that there are still people who recognize me and say, 'Boy, I wish the Rhinos were back. That stuff was really special.' It's pretty cool to hear."

"I'm telling you right now, of all the things I've done in my life, those four years I spent playing in that league, man, it didn't get any better than that," said former Anaheim Bullfrogs, Phoenix Cobras and Los Angeles Blades' star Bob McKillop. "That was the pinnacle of my career. That league was phenomenal to play in."

"I not only *loved* being a part of RHI, but I felt honored to experience everything I did," said Steve Pona. "This time in my life helped give formation and structure to where I am today. I will forever love Dennis Murphy. I will forever respect and admire all that he has accomplished and for the time he took to teach me about life, sports and how to bring a dream to life."

Perry Turnbull, the player/coach for the St. Louis Vipers who owns a roller hockey rink in St. Louis to this day, said that if RHI had today's skate and wheel technology, along with the young players who learned the game growing up, "We would still be out there playing professional roller hockey, and we would have had some nice crowds in the stands."

Turnbull added that the inline game has changed so much – it's faster, players have a greater ability to stop on a dime and go back the other direction in a hurry – that it would make for an exciting professional game today.

"The NHL has gone to 4-on-4 for overtime for one reason, and that's to open it up a little bit," Turnbull said. "I think we had something going there. It was a wonderful event. I wish today that somehow we could rekindle that. We should be in smaller buildings in a more intimate setting. We could reenergize that and have a pro league across America again. I think it would continue to grow the numbers of players that have an opportunity to play. There are lots of times at my rink I've walked up and tapped a player on the shoulder and said, 'That kid's pretty special, but there's no pro league anymore. I think we should use him on the ice.' "

A Second Chance?

I often wonder what would have happened if Roller Hockey International had been able to hang on a few years longer. Could it have solidified the financial standing of the league's teams, nailed down a long-term television contract and come to some sort of an agreement with the National Hockey League to have a pro roller hockey team in every NHL building in summertime?

"The only way [a professional roller hockey league] could happen again would be with the NHL's involvement," said Jeanie Buss. "The NHL has so many issues that they're dealing with in trying to make the NHL successful. A lot of the owners who don't own the arenas that their teams play in could care less about filling it during the summer time."

"It was exciting," said Larry King. "We were creating something out of nothing. A lot of us sacrificed a lot of money, but we could have easily been heroes if we'd gotten lucky and maybe the NHL had bought us, or we had gone to the single-entity concept earlier… who's to say? There are a lot of ways it could have gone and still been going today. But the problem is, I believe, all of our owners looked at the NHL as being the ultimate aim. Well, if you look at the NHL being your ultimate aim, then you're not promoting your own sport. We all were NHL wannabes, and that's probably why RHI doesn't exist. It's because the athletes, on the very basic level, wanted to be in the NHL. They were doing roller hockey because they couldn't make the NHL."

Ken Murchison, who runs the roller hockey side of the Anaheim Ducks amateur hockey leagues, maintains that a professional roller hockey league could one day return.

"It's hockey," Murchison said "We breed season-ticket holders. The kids don't recognize that they're on wheels versus blades, the bottom line is that they're playing hockey, and they still aspire to be Teemu Selanne, you know. In Southern California, I really think there's a possibility to really get this thing back to where it was, and I believe that there could be more roller hockey facilities again than the ice. It just makes a lot of sense."

"Never say never, because who knows what tomorrow's going to hold," said David Smallwood of sporting goods manufacturer Karhu USA. "But I think that now, especially in our economy and the way dollars are being stretched, the marketing and sponsorship and TV dollars are being stretched, I don't see something like that happening in the near future, if it happens at all."

"I don't see another [pro] roller hockey league ever making it," said David McLane. "The times are different, the NHL doesn't have the buzz it had back when it opened franchises in Anaheim, Phoenix, and Florida, plus its television ratings for professional hockey aren't great. Another factor is, when we started, ESPN was just about to launch its new network espn2 – this created a great opportunity for us to grow roller hockey. Third, the sales of inline skates and roller hockey products are at an all-time low. Fourth, the Buss family sold the Great Western Forum, and Jeanie Buss is now a vice president of the Los Angeles Lakers. Without a marquee venue and brains of a Jeanie Buss who knew every aspect to building a league and local team success, it is unlikely. And lastly, I haven't met another Dennis Murphy who has the Irish charm to pull all the parties together to make it happen again. Dennis Murphy was a guy that could sell a concept and get people excited about what could be. Dennis Murphy knew how to pick up the phone, make a cold call, and get someone to put money up for a dream. In retrospect, the stars were all aligned for great success, and I think that only happens once in life. Wow! It was a great ride!"

To focus solely on Roller Hockey International's demise is to miss the whole story, however. For several years, RHI was a wonderful professional sports league that brought excitement and pleasure to millions of fans across North America. Co-founded by four creative yet imperfect businessmen – Dennis Murphy, Larry King, Alex Bellehumeur and Ralph Backstrom – the league captured the imagination of a segment of the population and helped professional roller hockey have its short time in the spotlight.

David Smallwood said that what stood out to him about RHI's founders was their passion and their belief in what they were doing.

"They had very specific, grand plans, and even though RHI did not make it in the long run, which is a disappointment, I would still call it a success, because there were a number of years where we had great runs, and it was very instrumental for our brand in getting our consumer awareness, market share, where we stood in the marketplace," Smallwood said. "Attending games in L.A., in Anaheim and some other cities, having been in Vancouver for the All-Star Game, where they sold the rink out... They had grand plans and dreams, and although the thing did not ultimately live long term, I would still definitely classify it as a success."

For a brief moment in time, all of us involved in Roller Hockey International rode the crest of a wave, balanced on the leading edge of a sport that seemed to have limitless potential. And though that powerful wave crashed unexpectedly, it left little eddies and whirlpools reverberating. In Vancouver, roller hockey is one of the most popular summer recreational sports, with more than 7,000 participants. The North American Roller Hockey Championships, an amateur inline hockey tournament series, is still going strong, with Daryn Goodwin, who played for Team USA in RHI's inaugural tour, at its helm. The Buffalo Wings amateur inline hockey organization still exists and continues to win age-group championships. Various people in the sport continue to try to find the right ingredients to create a new professional inline hockey league. Whether one is ever successful, it will succeed or fail depending on the lessons it learns from the short and bittersweet history of Roller Hockey International, a fascinating story of wheelers, dealers, pucks and bucks.

CHAPTER 37

Crunching the Numbers

1993 RHI Final Standings

For more extensive Roller Hockey International statistics, please see www.rhistats.tripod.com

All Statistics courtesy of http://rhistats.tripod.com

1993 RHI Final Standings

MURPHY DIVISION

	GP	W	L	OTL	GF	GA	PTS
Toronto Planets	14	10	4	0	136	83	20
St. Louis Vipers	14	9	4	1	104	115	19
Connecticut Coasters	14	7	5	2	124	112	16
Florida Hammerheads	14	2	11	1	100	154	5

KING DIVISION

	GP	W	L	OTL	GF	GA	PTS
Vancouver VooDoo	14	11	2	1	160	91	23
Calgary Rad'z	14	8	6	0	125	104	16
Portland Rage	14	4	10	0	92	149	8
Utah Rollerbees	14	2	11	1	90	142	5

BUSS DIVISION

	GP	W	L	OTL	GF	GA	PTS
Anaheim Bullfrogs	14	13	0	1	130	83	27
Los Angeles Blades	14	8	6	0	110	107	16
Oakland Skates	14	5	9	0	112	122	10
San Diego Barracudas	14	5	9	0	109	130	10

1993 Top Scorers

Points	Team	GP	G	A	PTS
Charbonneau, Joe	VAN	14	25	43	68
Lawrence, Doug	OAK	14	12	48	60
Shank, Daniel	SD	14	28	31	59
Harrison, Ryan	VAN	14	27	32	59
Esselmont, Todd	VAN	14	26	31	57
Naud, Sylvain	OAK	14	31	20	51
Martin, Don	FLA	14	27	23	50
Ross, Steve	LA	14	11	38	49
Middendorf, Max	SD	14	29	18	47
Barahona, Ralph	LA	12	20	25	45
Rupp, Scott	STL	14	15	29	44
Fleetwood, Brent	POR	14	14	30	44
Hrytsak, Rob	CON	14	26	17	43
Clouston, Shaun	OAK	14	25	18	43
Hart, Myles	STL	14	22	20	42
Pachkevitch, Paul	CON	14	20	22	42
Richmond, James	TOR	14	12	28	40
Thompson, Mark	FLA	14	20	18	38
Gervais, Victor	ANA	14	14	24	38
Edgerton, Devin	ANA	13	18	19	37

1993 Leading Goaltenders
(Based on 4 or more games)

	Team	GPI	MIN	AVG	W	L	OTL	EN	SO	GA	Saves	SPCT
Jaycock, Randy	CGY	7	206	5.13	3	1	0	2	0	22	161	0.880
Legace, Manny	TOR	13	611	5.26	10	3	0	1	0	67	495	0.881
Laurie, Rob	ANA	7	312	5.38	7	0	0	0	0	35	208	0.856
Kinney, Ken	VAN	9	391	5.52	8	0	0	0	0	45	284	0.863
Horn, Bill	ANA	8	352	6.41	6	0	1	0	0	47	273	0.853
Humphrey, Scott	STL	6	285	6.74	4	1	1	0	0	40	194	0.829
O'Hara, Michael	LA	13	621	7.42	8	5	0	2	0	96	442	0.822
Ouellette, Francis	SD	9	406	7.57	4	4	0	2	0	64	323	0.835
Walsh, Neil	CON	10	374	7.57	6	2	0	1	0	59	282	0.827
Carlsen, Lance	VAN	7	280	7.71	3	2	1	0	0	45	188	0.807
Cox, Michael	CON	8	298	8.05	1	3	2	0	0	50	198	0.798
Flatt, Brian	OAK	9	364	8.31	3	5	0	0	0	63	293	0.823
Dadswell, Doug	CGY	10	377	8.66	5	4	0	0	1	68	289	0.810
Cohen, Paul	FLA	11	412	9.20	2	7	0	3	0	79	335	0.809
Seibel, Troy	OAK	7	306	9.25	2	4	0	0	0	59	233	0.798
Grimm, Rob	STL	8	304	9.32	5	2	0	0	0	59	209	0.780
Rougelot, Roger	UT	11	447	9.45	2	8	0	2	0	88	305	0.776
Mumford, Paul	POR	11	377	10.19	2	5	0	0	0	80	336	0.808
Skidmore, Paul	UT	7	221	10.86	0	3	1	1	0	50	147	0.746
Nein, Dennis	POR	10	294	11.27	2	5	0	0	0	69	256	0.788

1993 RHI Playoff Results

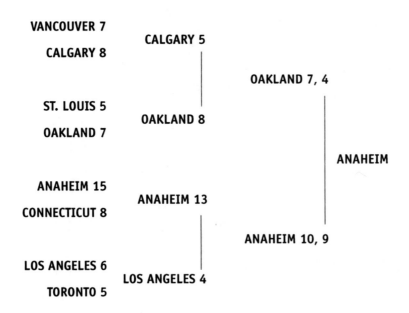

VANCOUVER 7
CALGARY 8
CALGARY 5

OAKLAND 7, 4

ST. LOUIS 5
OAKLAND 8
OAKLAND 7

ANAHEIM

ANAHEIM 15
ANAHEIM 13
CONNECTICUT 8

ANAHEIM 10, 9

LOS ANGELES 6
LOS ANGELES 4
TORONTO 5

1994 RHI Final Standings

EASTERN CONFERENCE

ATLANTIC DIVISION

	GP	W	L	OTL	PTS	PCT	GF	GA	PIM
Buffalo Stampede	22	15	3	4	34	.773	196	159	749
Montreal Roadrunners	22	13	9	0	26	.591	161	148	487
Philadelphia Bulldogs	22	12	10	0	24	.545	187	185	431
New Jersey Rockin Rollers	22	11	10	1	23	.523	158	165	622
Tampa Bay Tritons	22	11	11	0	22	.500	178	166	643
Florida Hammerheads	22	4	17	1	9	.205	139	188	647

CENTRAL DIVISION

	GP	W	L	OTL	PTS	PCT	GF	GA	PIM
Minnesota Arctic Blast	22	18	3	1	37	.841	260	187	407
Pittsburgh Phantoms	22	13	9	0	26	.591	207	193	424
Chicago Cheetahs	22	12	10	0	24	.545	182	190	368
Atlanta Fire Ants	22	10	10	2	22	.500	168	190	300
St. Louis Vipers	22	8	12	2	18	.409	154	173	495
New England Stingers	22	5	17	0	10	.227	173	219	344

WESTERN CONFERENCE

NORTHWEST DIVISION

	GP	W	L	OTL	PTS	PCT	GF	GA	PIM
Vancouver VooDoo	22	15	6	1	31	.705	188	157	412
Calgary Rad'z	22	12	8	2	26	.591	183	160	473
Phoenix Cobras	22	11	9	2	24	.545	174	187	616
Portland Rage	22	11	10	1	23	.523	197	173	523
Edmonton Sled Dogs	22	9	10	3	21	.477	164	170	328
Sacramento River Rats	22	5	17	0	10	.227	145	221	618

PACIFIC DIVISION

	GP	W	L	OTL	PTS	PCT	GF	GA	PIM
Los Angeles Blades	22	18	4	0	36	.818	180	133	406
San Jose Rhinos	22	13	7	2	28	.636	167	159	535
Anaheim Bullfrogs	22	13	8	1	27	.614	185	155	634
San Diego Barracudas	22	9	9	4	22	.500	171	178	319
Oakland Skates	22	10	12	0	20	.455	144	171	511
Las Vegas Flash	22	6	15	1	13	.295	152	186	558

1994 Leading Scorers

Points	Team	GP	G	A	PTS
Young, John	MIN	22	30	49	79
Skarda, Randy	MIN	21	18	59	77
Valicevic, Chris	POR	22	25	50	75
Woolf, Mark	SJ	22	40	34	74
St. Cyr, Gerry	POR	22	42	31	73
Hanson, John	MIN	22	35	37	72
Krakiwsky, Sean	CGY	22	30	42	72
Hanus, Tim	MIN	22	36	35	71
Hawley, Kent	PHL	22	29	37	66
Downey, Brian	POR	22	19	47	66
Vecchiarelli, John	BUF	22	32	33	65
Olimb, Larry	MIN	22	26	39	65
Clancey, Derek	PHL	21	18	45	63
Schuler, Alan	SJ	22	11	52	63
Harrison, Ryan	VAN	22	37	25	62
Rouleau, Guy	MON	21	31	31	62
Ingraham, Cal	NE	22	30	32	62
Wilcox, George	PIT	22	28	34	62
Rymsha, Andy	POR	22	16	46	62
Gruhl, Scott	SD	22	28	33	61

1994 Leading Goaltenders

(Based on 7 or more games)

	Team	GPI	MIN	AVG	W	L	OTL	EN	SO	GA	SAVES	SPCT
Mikhailovsky, Maxim	LA	19	856	5.60	15	3	0	0	0	100	628	0.863
Delorme, Marc	MON	18	522	6.16	9	5	0	1	0	67	344	0.837
Kinney, Ken	VAN	15	575	6.43	9	3	0	0	0	77	410	0.842
Carlsen, Lance	POR	18	736	6.58	9	4	2	1	0	101	548	0.844
Jaycock, Randy	CGY	11	476	6.65	6	3	0	2	0	66	333	0.835
Gordon, Chris	ANA	11	490	6.66	5	4	1	1	0	68	302	0.816
Sjerven, Grant	SJ	15	523	6.69	7	3	1	2	0	73	379	0.838
Humphrey, Scott	STL	13	473	6.89	5	4	1	1	0	68	412	0.858
Vitucci, Nick	BUF	22	1037	6.94	15	3	4	2	0	150	717	0.827
Bojcun, Todd	FLA	12	449	7.04	1	6	1	1	0	66	375	0.850
Berthiaume, Daniel	NJ	19	824	7.05	9	9	1	1	0	121	548	0.819
Slazyk, Jim	PHL	12	354	7.16	4	4	0	1	0	53	217	0.804
Perry, Alan	OAK	16	614	7.19	6	7	0	0	0	92	458	0.833
Micalef, Corrado	MON	18	527	7.19	4	4	0	1	0	79	350	0.816
Cowley, Wayne	LV	13	503	7.24	3	6	1	2	0	76	363	0.827
Laurie, Rob	ANA	13	563	7.24	8	4	0	0	0	85	418	0.831
McKinley, Rob	EDM	21	859	7.43	7	8	3	2	0	133	622	0.824
Sproxton, Dennis	TB	21	568	7.43	5	6	0	1	0	88	361	0.804
Gustafson, Jon	SJ	11	461	7.49	6	4	0	0	0	72	402	0.848
Ouellette, Francis	SD	20	791	7.58	8	8	2	3	0	125	531	0.809

1994 RHI Playoff Results

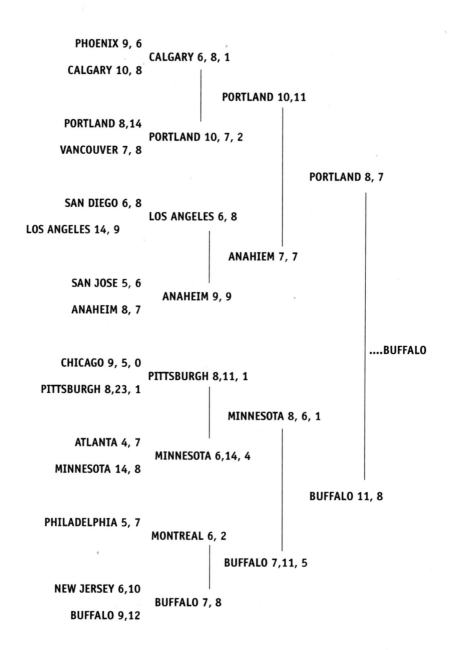

PHOENIX 9, 6
CALGARY 6, 8, 1
CALGARY 10, 8

PORTLAND 10,11

PORTLAND 8,14
PORTLAND 10, 7, 2
VANCOUVER 7, 8

PORTLAND 8, 7

SAN DIEGO 6, 8
LOS ANGELES 6, 8
LOS ANGELES 14, 9

ANAHIEM 7, 7

SAN JOSE 5, 6
ANAHEIM 9, 9
ANAHEIM 8, 7

....BUFFALO

CHICAGO 9, 5, 0
PITTSBURGH 8,11, 1
PITTSBURGH 8,23, 1

MINNESOTA 8, 6, 1

ATLANTA 4, 7
MINNESOTA 6,14, 4
MINNESOTA 14, 8

BUFFALO 11, 8

PHILADELPHIA 5, 7
MONTREAL 6, 2

BUFFALO 7,11, 5

NEW JERSEY 6,10
BUFFALO 7, 8
BUFFALO 9,12

1995 RHI Division Standings

EASTERN CONFERENCE

ATLANTIC DIVISION

	GP	W	L	OTL	PTS	PCT	GF	GA	PIM
Montreal Roadrunners	24	15	6	3	33	.688	175	133	596
Ottawa Loggers	24	14	9	1	29	.604	181	155	351
New Jersey Rockin Rollers	24	13	11	0	26	.542	172	167	653
Philadelphia Bulldogs	24	12	10	2	26	.542	179	165	437
Orlando RollerGators	23	7	16	0	14	.304	135	184	481

CENTRAL DIVISION

	GP	W	L	OTL	PTS	PCT	GF	GA	PIM
St. Louis Vipers	22	13	7	2	28	.636	166	157	520
Minnesota Blue Ox	24	13	11	0	26	.542	175	209	496
Detroit Motor City Mustangs	24	11	9	4	26	.542	177	181	429
Chicago Cheetahs	24	10	12	2	22	.458	194	194	461
Buffalo Stampede	23	10	13	0	20	.435	169	178	520

WESTERN CONFERENCE

NORTHWEST DIVISION

	GP	W	L	OTL	PTS	PCT	GF	GA	PIM
Vancouver VooDoo	24	13	10	1	27	.563	203	185	459
Sacramento River Rats	24	12	9	3	27	.563	185	174	510
San Jose Rhinos	24	13	11	0	26	.542	174	174	819
Oakland Skates	24	10	10	4	24	.500	157	173	535

PACIFIC DIVISION

	GP	W	L	OTL	PTS	PCT	GF	GA	PIM
Anaheim Bullfrogs	24	19	4	1	39	.813	219	157	558
Phoenix Cobras	24	13	11	0	26	.542	158	161	466
San Diego Barracudas	24	12	11	1	25	.521	167	172	521
Los Angeles Blades	24	9	10	5	23	.479	147	164	458
Oklahoma Coyotes	24	7	17	0	14	.292	159	209	333

1995 Leading Scorers

Points	Team	GP	G	A	PTS
Lawrence, Doug	OKL	24	23	68	91
Rouleau, Guy	MON	24	37	46	83
Szabo, Tony	DET	24	50	32	82
Gervais, Victor	ANA	21	23	55	78
Shank, Daniel	ANA	19	24	48	72
York, Harry	CHI	24	24	47	71
Martens, Michael	CHI	24	30	40	70
Woolf, Mark	SJ	24	29	40	69
Palmer, Chris	OTT	22	35	33	68
Vecchiarelli, John	BUF	23	31	37	68
Wetzel, Todd	ANA	23	40	27	67
Ricci, Angelo	CHI	24	33	33	66
Burfoot, Scott	DET	21	17	48	65
Hanson, John	MIN	24	37	27	64
Harrison, Ryan	VAN	24	31	32	63
Reynolds, Bobby	DET	24	27	35	62
Lacroix, Martin	MON	24	27	35	62
Ast, Doug	VAN	23	34	27	61
Rohlicek, Jeff	CHI	22	20	41	61
Drevitch, Scott	OKL	24	21	38	59

1995 Leading Goaltenders
(Based on 7 or more games)

	Team	GPI	MIN	AVG	W	L	OTL	EN	SO	GA	SAVES	SPCT
Micalef, Corrado	MON	13	565	5.17	7	3	1	1	0	61	313	0.837
Gravel, Francois	MON	12	516	5.29	8	2	2	0	0	57	345	0.858
Bernard, Mark	PHL	11	482	5.67	6	3	0	3	0	57	332	0.853
Rodrigue, Sylvain	OTT	17	712	6.06	10	6	1	2	0	90	465	0.838
Hamelin, Hugo	PHX	14	629	6.10	7	6	0	0	0	80	440	0.846
Gauthier, Sean	LA	22	1022	6.24	8	9	5	3	0	133	692	0.839
Gordon, Chris	ANA	11	527	6.28	10	1	0	0	0	69	328	0.826
DelGuidice, Matt	NJ	11	471	6.41	5	4	0	1	0	63	266	0.809
DelGuidice, Matt	OTT	8	355	6.48	3	3	0	1	0	48	203	0.809
Cavallin, Mark	OAK	17	743	6.51	8	4	3	0	0	101	601	0.856
Rogles, Chris	STL	17	735	6.53	10	5	1	0	0	100	514	0.837
Ouellette, Francis	SD	18	765	6.58	9	6	1	0	0	105	554	0.841
Gustafson, Jon	SJ	14	669	6.59	8	6	0	1	0	92	426	0.822
Laurie, Rob	ANA	13	623	6.70	9	3	1	0	0	87	439	0.835
Naumov, Sergei	SAC	15	524	7.04	6	3	2	0	0	77	381	0.832
Mazzoli, Pat	NJ	17	732	7.07	7	9	0	0	0	108	508	0.825
Sproxton, Dennis	SAC	16	624	7.08	6	6	1	2	0	92	413	0.818
Butt, Kevin	DET	7	232	7.21	1	2	2	1	0	35	151	0.812
Bell, Bob	VAN	14	561	7.26	5	6	1	3	0	85	332	0.796
Berthiaume, Daniel	DET	20	916	7.28	10	7	2	2	0	139	686	0.832

1995 RHI Playoff Results

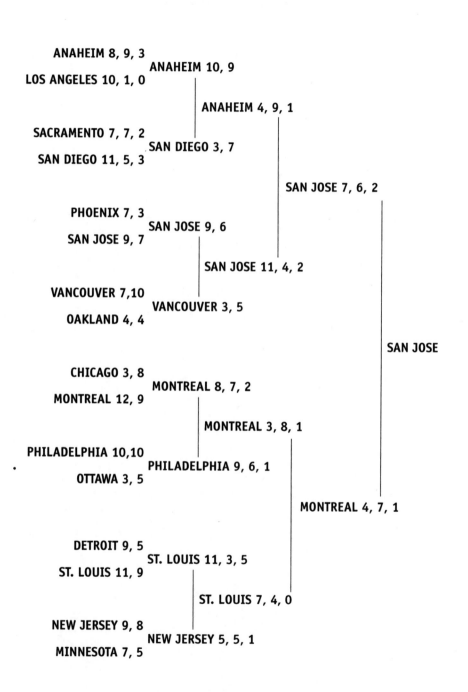

ANAHEIM 8, 9, 3
ANAHEIM 10, 9
LOS ANGELES 10, 1, 0

ANAHEIM 4, 9, 1

SACRAMENTO 7, 7, 2
SAN DIEGO 3, 7
SAN DIEGO 11, 5, 3

SAN JOSE 7, 6, 2

PHOENIX 7, 3
SAN JOSE 9, 6
SAN JOSE 9, 7

SAN JOSE 11, 4, 2

VANCOUVER 7,10
VANCOUVER 3, 5
OAKLAND 4, 4

SAN JOSE

CHICAGO 3, 8
MONTREAL 8, 7, 2
MONTREAL 12, 9

MONTREAL 3, 8, 1

PHILADELPHIA 10,10
PHILADELPHIA 9, 6, 1
OTTAWA 3, 5

MONTREAL 4, 7, 1

DETROIT 9, 5
ST. LOUIS 11, 3, 5
ST. LOUIS 11, 9

ST. LOUIS 7, 4, 0

NEW JERSEY 9, 8
NEW JERSEY 5, 5, 1
MINNESOTA 7, 5

1996 Division Standings

EASTERN CONFERENCE

ATLANTIC DIVISION

	GP	W	L	OTL	PTS	PCT	GF	GA	PIM
Empire State Cobras	28	16	7	5	37	.661	202	168	462
Orlando Jackals	28	17	9	2	36	.643	231	201	448
Long Island Jawz	28	16	9	3	35	.625	246	211	513
Philadelphia Bulldogs	28	16	9	3	35	.625	202	199	570
New Jersey Rockin Rollers	28	7	17	4	18	.321	167	227	374

CENTRAL DIVISION

	GP	W	L	OTL	PTS	PCT	GF	GA	PIM
Minnesota Arctic Blast	28	22	6	0	44	.786	246	200	370
St. Louis Vipers	28	15	12	1	31	.554	207	209	520
Montreal Roadrunners	28	14	11	3	31	.554	177	174	463
Ottawa Loggers	28	3	22	3	9	.161	174	263	463

WESTERN CONFERENCE

NORTHWEST DIVISION

	GP	W	L	OTL	PTS	PCT	GF	GA	PIM
Vancouver VooDoo	28	18	7	3	39	.696	217	162	665
Oakland Skates	28	15	11	2	32	.571	187	181	456
San Jose Rhinos	28	15	12	1	31	.554	189	180	764
Sacramento River Rats	28	10	17	1	21	.375	185	229	456

PACIFIC DIVISION

	GP	W	L	OTL	PTS	PCT	GF	GA	PIM
Anaheim Bullfrogs	28	22	4	2	46	.821	215	159	495
Los Angeles Blades	28	16	11	1	33	.589	160	155	438
Oklahoma Coyotes	28	13	12	3	29	.518	174	174	524
San Diego Barracudas	28	9	18	1	19	.339	183	233	553
Denver Daredevils	28	8	17	3	19	.339	173	210	467

1996 Leading Scorers

Points	Team	GP	G	A	PTS
Belanger, Hugo P.	LI	25	48	53	101
Ast, Doug	VAN	28	50	41	91
St. Cyr, Gerry	SAC	28	48	41	89
Laylin, Cory	MIN	28	42	47	89
Woolf, Mark	SJ	27	32	53	85
Palmer, Chris	EMP	25	37	47	84
Gervais, Victor	ANA	25	29	55	84
Shank, Daniel	ORL	28	31	50	81
Skoryna, Christian	STL	28	36	44	80
Young, John	MIN	28	24	55	79
Larin, Daniel	ORL	26	32	46	78
Parsons, Don	LI	26	40	36	76
Lawrence, Doug	ORL	28	21	52	73
Hanson, John	MIN	27	37	35	72
Hamr, Radek	OKL	28	21	51	72
Metropolit, Glen	LI	28	32	39	71
Burton, Joe	OKL	28	42	28	70
Slivchenko, Vadim	SAC	28	28	42	70
Cirone, Frank	STL	28	37	32	69
Colbourne, Darren	SJ	28	36	33	69

1996 Leading Goaltenders
(Based on 8 or more games)

	Team	GPI	MIN	AVG	W	L	OTL	EN	SO	GA	SAVES	SPCT
Ferguson, Jeff	LA	16	606:56	4.82	10	3	0	0	0	61	434	0.877
Raymond, Eric	ANA	9	418:41	5.04	7	2	0	1	0	44	245	0.848
Humphrey, Scott	VAN	17	691:30	5.41	10	3	2	0	0	78	525	0.871
Horn, Bill	ORL	11	480:51	5.59	8	2	0	1	0	56	300	0.843
Vitucci, Nick	EMP	15	717:07	5.69	10	2	3	1	0	85	468	0.846
Goverde, David	EMP	13	622:05	5.71	6	5	2	3	0	74	480	0.866
Mazzoli,	LI	8	374:52	5.76	4	1	2	1	0	45	228	0.835
Laurie, Rob	ANA	21	922:18	5.83	15	2	2	0	0	112	583	0.839
Bell, Robert	VAN	13	600:42	5.83	8	3	1	1	0	73	361	0.832
Sjervin, Grant	SJ	10	382:59	5.89	4	3	1	1	0	47	236	0.834
Skudra, Peter	OKL	18	720:44	5.99	10	4	1	1	0	90	492	0.845
Gauthier, Sean	LA	19	733:00	6.02	6	8	1	1	0	92	475	0.838
Morissette, Alain	MON	14	642:45	6.05	5	8	1	1	0	81	433	0.842
Herlofsky, Derek	MIN	15	585:03	6.07	9	3	0	1	0	74	400	0.844
Cavallin, Mark	OAK	23	986:16	6.13	10	6	2	0	0	126	742	0.855
Gravel, Francois	MON	16	696:27	6.13	9	3	2	0	0	89	517	0.853
Bonvie, Joe	SJ	21	883:05	6.14	10	9	0	6	0	113	583	0.838
Filiatrault, Jean	OKL	16	613:18	6.18	3	8	2	1	0	79	455	0.852
Richards, Mark	PHL	20	814:36	6.19	11	6	0	2	0	105	579	0.846
Cadden, Corey	DEN	20	805:45	6.43	5	10	2	0	0	108	570	0.841

1996 RHI Playoff Results

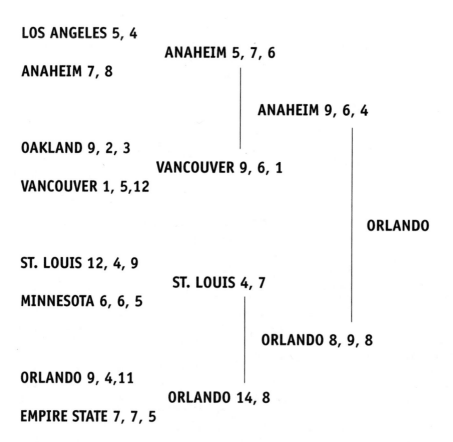

LOS ANGELES 5, 4

ANAHEIM 5, 7, 6

ANAHEIM 7, 8

ANAHEIM 9, 6, 4

OAKLAND 9, 2, 3

VANCOUVER 9, 6, 1

VANCOUVER 1, 5,12

ORLANDO

ST. LOUIS 12, 4, 9

ST. LOUIS 4, 7

MINNESOTA 6, 6, 5

ORLANDO 8, 9, 8

ORLANDO 9, 4,11

ORLANDO 14, 8

EMPIRE STATE 7, 7, 5

1997 RHI Final Standings

EASTERN CONFERENCE

	GP	W	L	OTL	PTS	PCT	GF	GA	PIM
Orlando Jackals	24	20	4	0	40	.833	229	145	513
New Jersey Rockin Rollers	24	16	8	0	32	.667	195	174	625
Montreal Roadrunners	24	9	10	5	23	.479	161	164	679
Ottawa Wheels	24	10	12	2	22	.458	162	181	304
Buffalo Wings	24	6	18	0	12	.250	127	208	530

WESTERN CONFERENCE

	GP	W	L	OTL	PTS	PCT	GF	GA	PIM
San Jose Rhinos	24	15	7	2	32	.667	175	148	553
Anaheim Bullfrogs	24	15	9	0	30	.625	173	156	435
Los Angeles Blades	24	11	8	5	27	.563	166	155	405
St. Louis Vipers	24	12	10	2	26	.542	174	169	339
Sacramento River Rats	24	6	16	2	14	.292	123	185	438

1997 Leading Scorers

Points	Team	GP	G	A	PTS
Lund, Bill	ORL	24	32	46	78
Hamr, Radek	SJ	24	19	56	75
Cirone, Frank	STL	24	34	39	73
Reeves, Kyle	ORL	24	41	29	70
Skoryna, Christian	STL	23	27	43	70
Shank, Daniel	ORL	17	19	47	66
Woolf, Mark	SJ	24	35	29	64
Bouchard, Robin	OTT	24	28	35	63
Gervais, Victor	ANA	17	17	45	62
Ast, Doug	LA	21	32	27	59
Elders, Jason	SJ	24	36	21	57
Hanson, John	ORL	22	33	24	57
LaCroix, Martin	MON	23	22	32	54
Larin, Daniel	ORL	21	23	30	53
Brown, Jim	STL	24	21	32	53
Szabo, Tony	NJ	20	30	21	51
St. Jacques, Kevin	LA	19	17	32	49
Spoltore, John	NJ	24	16	32	48
Cooke, Jamie	ORL	20	14	34	48

1997 Leading Goaltenders

(Based on 7 or more games)

	Team	GPI	MIN	AVG	W	L	OTL	EN	SO	GA	SAVES	SPCT
Naumov, Sergei	ORL	10	383:29	4.50	6	2	0	0	0	36	211	0.854
Micalef, Corrado	SJ	16	591:32	5.84	8	4	1	1	0	72	408	0.850
Pye, Bill	LA	11	400:10	6.00	5	2	2	0	0	50	224	0.818
Bonvie, Joe	SJ	12	555:05	6.14	7	3	1	2	0	71	355	0.833
Shepard, Ken	STL	15	542:15	6.20	5	5	2	1	0	70	352	0.834
Goverde, David	ANA	13	505:32	6.26	6	4	0	2	0	66	345	0.839
Ferguson, Jeff	LA	18	740:18	6.29	6	6	3	2	0	97	463	0.827
Richards, Mark	NJ	16	658:19	6.63	10	4	0	0	0	91	424	0.823
Ouellette, Francis	ORL	15	655:34	6.81	13	1	0	0	0	93	321	0.775
Morissette, Alain	MON	19	807:52	6.83	7	8	2	1	0	115	486	0.809
Laurie, Rob	ANA	15	594:46	6.94	9	4	0	1	0	86	410	0.827
Seibel, Troy	SAC	18	605:36	7.05	3	10	0	5	0	89	413	0.823
Hamelin, Hugo	OTT	8	352:02	7.09	3	4	0	1	0	52	236	0.819
Vitucci, Nick	NJ	18	714:39	7.12	8	9	0	1	0	106	513	0.829
Vezina, Steve	OTT	14	414:21	7.18	4	5	0	1	0	62	272	0.814
Cavallin, Mark	STL	15	575:52	7.58	7	4	0	2	0	91	421	0.822
Delorme, Marc	MON	11	402:09	7.64	3	5	1	2	0	64	241	0.790
Dorosh, David	OTT	11	383:00	7.90	3	3	2	0	0	63	235	0.789
Bernard, Mark	BUF	10	321:02	10.32	1	6	0	0	0	69	210	0.753
Rheaume, Manon	SAC	8	157:08	10.38	0	2	1	0	0	34	106	0.757

1997 Playoff Results

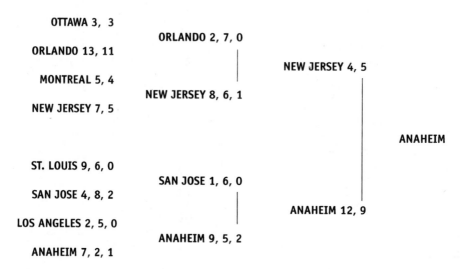

```
OTTAWA 3,  3
                    ORLANDO 2, 7, 0
ORLANDO 13, 11
                                        NEW JERSEY 4, 5
MONTREAL 5, 4
                    NEW JERSEY 8, 6, 1
NEW JERSEY 7, 5
                                                            ANAHEIM

ST. LOUIS 9, 6, 0
                    SAN JOSE 1, 6, 0
SAN JOSE 4, 8, 2
                                        ANAHEIM 12, 9
LOS ANGELES 2, 5, 0
                    ANAHEIM 9, 5, 2
ANAHEIM 7, 2, 1
```

Major League Roller Hockey 1998 Regular Season

Final Standings

COASTAL DIVISION

	GP	W	L	OTL	GF	GA	PTS
Anaheim Bullfrogs	20	19	0	1	263	84	39
Washington Power	20	9	11	0	135	212	18
New York Riot	20	7	12	1	143	174	15
Philadelphia Sting	20	7	13	0	91	242	14

GREAT LAKES DIVISION

	GP	W	L	OTL	GF	GA	PTS
2 ptOrlando Surge	20	18	1	1	237	93	37
Virginia Vultures	20	16	4	0	264	119	32
Tampa Bay Rollin' Thunder	20	10	8	2	168	160	22
South Carolina Fire Ants	20	8	11	1	142	152	17
Carolina Crushers	20	0	19	1	70	226	1

SOUTHERN DIVISION

	GP	W	L	OTL	GF	GA	PTS
2 ptColumbus Hawks	20	17	2	1	172	82	35
Buffalo Wings	20	11	8	1	174	125	23
Port Huron North Americans	20	9	9	2	129	183	20
Toronto Torpedoes	20	5	13	2	134	176	12
Pennsylvania Posse	20	4	16	0	96	190	8

RHI 1999 Final Standings

EASTERN CONFERENCE

	GP	W	L	OTL	PTS	PCT	GF	GA	PIM
St. Louis Vipers	26	17	8	1	35	.673	221	168	297
Buffalo Wings	26	13	13	0	26	.500	185	193	440
Minnesota Blue Ox	26	11	15	0	22	.423	159	197	294
Chicago Bluesmen	26	7	17	2	16	.308	146	209	223

WESTERN CONFERENCE

	GP	W	L	OTL	PTS	PCT	GF	GA	PIM
Anaheim Bullfrogs	26	21	3	2	44	.846	197	127	403
Las Vegas Coyotes	26	16	7	3	35	.673	144	123	280
San Jose Rhinos	26	12	11	3	27	.519	144	137	485
Dallas Stallions	26	7	17	2	16	.308	117	159	337

1999 Leading Scorers

Points	Team	GP	G	A	PTS
Belanger, Hugo	ANA	23	37	43	80
Blum, Ken	BUF	26	36	39	75
Vecchiarelli, John	BUF	24	28	43	71
Martens, Michael	STL	24	34	36	70
Skoryna, Christian	STL	22	36	33	69
St. Jacques, Kevin	ANA	22	21	46	67
Langlois, Jocelyn	STL	25	32	29	61
Stewart, Glenn	MIN	26	29	32	61
Major, Mark	BUF	23	24	34	58
Hanson, John	MIN	21	31	20	51
Neal, Jay	LVG	25	19	32	51
Laylin, Cory	MIN	23	17	34	51
Yoder, C.J.	STL	18	15	34	49
Menicci, Tom	ANA	25	20	28	48
Cooke, Jamie	LVG	23	19	29	48
Gorewich, Ben	STL	25	25	22	47
Elders, Jason	SJO	25	22	23	45
St. Cyr, Gerry	LVG	21	21	24	45
Lund, Bill	MIN	21	14	31	45

Several Players Tied at 43

1999 Leading Goaltenders

(Based on 450 or more minutes)

	Team	GPI	MIN	AVG	W	L	OTL	EN	SO	GA	SAVES	SPCT
Guzda, Brad	LVG	17	700:14	4.46	8	3	3	0	0	65	442	0.872
Simchuk, Konstantin	LVG	14	537:42	4.73	8	4	0	2	0	53	302	0.851
Laurie, Rob	ANA	19	825:36	4.88	16	2	1	0	0	84	442	0.840
Ferguson, Jeff	SJO	19	827:03	5.22	9	7	2	1	0	90	467	0.838
Bonvie, Joe	DAL	15	569:03	5.48	5	6	1	0	0	65	380	0.854
Smith, Greg	DAL	15	588:53	5.70	2	9	1	3	0	70	337	0.828
Jensen, James	STL	21	932:33	6.48	13	8	0	3	0	126	604	0.827
Vezina, Steve	BUF	20	871:15	6.83	11	8	0	1	0	124	615	0.832
St. Pierre, Kevin	CHI	23	973:17	6.95	7	11	2	5	0	141	723	0.837
Naumov, Sergei	MIN	26	1220:37	7.35	11	15	0	4	0	187	890	0.826

1999 RHI Playoff Results

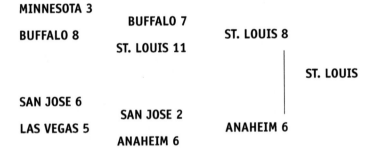

MINNESOTA 3

BUFFALO 8

BUFFALO 7

ST. LOUIS 11

ST. LOUIS 8

ST. LOUIS

SAN JOSE 6

LAS VEGAS 5

SAN JOSE 2

ANAHEIM 6

ANAHEIM 6

RHI Championship Winners

1993 Anaheim Bullfrogs def. Oakland Skates
1994 Buffalo Stampede def. Portland Rage
1995 San Jose Rhinos def. Montreal Roadrunners
1996 Orlando Jackals def. Anaheim Bullfrogs
1997 Anaheim Bullfrogs def. New Jersey Rockin Rollers
1998 No season (MLRH Champion: Anaheim Bullfrogs)
1999 St. Louis Vipers def. Anaheim Bullfrogs (Ralph Backstrom Cup)

CPSIA information can be obtained at www.ICGtesting.com
Printed in the USA
LVOW06s0133201113

362033LV00013B/372/P